The
REALLY USEFUL BOOK OF SCIENCE EXPERIMENTS

The Really Useful Book of Science Experiments contains 100 simple-to-do science experiments that can be confidently carried out by any teacher in a primary school classroom with minimal (or no!) specialist equipment needed.

The experiments in this book are broken down into easily manageable sections including:

- **It's alive**: experiments that explore our living world, including the human body, plants, ecology and disease
- **A material world**: experiments that explore the materials that make up our world and their properties, including metals, acids and alkalis, water and elements
- **Let's get physical**: experiments that explore physics concepts and their applications in our world, including electricity, space, engineering and construction
- **Something a bit different**: experiments that explore interesting and unusual science areas, including forensic science, marine biology and volcanology.

Each experiment is accompanied by a 'subject knowledge guide', filling you in on the key scientific concepts behind the experiment. There are also suggestions for how to adapt each experiment to increase or decrease the challenge.

The text does not assume a scientific background, making it incredibly accessible, and links to the new National Curriculum programme of study allow easy connections to be made to relevant learning goals. This book is an essential text for any primary school teacher, trainee teacher or classroom assistant looking to bring the exciting world of science alive in the classroom.

Tracy-ann Aston is Lecturer in Education and Teacher Training at the University of Bedfordshire, UK.

The Really Useful Series

The

REALLY USEFUL BOOK OF SCIENCE EXPERIMENTS

100 easy ideas for primary school teachers

Tracy-ann Aston

Routledge
Taylor & Francis Group

LONDON AND NEW YORK

Please visit the eResources site at www.routledge.com/9781138784147

First published 2016
by Routledge
2 Park Square, Milton Park, Abingdon, Oxon OX14 4RN

and by Routledge
711 Third Avenue, New York, NY 10017

Routledge is an imprint of the Taylor & Francis Group, an informa business

© 2016 Tracy-ann Aston

British Library Cataloguing in Publication Data
A catalogue record for this book is available from the British Library

Library of Congress Cataloging in Publication Data
Aston, Tracy-Ann.
  The really useful book of science experiments: 100 easy ideas for primary school teachers/Tracy-Ann Aston.
  pages cm
  1. Science – Experiments. 2. Science – Study and teaching (Primary) – Activity programs. I. Title.
  Q164.A78 2016
  372.35'044–dc23
  2015012991

ISBN: 978-1-138-78413-0 (hbk)
ISBN: 978-1-138-78414-7 (pbk)
ISBN: 978-1-315-76830-4 (ebk)

Typeset in Palatino and Gill Sans
by Florence Production Ltd, Stoodleigh, Devon, UK
Printed in Great Britain by Ashford Colour Press ltd

Contents

Introduction

about the programmes and investigations that have taken place, which is particularly good for some of the more experimental or exploratory investigations as well (of course in line with school safeguarding policies). Some of these have links and when pressed, will direct the reader of the book and they can then find out and understand by just seeing the pictures of the activities taking place.

ABOUT THIS BOOK

This book is designed for all teachers, trainee teachers, classroom assistants and parents who want to create 'wow' moments for children as they discover, first-hand, how the world around them works. Science can be taught through books and worksheets (and often is), but for children to really experience science they must have the chance to regularly carry out experimental work that not only challenges their thinking but also increases their enjoyment of science as a subject. This book presents 100 science investigations that can be carried out with primary school-level children in order to foster their love of this vital subject. There is a mixture of classic experiments that have stood the test of time along with new experiments that may be less familiar to teachers. I hope that teachers and students will find the investigations in the book inspiring, and that it will encourage teachers to expand the range and amount of science investigations that they carry out in their classroom

WHY SCIENCE INVESTIGATIONS ARE CRUCIAL IN SCIENCE LESSONS

The decline of students studying STEM (science, technology, engineering and mathematics) subjects at university is contributing to a skills shortage in the labour force. We are living in an increasingly scientific world and we need individuals with knowledge of the science subjects. Unfortunately, children often have a very narrow idea of what a 'scientist' and 'science' mean, with images of old men with crazy hair, wearing lab coats, carrying out investigations by themselves in a laboratory (Silver and Rushton, 2008). The truth, however, is very different. Scientists come from all walks of life and work in an incredibly diverse field: from pharmacists developing the latest drugs, marine biologists exploring the deepest oceans and astrophysicists designing new and better telescopes. Science is a multi-disciplinary subject; the days of scientists working away for hours on end by themselves in their own laboratory are gone, and research is now shared across teams from around the world who are working together to create the next breakthrough. The investigations in this book allow students to work together collaboratively, discovering scientific ideas and principles for themselves in meaningful and relevant contexts. Through undertaking a broad-range of scientific enquiries, students not only develop a greater knowledge and enjoyment of science but they also develop key practical skills such as observation, measuring, handling data, communicating, etc., all of which are highly transferable to other subjects.

In order to create the next generation of scientists and science-literate individuals, we need to inspire pupils with exciting, relevant and hands-on science experiences. Science investigations can play a big part in this endeavour. Research has consistently shown that children's interest in science declines as they move up through primary school (Murphy and Beggs, 2003). This decline has often been attributed to the lack of quality experimental work taking place in science lessons. Primary school pupils frequently say that their favourite part of science is the investigations they get to partake in; however, there is often a lack of regular, high-quality, practical science taking place in lessons. In order to sustain pupils' interest in science, there must be ample opportunities for them to undertake science experiments. To achieve successful science investigations in the classroom, teachers need to have sufficient confidence and knowledge on how to carry out a range of different science investigations. Having worked with trainee teachers, this confidence and knowledge has often been citied as lacking, due to the shortage of training and support given to teachers and trainee teachers in the subject of science. This book aims to provide teachers and trainee teachers with a wealth of ideas that they can choose from, secure in the knowledge that they are being fully supported in terms of what they need to know and carry out. The investigations in this book have all been tried and tested, and prove popular with both teachers and students. Specialised and expensive equipment is not required in order to carry out high-quality science investigations, and this book presents experiments that can be conducted using standard classroom equipment and household items. Health and safety concerns have also played a part in reducing the number and range of science investigations being carried out in schools, particularly in primary schools. However, a number of exciting science investigations can still be carried out in primary school science lessons as long as some basic health and safety rules are followed. This book sets out the simple steps that need to be taken by teachers in order to carry out fun and safe science lessons in their classrooms.

THE NEW NATIONAL CURRICULUM FOR SCIENCE

The National Curriculum for science (DfE, 2013a) provides a framework for the teaching of science at primary school level. The primary National Curriculum is divided into two key stages, Key Stage 1 (for years 1 and 2) and Key Stage 2 (for years 3 to 6). The topics now covered include plants, animals including humans, living things and their habitats, evolution and inheritance (a new addition to the primary science curriculum), everyday materials, uses of everyday materials, properties and changes of materials, seasonal changes, rocks, states of matter, light, forces and magnets, sound, electricity, and Earth and space. Working scientifically sets out the practical, investigative skills that students need to develop while studying science. Although this area of the science curriculum has its own set of standards, it is expected to be taught alongside the content areas of the science curriculum rather than as a discrete body of knowledge. The investigations in this book will allow teachers to achieve the standards of 'working scientifically' while also achieving the content areas of the science curriculum.

Although the investigations in this book have been linked with the new National Curriculum (2014) for science, teachers should not feel that they may only carry out specific investigations at certain times throughout the year. The new National Curriculum provides more freedom for teachers in terms of what and how they teach, and all the investigations in this book include ways they can be adapted in order to increase or decrease the challenge for different ages or abilities of children. The National Curriculum sets out the minimum statutory requirement for science, so there is scope for teachers and schools to develop their own curricula and schemes of work. Remember: science investigations don't have to just remain in science lessons either. These investigations would also be suitable for after-school science clubs or could be incorporated into other subject lessons to facilitate cross-curricular learning.

THE TEACHERS' STANDARDS

The new Teachers' Standards, as set out by the Department for Education (DfE, 2013b), are the minimum requirements that all trainee teachers and qualified teachers are expected to achieve. The current standards state that teachers must:

1 Set high expectations that inspire, motivate and challenge pupils.
2 Promote good progress and outcomes by pupils.
3 Demonstrate good subject and curriculum knowledge.
4 Plan and teach well-structured lessons.
5 Adapt teaching to respond to the strengths and needs of all pupils.
6 Make accurate and productive use of assessment.
7 Manage behaviour effectively to ensure a good and safe learning environment.
8 Fulfil wider professional responsibilities.

The investigations in this book will help trainee teachers and qualified teachers to achieve the Teachers' Standards by presenting well-planned and structured investigations that will excite and motivate students. Assessment ideas for each investigation are suggested along with useful questions to ask pupils in order to assess and extend their learning. Opportunities for incorporating ICT into the investigations have been highlighted and there are suggestions on how to extend the investigations, either through homework or cross-curricular work.

REFERENCES

DfE (2013a) *National Curriculum in England: Science programmes of study*. London: DfE.

DfE (2013b) *Teachers' Standards*. London: DfE.

Murphy, C. and Beggs, J. (2003) Children's perceptions of school science. *School Science Review*, 84(308): 109–116.

Silver, A. and Rushton, B. (2008) Primary school children's attitudes towards science, engineering and technology and their images of scientists and engineers. *International Journal of Primary, Elementary and Early Years Education*, 36(1): 51–67.

How to use this book

This book presents 100 science experiments that are suitable for primary school-aged pupils. This book has been guided by the new (2014) National Curriculum for science but is not limited to the statutory programme of study. These experiments could be carried out in the primary school classroom as part of the science teaching, but could also be utilised in science clubs or by parents looking to challenge and excite their children at home. The experiments are divided into four sections: 'its alive', 'a material world', 'let's get physical' and 'something a bit different'. Each experiment in the book is broken down into the following sections:

- **Learning objectives**: The objective for the investigation.

- **Introduction**: A brief overview of the science experiment.

- **Useful prior work**: What the children should ideally already know before completing the experiment.

- **Background science**: A brief overview of the science behind the experiment. This is intended for teachers and is not indicative of what the children would need to know.

- **National Curriculum links**: Ideas of where the experiment fits into the National Curriculum for science.

- **Materials needed**: A list of the materials required for the experiment.

- **Safety and technical notes**: An overview of the safety considerations needed for the experiment and any particular technical issues for the experiment. Some of the experiments in this book use common allergens, for example egg, dairy, strawberries, etc. Teachers should remember to check for any allergies before completing these experiments. Some experiments will require parental permission (these experiments are identified in the book). Teachers should ensure they have permission for the specific lesson or are covered by the school's general permissions policy for science lessons.

- **Method**: The method needed for the children to carry out the experiment.

- **Data collection ideas**: Ideas for how the results from the experiment can be presented.

- **Differentiation**: Ideas for how the experiment could be made more or less challenging.

- **Useful questions to ask the children**: Some suggestions for questions that you could ask the children during and after the experiment.

- **Further work**: Ideas for further work based on the experiment that could be carried out in another lesson or set as homework.

All tables are available to download from the eResources site at www.routledge.com/9781138784147

EXPERIMENTS 1–100

EXPERIMENT 1

Reaction times

LEARNING OBJECTIVES:
Measuring our reaction times!

INTRODUCTION:
The children investigate their reaction times by catching a ruler as another person drops it. The distance at which it is caught can then be converted into a 'reaction time'.

USEFUL PRIOR WORK:
The children do not need to have any particular prior knowledge before completing this investigation.

 BACKGROUND SCIENCE:
A reaction time is how long an organism takes to respond to a particular stimulus. This is made up of both 'thinking time' (how long it takes your brain to realise that something has happened that it needs to respond to) and the speed of the nervous system in responding to the stimulus. In humans, the nervous system is made up of the brain and neurones (nerve cells). Nervous impulses travel very fast around the body, meaning that we can react to stimuli quickly. This is important for survival, for example moving your hand away when you touch something hot. However your body does not react instantly to stimuli. There is usually some delay between the stimulus and your body's reaction. This delay is the *reaction time*. Certain factors can increase or decrease your reaction times. Alcohol, for instance, is a depressant drug that slows down your nervous system, therefore increasing your reaction times. Certain diseases of the nervous system such as multiple sclerosis can also increase reaction times.

NATIONAL CURRICULUM LINKS:
- **Year 3 programme of study**: Animals, including humans
  - Identify that humans and some other animals have skeletons and muscles for support, protection and movement.

MATERIALS NEEDED:
- Rulers: 30cm or metre rulers

 SAFETY AND TECHNICAL NOTES:
- Use smaller rulers, for example 30cm long, if doing this investigation with younger children. Older children could use metre rulers.
- It is worth demonstrating the technique of dropping and catching the ruler with the children. The child dropping the ruler should not tell the child catching the ruler when they will drop it. The children should try to catch the ruler using just their dominant hand.

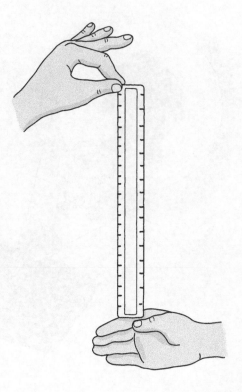

METHOD:

TO BE DONE IN ADVANCE BY THE TEACHER:
Have the 'calculating your reaction time table' prepared, either on a worksheet or on a whiteboard.

 CHILDREN:
1 Stand facing each other.
2 Have your partner hold the ruler out at arm's length with the number '0' at the bottom end of the ruler.
3 Hold your arm out so that your dominant hand is just below the ruler (but not touching the ruler!)
4 Have your partner let go of the ruler when they are ready. Try to catch it as quickly as you can.
5 When you have caught the ruler, write down the number on the ruler closest to your thumb.
6 Repeat the experiment five times before swapping roles with your partner.

 DATA COLLECTION IDEAS:

| | [Name] | | [Name] | |
	Length (cm)	Time (s)	Length (cm)	Time (s)
Trial 1				
Trial 2				
Trial 3				
Trial 4				
Trial 5				
Average				

DIFFERENTIATION:
* **Decrease the challenge:** The children can be helped when reading off where they have caught the ruler.
* **Increase the challenge:** The children could repeat the investigation with their non-dominant hand and compare the results.

USEFUL QUESTIONS TO ASK THE CHILDREN:
* Do you think there is anything we could do to improve our reaction times?
* Can you think of anything that might slow down our reaction times?
* What jobs need people to have fast reaction times?

FURTHER WORK:
The investigation could be repeated regularly over a few weeks to see if the children's reaction times improve. This could be related to athletes who need to improve their reaction times – for example, runners who need to start as soon as the starting pistol is fired. They usually achieve this by regular practice in order to improve their reaction times.

EXPERIMENT 2

Decomposing

LEARNING OBJECTIVES:
Investigating which materials will decompose and how they decompose.

INTRODUCTION:
Children investigate which materials decompose and the rate of decay by burying different materials in the ground. The materials will be observed over a period of time to see the changes that occur.

USEFUL PRIOR WORK:
The children should know what the word 'decay' or 'decomposition' means (they may use the word 'rotting' instead).

 BACKGROUND SCIENCE:
Decay occurs due to bacteria (and some fungi) that live in soil. Bacteria are living organisms, which means that they require certain conditions in order to live. One of these conditions is that they must have a source of nutrition. For bacteria living in the soil, this nutrition usually comes from the breakdown of organic (living) material. The bacteria break down the organic matter by releasing enzymes. All organic material will eventually decay, including materials made from previously living organisms, for example paper. Most man-made materials will not decay, or will take a very long time to break down (hundreds of years, for example). Rates of decay are affected by factors such as temperature (because enzymes are involved, the temperature cannot be too hot or too cold), the amount of water and oxygen present, and the presence of other organisms that can assist decay – for example, worms and flies.

NATIONAL CURRICULUM LINKS:
- **Year 1 programme of study**: Everyday materials
  - Compare and group together a variety of everyday materials on the basis of their simple physical properties.
- **Year 4 programme of study**: Living things and their habitats
  - Recognise that environments can change and that this can sometimes pose dangers to living things.
- **Year 5 programme of study**: Properties and changes of materials
  - Compare and group together everyday materials on the basis of their properties, including their hardness, solubility, transparency, conductivity (electrical and thermal) and response to magnets.
  - Give reasons, based on evidence from comparative and fair tests, for the particular uses of everyday materials, including metals, wood and plastic.

MATERIALS NEEDED:
- Suitable materials for decomposing – for example newspaper, cardboard, tin foil, plastic bottle, tin can, banana peel, metal spoon, apple core, used tea bag
- Suitable digging tools, for example a hand trowel
- Markers for where the items are buried, for example plant labels or lolly sticks
- Digital camera

 SAFETY AND TECHNICAL NOTES:
- Do not bury meat, fish, cooked food or eggs/eggshells as they may attract vermin.
- Ensure any containers that previously contained food items have been washed thoroughly.

- Supervise children when they are using garden tools. Use tools that are a suitable size for the children.
- The children should wash their hands after carrying out the investigation.

METHOD:

TO BE DONE IN ADVANCE BY THE TEACHER:

Collect the items that will be buried and locate a suitable site for the investigation. Before each item is buried, take a photograph to act as a reminder for the children. You could also have them make detailed observations of each item, including what it looks like, smells like, feels like, etc.

 CHILDREN:

1 Choose the first item you will be burying in the soil.
2 Use the hand trowel to dig a hole in the compost. Make sure it is big enough to fit the whole item into.
3 Place the item you are burying into the hole and cover it with the soil you removed. Pat the soil down to make it as smooth as possible on top.
4 Place a labelled marker by your item to show where it is buried.
5 Repeat with the rest of the items. Try to make your holes the same depth from the surface each time.

Returning to examine your items:

1 Find one of your labelled markers. Carefully dig up the item using the hand trowel. Do not remove the item from the hole or touch the item unless your teacher has said you can.
2 Take a photo of the item and write down any observations. Think about what you can see, smell, feel and hear.
3 Carefully cover the item with the soil again and replace the marker.
4 Repeat with the other items that you buried.

 DATA COLLECTION IDEAS:

The children can take photographs of the items every time they are examined using a digital camera. These photos can then be used as a 'timeline' of decomposition and will help to remind the children of what has taken place. The children can also write down their observations each time they examine the items.

DIFFERENTIATION:

- **Decrease the challenge:** This could be carried out as a whole class investigation, with different children taking on different roles over the course of the investigation.
- **Increase the challenge:** The children could investigate additional factors that affect decomposing. For example, they could bury the same items in dry compost in pots in the classroom and compare these with the items buried outside. The lack of water for the bacteria will mean the material decomposes very slowly if at all.

USEFUL QUESTIONS TO ASK THE CHILDREN:

- What did the materials that decayed/did not decay have in common?
- Why do you think some materials did not decay?
- Why is it important to know if a material will decay?

FURTHER WORK:

This investigation can be linked to work on recycling and sustainability. For example, the children could design an object (for example a bag) that will be able to decompose after it has been used and compare it with the same object made from materials that would not decompose.

Keeping warm

LEARNING OBJECTIVES:
Investigate which materials are best at keeping us warm.

INTRODUCTION:
The children investigate which material is best at keeping us warm by seeing how well different materials insulate a beaker of warm water. The temperature of the water will be measured over a set period of time to see the change in the temperature.

USEFUL PRIOR WORK:
The children should be able to use thermometers or data-loggers.

 BACKGROUND SCIENCE:
A beaker of hot water will lose heat by the processes of conduction, convection and radiation. Heat is a form of energy that can only travel in one direction – from an area that is hot to an area that is cold. In conduction and convection, the energy is transferred when particles bump into each other, causing energy to pass from the 'hot' particle to the 'cold' particle. In radiation, the energy is transferred when heat is given off as infrared radiation, a type of electromagnetic wave. An insulator is something that prevents or slows down this transfer of energy. Some materials prevent the loss of heat from the processes of conduction and convection. These materials tend to be ones where there are pockets of trapped air, for example polystyrene. Air, especially trapped air, is a good insulator due to its particles being very far apart. Other materials, such as foil, prevent heat loss from the process of radiation as they 'radiate' the heat back to the source.

NATIONAL CURRICULUM LINKS:
- **Year 1 programme of study**: Everyday materials
  - Compare and group together a variety of everyday materials on the basis of their simple physical properties.
- **Year 2 programme of study**: Animals, including humans
  - Find out about and describe the basic needs of animals, including humans, for survival (water, food and air).
- **Year 2 programme of study**: Uses of everyday materials
  - Identify and compare the suitability of a variety of everyday materials – including wood, metal, plastic, glass, brick, rock, paper and cardboard – for particular uses.
- **Year 5 programme of study**: Properties and changes of materials
  - Compare and group together everyday materials on the basis of their physical properties including their hardness, solubility, transparency, conductivity (electrical and thermal) and response to magnets.

MATERIALS NEEDED:
- A selection of different materials to test, for example fabric, tin foil, cotton wool, newspaper, tissue paper
- Beakers
- Thermometers or data-loggers
- Elastic bands
- Timers
- Water

SAFETY AND TECHNICAL NOTES:

- Supervise children when they are using hot water. Boiling water is not necessary for this investigation. Water from the hot tap will be sufficient.
- Ensure that the beakers are not in danger of being knocked over, especially when the thermometers are placed in them.
- Children should stand up during the investigation to reduce the risk if the water is spilled.
- Avoid using mercury thermometers if possible.

METHOD:

TO BE DONE IN ADVANCE BY THE TEACHER:

Prepare the materials to be used ensuring that they are as similar a size as possible. This is a 'fair test' investigation, so encourage the children to think about the variables they will need to control.

 CHILDREN:

1 Wrap your beaker with one of the materials you have been given. Try to wrap the material around the beaker evenly. Hold it in place with an elastic band.
2 Fill the beaker with the warm water.
3 Take the temperature of the water and record this in your results table.
4 Start the timer. Take the temperature of the water every minute for 5 minutes.
5 Repeat the investigation with the rest of the materials.

 DATA COLLECTION IDEAS:

Material	Starting temperature (°C)	Temperature of the water (°C)					Difference between starting temperature and the temperature after 5 mins
		1 min	2 mins	3 mins	4 mins	5 mins	

DIFFERENTIATION:

- **Decrease the challenge:** Some children may find it difficult taking the temperature every minute. Data-loggers can often be set up to automatically take and record temperatures at set intervals.
- **Increases the challenge:** The children could investigate whether the materials are just as good at insulating cold objects by, for example, wrapping up a beaker that contains ice cubes. The results could then be compared.

USEFUL QUESTIONS TO ASK THE CHILDREN:

- Which material was the best/worst insulator? How do you know this?
- Why do you think these materials were good/bad insulators?
- Which items of clothing are usually designed to be good insulators?

FURTHER WORK:

The results from this investigation could be linked with the idea of insulated clothing and the additional properties the clothes would need. For example, cotton wool is a good insulator but it is not waterproof. Children could consider how they could make a suitable, insulating, item of clothing.

Heartbeats

LEARNING OBJECTIVES:
Investigating how our heart rate changes when we exercise.

INTRODUCTION:
The children investigate their heart rates at rest and when exercising. After measuring their heartbeat while sitting down, the children will then undergo different types of physical activity in order to see the effect it has on their heart rate.

USEFUL PRIOR WORK:
The children should know the basic role of the heart in the body and that your pulse rate tells you how fast your heart is beating.

 BACKGROUND SCIENCE:
The role of the heart is to pump blood around your body. The blood contains oxygen, broken down food and waste products produced by the body. The heart needs to beat faster during exercise because your muscles need oxygen (carried in the red blood cells) for respiration (the process by which energy is made from the food we eat). The more work the muscles have to do, the more energy they require. Your muscles also produce carbon dioxide as a waste product in respiration, which needs to be taken to the lungs via the blood (carbon dioxide is dissolved in the bloodstream). The muscles may also produce lactic acid (the substance that gives you a 'stitch'), which needs to be taken to the liver to be broken down. These additional factors also mean that the heart has to beat faster to carry these substances around the body quickly.

NATIONAL CURRICULUM LINKS:
- **Year 2 programme of study**: Animals, including humans
  - Describe the importance for humans of exercise, eating the right amounts of different types of food and hygiene.
- **Year 6 programme of study**: Animals, including humans
  - Identify and name the main parts of the human circulatory system and describe the functions of the heart, blood vessels and blood.
  - Recognise the impact of diet, exercise, drugs and lifestyle on the way their bodies function.
  - Describe the way in which nutrients and water are transported within animals, including humans.

MATERIALS NEEDED:
- Suitable exercise equipment, for example balls, skipping ropes, hula-hoops, gym mats, etc.
- Timers

 SAFETY AND TECHNICAL NOTES:

- Keep the exercise level to the same as that in a PE lesson.
- Ensure children are wearing suitable footwear and clothing.
- Do not allow children to run up and down stairs.
- Be sensitive to children who may be embarrassed about being physically active.
- Be aware of children with any health problems that will impact on them exercising.
- It is best if you time the children as a whole class while doing this activity.

METHOD:

TO BE DONE IN ADVANCE BY THE TEACHER:

Ensure that a suitable space is set up for the investigation and that the children have access to a range of suitable sports equipment.

 CHILDREN:

1 Measure your pulse while you are sitting down resting. Write the result onto your result table.
2 Exercise for 1 minute using your chosen form of exercise. Your teacher will time you and tell you when to stop.
3 When 1 minute is up, take your pulse again. Write the result onto your table.
4 Sit down again for 1 minute. Take your pulse again. If it has reached your resting heart rate again you can carry on. If not, wait for another 30 seconds and then take your pulse again.
5 Repeat the investigation with a different type of exercise.

✎ DATA COLLECTION IDEAS:

'My resting heart rate is:_____.'

Type of exercise	Heart rate after 1 min of exercise

DIFFERENTIATION:

• **Decrease the challenge:** Students could simply record how tired they feel after each type of exercise on a scale from 1–10.
• **Increase the challenge:** The children could also investigate how long it takes their heart to return to their resting pulse rate after exercising for 1 minute and whether this varies with the type of exercise.

USEFUL QUESTIONS TO ASK THE CHILDREN:

• Which type of exercise increased your heart rate the most/least? Why do you think this was?
• What other types of exercise do you think would increase your heart rate a lot?
• Why do you think your heart beats faster when you are exercising?

FURTHER WORK:

This work can be linked to having a healthy lifestyle. Children could investigate what else they need to do in order to have a 'healthy heart', for example having a healthy diet low in salt and cholesterol, not smoking, not drinking excess alcohol, etc.

EXPERIMENT 5

Big feet, big hands?

LEARNING OBJECTIVES:
Investigate the relationship between different parts of our body.

INTRODUCTION:
The children investigate different parts of their body to see if there is any relationship between them. They can be provided with the relationships to investigate or can be encouraged to come up with their own.

USEFUL PRIOR WORK:
The children do not need to have any particular prior knowledge for this investigation but they should be able to use simple measuring equipment, for example tape-measures.

 BACKGROUND SCIENCE:
The human body tends to be in proportion for most people. This is because genes, which are one factor in determining our body characteristics, can influence how long bones grow in our body. These genes will impact on all of the bones in the body in the same way. Therefore, for example, people who are taller will generally have bigger feet than smaller people. Other factors such as diet will impact on the human body, potentially causing more or less bone or muscle development. Having certain body characteristics can also influence how well you perform certain tasks. For example, people who have longer legs can usually jump further than people with shorter legs, and people with larger hands usually have a bigger 'grab-size' than people with smaller hands.

NATIONAL CURRICULUM LINKS:
- **Year 3 programme of study**: Animals, including humans
  - Identify that humans and some other animals have skeletons and muscles for support, protection and movement.
- **Year 5 programme of study**: Animals, including humans
  - Describe the changes as humans develop to old age.
- **Year 6 programme of study**: Animals, including humans
  - Recognise the impact of diet, exercise, drugs and lifestyle on the way their bodies function.
- **Year 6 programme of study**: Evolution and inheritance
  - Recognise that living things produce offspring of the same kind, but normally offspring vary and are not identical to their parents.

MATERIALS NEEDED:
A selection of simple measuring equipment, for example tape-measures, rulers, string

 SAFETY AND TECHNICAL NOTES:
- Avoid any activity that involves weighing the children as this may upset some children.
- In order to obtain reliable results, it is good idea to measure at least twenty people. Results can always be 'pooled' from different groups doing the same investigation.

METHOD:

TO BE DONE IN ADVANCE BY THE TEACHER:
Decide on some body-relationships that the class can choose from or allow the children to come up with their own investigations.

 CHILDREN:

1 Decide which body-relationship you want to investigate.
2 Decide what equipment you will need for your investigation.
3 Carry out your investigations, using as many people in the class as possible.
4 Record your results on your results table.

 DATA COLLECTION IDEAS:
The children can record their results on basic tables and then produce a histogram, bar-chart or scatter-graph, depending on what they choose to investigate.

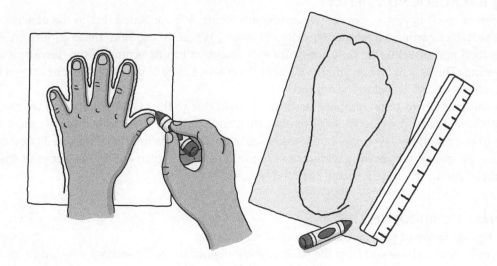

DIFFERENTIATION:
• **Decrease the challenge:** The children could record their results visually, for example drawing around hands/feet and sticking these onto a pre-prepared class graph.
• **Increase the challenge:** The children could investigate body parts that are harder to measure for example head circumference or length of index finger. They could also be introduced to the idea of a 'line of best fit' on a scatter-graph and what this is used for.

USEFUL QUESTIONS TO ASK THE CHILDREN:
• What did you find out about your body-relationship? Did this surprise you?
• Why did we need to measure lots of people in our investigations?
• Do you think you would get the same results if you measured older/younger people?

FURTHER WORK:
The children could choose one of their body-relationships to investigate with another class of older or younger pupils to see if the relationship stays the same.

EXPERIMENT 6

Taste vs. smell

LEARNING OBJECTIVES:
Investigate the effect of using just our sense of taste when eating.

INTRODUCTION:
Children investigate the effect of using just their sense of taste when eating. Children will try to distinguish the flavour of different fruit while blindfolded and not using their sense of smell.

USEFUL PRIOR WORK:
Children should know the name and role of the five senses.

 BACKGROUND SCIENCE:
Your sense of smell is very important when you are eating. We can smell due to the olfactory region of the nose, which contains neurones that detect odours. When we eat food, these odours are released from the food and travel to the nose. They are very important in determining the flavour of the food we are eating. This is why, when you have a cold, food tastes very bland because your nose is blocked and the odours cannot travel to the neurones.

It is still possible to taste without the sense of smell due to the taste buds located on the tongue. Chemicals from the food we eat dissolve in our saliva and stimulate these taste buds to send a nervous impulse to our brain; however, these taste buds are only able to distinguish the main 'tastes' of sweet, salty, sour, bitter and the recently added umami (savouriness), which is why the sense of smell is so important in enhancing the flavour of the food we eat.

NATIONAL CURRICULUM LINKS:
- **Year 1 programme of study**: Animals, including humans
  - Identify, name, draw and label the basic parts of the human body and say which part of the body is associated with each sense.
- **Year 2 programme of study**: Animals, including humans
  - Find out about the basic needs of animals, including humans, for survival (water, food and air).
- **Year 3 programme of study**: Animals, including humans
  - Identify that animals, including humans, need the right types and amount of nutrition, and that they cannot make their own food; they get nutrition from what they eat.
- **Year 4 programme of study**: Animals, including humans
  - Describe the simple functions of the basic parts of the digestive system in humans.

MATERIALS NEEDED:
- A selection of strongly flavoured, cut-up fruit, for example apple, strawberry, banana
- Blindfolds

 SAFETY AND TECHNICAL NOTES:
- Place the cut-up fruit on paper towels or in small, clean pots.
- Children should wash their hands before the investigation.
- Be aware of any allergies.
- Ensure parental permission has been given for this experiment.

METHOD:

TO BE DONE IN ADVANCE BY THE TEACHER:
Separate the fruits and place each flavour into a different pot or onto paper towels.

 ### CHILDREN:
1 Put on the blindfold.
2 Have your partner choose a piece of fruit for you. (Do not let them tell you what the fruit is!)
3 Hold your nose then chew the fruit (don't swallow!).
4 Tell your partner what flavour you think the fruit is. Have them write this down on the results table.
5 Now, let go of your nose and finish eating the fruit. What flavour do you think it is now? Have your partner write this down on the results table.

 ### DATA COLLECTION IDEAS:

Fruit flavour	Flavour I guessed while holding my nose	Flavour I guessed while not holding my nose

DIFFERENTIATION:
- **Decrease the challenge:** The children could use just two types of fruit and see how many times they are able to correctly identify the fruit.
- **Increase the challenge:** The children could extend this investigation by coming-up with their own 'taste vs. smell' investigation. They could, for example, try to identify different types of crisps, vegetables, etc. and see which type of food is most difficult to 'taste' without their sense of smell.

USEFUL QUESTIONS TO ASK THE CHILDREN:
- Was any flavour easier to detect than the others? Why do you think this was?
- Was any flavour harder to detect than the others? Why do you think this was?
- Why do you think it was easier to 'taste' the fruit when you were not holding your nose?

FURTHER WORK:
This investigation could be linked to cross-curricular work on cooking. The children could cook or bake food items that contain strong smells, for example vanilla, strawberry and peppermint.

Catch the ball!

LEARNING OBJECTIVES:
Investigate the effects of having just one eye instead of two!

INTRODUCTION:
The children investigate the effect of using just one eye when attempting to catch a ball by first throwing and catching the ball with both eyes open and then throwing and catching the ball with one eye covered.

USEFUL PRIOR WORK:
Children should know the name and role of the five senses.

 BACKGROUND SCIENCE:
Humans have two eyes that are close together on the front of our heads. The fields of vision from our two eyes therefore overlap. This gives us something called binocular vision, which means we have very good depth perception and are able to judge distances easily. Closing one eye removes this depth perception, which makes it harder for us to judge the distance and location of objects. Some animals have monocular vision. They have two eyes but the fields of vision do not overlap. They can control the eyes separately and receive different messages from each eye. This allows them to look in two different directions at once. This means that their field of vision is greater, but their depth perception is reduced. In nature, most predators have binocular vision, allowing them to home in on their prey, whereas prey animals tend to have monocular vision, allowing them to look out for predators.

NATIONAL CURRICULUM LINKS:
- **Year 1 programme of study**: Animals, including humans
  - Identify, name, draw and label the basic parts of the human body and say which part of the body is associated with each sense.

MATERIALS NEEDED:
- Soft balls
- Blindfolds or eyepatches

 SAFETY AND TECHNICAL NOTES:
- Use a soft ball to prevent any injuries.
- Ensure there is plenty of space for children to throw the ball safely. Ideally use a hall or the playground.
- The children may struggle with covering just one eye with the blindfold. Eyepatches can be used instead. These could be made by the children at the start of the investigation.
- Be aware and sensitive of any children who may have sight problems. For children who wear glasses, blindfolds or eyepatches should be placed underneath the glasses.

METHOD:

TO BE DONE IN ADVANCE BY THE TEACHER:
Select a suitable space for the investigation. Have materials ready if the children are making their eyepatches.

CHILDREN:

Both eyes:

1 Have your partner stand five steps away from you.
2 When you are ready, have your partner throw the ball to you. Try to catch the ball.
3 Record in your results table whether you caught the ball.
4 Repeat this ten times.

One eye:

1 Cover one eye with the blindfold or eyepatch. If you are right-handed, cover your right eye. If you are left-handed, cover your left eye.
2 Have your partner stand five steps away from you.
3 When you are ready, have your partner throw the ball to you. Try to catch the ball.
4 Record in your results table whether you caught the ball.
5 Repeat this ten times.

 DATA COLLECTION IDEAS:

Trial	Both eyes open	One eye covered
1		
2		
3		
4		
5		

DIFFERENTIATION:
- **Decrease the challenge:** If the children are struggling with catching the ball, you can vary the distance between the two children.
- **Increase the challenge:** The children could also investigate if it makes a difference which eye is covered, or try to catch the ball with one hand.

USEFUL QUESTIONS TO ASK THE CHILDREN:
- Was it easier or harder to catch the ball with one eye compared to two eyes? Why do you think this was?
- Do you think it makes any difference which eye is covered?
- Why is it useful for humans to be able to judge distances?

FURTHER WORK:
The children could investigate animals that have binocular vision and animals that have monocular vision and why this is advantageous for them.

How sensitive are you?

LEARNING OBJECTIVES:
Investigate how sensitive our skin is to touch.

INTRODUCTION:
The children investigate how sensitive different parts of the body are at detecting two separate points touching their skin.

USEFUL PRIOR WORK:
Children should know the name and role of the five senses.

 BACKGROUND SCIENCE:
The skin is a highly sensitive organ. The middle layer of the skin, the dermis, contains the touch receptors that respond to pressure. When something stimulates the skin, the touch receptors send a nervous impulse to the brain that then interprets the impulse. Some areas of our body have more sensitive skin then other areas. For example, the skin on our fingertips is very sensitive as it contains more nerve endings than, for example, the skin on our arms. This is because it is advantageous for our fingers to be very sensitive so that we can use objects in our hands easily. The ability to distinguish two separate points touching our skin is called point discrimination. The more sensitive parts of our skin are able to detect two distinct 'touch points', even if those points are very close together. Less sensitive areas of our skin will only be able to detect one touch point when the points are close together. The distance at which the two points can be felt as two separate points will vary on different parts of the body.

NATIONAL CURRICULUM LINKS:
- **Year 1 programme of study**: Animals, including humans
  - Identify, name, draw and label the basic parts of the human body and say which part of the body is associated with each sense.

MATERIALS NEEDED:
- Blindfold
- Opened paperclips with Blu-Tack on each end

 SAFETY AND TECHNICAL NOTES:
- In order to reduce the risk of injury, do not use implements with a sharp point.
- Supervise the children at all times.
- The children may need help with measuring the distance of the opened paperclip.
- Only carry out the test on safe parts of the body – for example palm of hand, back of hand, fingertip, lower arm, lower leg.

METHOD:

TO BE DONE IN ADVANCE BY THE TEACHER:
Prepare the opened paperclips so that the ends are covered with Blu-Tack. Try not to use too much Blu-Tack or create a 'ball' of Blu-Tack on the ends. You just need enough to take away the sharpness of the point.

CHILDREN:

1 Put on the blindfold.
2 Have your partner touch you with the opened paperclip on the first place you are testing.
3 Have your partner slowly move the two ends of the paperclip closer together (do not drag them but lift them up and move them closer together).
4 Keep doing this until you can no longer feel two separate ends touching your skin but instead it feels like only one paperclip end is touching you.
5 Have your partner keep the paperclip still and carefully remove it from your skin. Measure the distance between the two points of the paperclip. Record this result on your results table. If the two ends are touching each other write 'touching'.
6 Repeat on the other areas you are testing.

 DATA COLLECTION IDEAS:

Part of body	Distance at which it felt like just one end of a paperclip
Back of hand	
Palm of hand	
Fingertip	
Lower arm	
Lower leg	

DIFFERENTIATION:

- **Decrease the challenge:** The children may need to work with an adult who can then measure the distance between the paperclip ends.
- **Increase the challenge:** The children could carry out a systematic investigation into whether all fingertips are as sensitive as each other.

USEFUL QUESTIONS TO ASK THE CHILDREN:

- Which part of your body was the most/least sensitive? Why do you think this was the case?
- Why is it useful for our skin to be sensitive to touch?
- What else is our skin able to detect?

FURTHER WORK:

The children could investigate Braille, and how having sensitive fingertips allows people to be able to read Braille.

Time to get sweaty

LEARNING OBJECTIVES:
Investigating how sweat helps us to stay cool.

INTRODUCTION:
The children investigate how sweat keeps us cool by using beakers of water wrapped in dry cotton wool and damp cotton wool and seeing how quickly they cool down.

USEFUL PRIOR WORK:
The children should know that we sweat when we are hot.

 BACKGROUND SCIENCE:
Our ideal internal body temperature is 37°C. Sometimes we become too hot and therefore our body needs to cool us down. This is because our bodies rely on enzymes to carry out different activities and the enzymes can only work in a very limited temperature range. Exercise is an example of something that can increase our body temperature. This is because respiration, the process by which we release energy from the food we eat, releases heat. If we are performing exercise, our muscles need more energy therefore our body carries out more respiration, releasing more heat. Sweat is one way in which our body attempts to cool us down. Sweat cools us down because the water on the surface of our skin evaporates, using the excess heat from our body in order to do so.

NATIONAL CURRICULUM LINKS:
* **Year 2 programme of study**: Animals, including humans
  - Find out about and describe the basic needs of animals, including humans, for survival (water, food and air).
* **Year 4 programme of study**: States of matter
  - Identify the part played by evaporation and condensation in the water cycle and associate the rate of evaporation with temperature.
* **Year 6 programme of study**: Animals, including humans
  - Recognise the impact of diet, exercise, drugs and lifestyle on the way their bodies function.

MATERIALS NEEDED:
* Beakers or plastic pots
* Thermometers or data-loggers
* Cotton wool
* Elastic bands
* Water

 SAFETY AND TECHNICAL NOTES:
* Supervise children when they are using hot water. Boiling water is not necessary for this experiment. Water from the hot tap would be sufficient.
* Ensure that the beakers are not in danger of being knocked over, especially when the thermometers are placed in them.
* Children should stand up during the experiment to reduce the risk if the water is spilled.
* Avoid using mercury thermometers if possible.

METHOD:

TO BE DONE IN ADVANCE BY THE TEACHER:
Cut up pieces of cotton wool so that they are the same size and will fit around the beakers or pots.

 CHILDREN:

1 Wrap the dry cotton wool around one of your beakers and the damp cotton wool around the other beaker. Try to evenly cover the beakers. Hold the cotton wool in place with an elastic band.
2 Carefully fill the beakers with the warm water.
3 Use the thermometer or data-logger to take the temperature of the beakers. Record this on your results table. Keep the thermometer or data-logger in the beaker.
4 Start the timer.
5 Record the temperature of the beakers every minute for 10 minutes.
6 Write the results in your results table.

 DATA COLLECTION IDEAS:

Time (m)	Temperature of the water °C	
	Dry cotton wool	Damp cotton wool
0 (starting temperature)		
1		
2		
3		
4		
5		

DIFFERENTIATION:
- **Decrease the challenge:** The children may find it difficult taking the temperature every minute. Some data-loggers can be set up to automatically take and record the temperature at set intervals.
- **Increase the challenge:** The children could investigate whether the amount of sweat makes any difference by comparing cotton wools of different wetness.

USEFUL QUESTIONS TO ASK THE CHILDREN:
- Which beaker cooled down the quickest? Why do you think this was?
- Why is it important for us to be able to sweat?
- How do you think sweat cools us down?

FURTHER WORK:
This investigation could be linked to cross-curricular work in PE. The children can be encouraged to think about what activity in PE makes them sweat the most and why this might be.

Food testing

LEARNING OBJECTIVES:
Investigate which foods contain starch and fats.

INTRODUCTION:
The children investigate which foods contain starch and fat by using iodine to test for the presence of starch and filter paper to test for the presence of fat.

USEFUL PRIOR WORK:
The children should know the names of the main food groups.

 BACKGROUND SCIENCE:
Starch and fats are two examples of organic molecules. Starch is a type of carbohydrate and is found in most plant-based foods for example, wheat, vegetables, grains. Fats can be solid (for example butter), and liquid (for example olive oil). Fats can be found in many different types of food, especially meat and dairy, but are not usually found in fruit and vegetables. Starch can be tested for using iodine. When iodine is added to the food being tested, it will turn a dark blue/black colour if starch is present. Fats can be tested for using filter paper. The filter paper is rubbed onto the food, and if it goes see-through then fats are present. Although these tests will detect the presence of either starch or fat they are not able to provide information on how much starch or fat is present.

NATIONAL CURRICULUM LINKS:
- **Year 2 programme of study**: Animals, including humans
  - Describe the importance for humans of exercise, eating the right amounts of different types of food and hygiene.
- **Year 3 programme of study**: Animals, including humans
  - Identify that animals, including humans, need the right types and amount of nutrition, and that they cannot make their own food; they get nutrition from what they eat.
- **Year 6 programme of study**: Animals, including humans
  - Recognise the impact of diet, exercise, drugs and lifestyle on the way their bodies function.

MATERIALS NEEDED:
- A selection of foods to test – for example, bread, butter, chocolate, cereal, fruits and vegetables
- Iodine solution
- Filter paper cut into small squares or circles
- Beakers or plastic pots

 SAFETY AND TECHNICAL NOTES:
- Care needs to be taken when using iodine solution – it can stain clothing and skin. Ensure children are supervised at all times when using the iodine solution. Follow all safety instructions on the bottle.
- The children should be told to not eat the food used in the investigation.

METHOD:

TO BE DONE IN ADVANCE BY THE TEACHER:

Cut up the filter paper into suitable test-sized pieces (about 2cm squares is fine).
Cut up any large pieces of food to be tested.

 CHILDREN:

1 Choose the first food you want to test.
2 Take two beakers and put a piece of this food into each of them.
3 Add a few drops of the iodine solution onto the food in one of the beakers. Be careful not to get any iodine on your hands or clothes.
4 Write down what colour the iodine goes on your results table. If it turns dark blue/black, there is starch in the food.
5 Now rub the filter paper over the food in the other beaker. You may have to take the food out of the beaker to do this.
6 Hold the filter paper up to light. Record in your results table if the paper has gone see-through. If it has then there is fat in the food.
7 Repeat the investigation with the rest of the foods to be tested. Wash out your beakers or use a new beaker each time.

 DATA COLLECTION IDEAS:

Type of food	Colour of the iodine	Does the food contain starch?	Did the filter paper go see-through?	Does the food contain fat?

DIFFERENTIATION:

* **Decrease the challenge:** The children may find it easier testing larger pieces of food that are not in beakers. Wipe-clean tiles could be used instead.
* **Increase the challenge:** The children could test different parts of vegetables and fruit for starch to see if all of the parts contain starch. For example, leaves, stems, roots, etc.

USEFUL QUESTIONS TO ASK THE CHILDREN:

* Which foods contained starch/fats? How do you know this?
* Were you surprised by any results?
* Why is it important for us to eat lots of different types of food?

FURTHER WORK:

This investigation could be linked to further work on healthy eating and healthy lifestyles. The children could construct meal plans or menus with appropriate amounts of food from the different food groups.

All about yeast

LEARNING OBJECTIVES:
Investigate what temperature of water yeast prefers.

INTRODUCTION:
The children investigate whether yeast prefers warm or cold water by measuring the height of the froth produced by yeast in different temperatures of water.

USEFUL PRIOR WORK:
The children do not need to have any particular prior knowledge before completing this investigation.

 BACKGROUND SCIENCE:
Yeast is a single-celled micro-organism that is classified in the fungus kingdom of life. It is therefore a living organism and requires a food source to survive. This food source is usually a sugar. Yeast performs respiration using the sugar – similar to human respiration except yeast perform anaerobic respiration (without oxygen) rather than aerobic respiration (with oxygen). As it respires, it produces carbon dioxide gas. This is why yeast is used in such processes as brewing and bread making. The carbon dioxide gas makes bread rise and beer fizzy. Like all living organisms, yeast prefers certain conditions and certain food sources. For example, warm conditions are better for yeast than cold conditions, and certain sugars are better than others.

NATIONAL CURRICULUM LINKS:
- **Year 2 programme of study**: Living things and their habitats
  - Explore and compare the differences between things that are living, dead and things that have never been alive.
- **Year 6 programme of study**: Living things and their habitats
  - Describe how living things are classified into broad groups according to common observable characteristics and based on similarities and differences, including micro-organisms, plants and animals.

MATERIALS NEEDED:
- Packets of dried yeast (easy active is the best type to use)
- Clear plastic tubs or beakers
- Sugar
- Timers
- Teaspoons
- Measuring cylinder
- Rulers
- Water

 SAFETY AND TECHNICAL NOTES:
- Yeast produces carbon dioxide, so do not carry out any investigations in a sealed container as the pressure of the gas may lead to explosions.
- Children should wash their hands after the investigation.

METHOD:

TO BE DONE IN ADVANCE BY THE TEACHER:
Have the bowls of yeast and sugar ready for the children

 CHILDREN:

1 Put a teaspoon of yeast into two beakers.
2 Add 100ml of cold water to one beaker and 100ml of warm water to the other beaker.
3 Add 1 teaspoon of sugar to each beaker and stir for a few seconds using your teaspoon to dissolve the sugar.
4 Start your timer. Leave the beakers for 2 minutes.
5 Watch what is happening in the beakers and make notes on what you can see.
6 When the 2 minutes are up use the ruler to measure how high the froth is on top of each beaker. Write this down on your results table.
7 Repeat the investigation 2 more times. Wash out your beakers first or use new beakers.

 DATA COLLECTION IDEAS:

What I can see happening in the beakers:

Trial	Height of the froth (cm)	
	Warm water	Cold water
1		
2		
3		

DIFFERENTIATION:
- **Decrease the challenge:** The children may need help with measuring the height of the froth in the beakers.
- **Increase the challenge:** The children could carry out a systematic investigation over a range of temperatures rather than just two.

USEFUL QUESTIONS TO ASK THE CHILDREN:
- What did you observe happening in your beakers?
- Which temperature of water did the yeast prefer? How did you know this?
- What do we use yeast for?

FURTHER WORK:
A demonstration could be carried out by the teacher using boiling water to show that yeast will not be active in this temperature as the heat kills the yeast.

This work could also lead on to the children making their own bread using yeast with cross-curricular links to design and technology.

EXPERIMENT 12

What do plants need to grow?

LEARNING OBJECTIVES:
Investigate what plants need in order to grow healthily.

INTRODUCTION:
The children investigate the factors that plants need to grow by planting seeds under different conditions and observing how well they grow.

USEFUL PRIOR WORK:
The children should know that plants are living organisms and that they come from seeds or bulbs planted in the ground.

 BACKGROUND SCIENCE:
In order for plants to grow they require a source of light, water and carbon dioxide for photosynthesis. Plants are able to germinate (begin growing) in the dark as they do not need to make their own food via photosynthesis at this point. This is because they have a food source in the seed that they can use in the initial stages of growth. Plants germinated in the dark will often have taller stems then those germinated in the light because the plant is trying to grow towards a light source. However, the stems of plants grown in the dark will often be weak and spindly compared to the healthy stems of plants grown in the light. Plants grown without water will be weak and liable to wilt. This is because the plant cells will become flaccid due to there being little water in the cell. The water would normally fill the space inside the cell called a vacuole, which 'pushes against' the cell walls, keeping the cell rigid and the plant upright.

Temperature can also affect how well a plant grows, with most plants preferring warm conditions. This is because the enzymes in the plant need a certain temperature in order to work.

NATIONAL CURRICULUM LINKS:
* **Year 1 programme of study**: Plants
  – Identify and describe the basic structure of a variety of common flowering plants, including trees.
* **Year 2 programme of study**: Plants
  – Observe and describe how seeds and bulbs grow into mature plants.
  – Find out and describe how plants need water, light and a suitable temperature to grow and stay healthy.
* **Year 3 programme of study**: Plants
  – Explore the requirements of plants for life and growth (air, light, water, nutrients from soil and room to grow) and how they vary from plant to plant.

MATERIALS NEEDED:
* Easy-to-grow seeds, for example cress or runner beans
* Suitable container for growing the plants
* Compost
* Water
* Digital camera

SAFETY AND TECHNICAL NOTES:

- Tell children not to eat the seeds.
- Use seeds that have not been treated with pesticides. It should say on the packet.
- Children should wash their hands after the investigation.

METHOD:

TO BE DONE IN ADVANCE BY THE TEACHER:

Prepare spaces for the plants to be grown in, for example, a dark cupboard, a windowsill, on or near a radiator, in a cool box or fridge.

Decide what factors will be investigated, or let the children choose which one they want to investigate.

 CHILDREN:

1 Prepare your seed pots by filling each pot with some compost. Pat the compost down so that it fills the pot.
2 Depending on which seeds you chose, either sprinkle a few cress seeds on top of each pot or put one runner bean seed in each pot. Gently pat the seeds down into the compost. Do not push them down too far. They just need to be covered by the compost.
3 Water each pot gently (unless you are investigating the effect of not watering the seeds).
4 Choose where to put your pots. Make sure your pots are labelled.
5 Check on your pots every day to see what is happening.

 DATA COLLECTION IDEAS:

The children could take photographs of their pots or draw what they see each day. These pictures can then be arranged into a 'timeline of growth'.

DIFFERENTIATION:

- **Decrease the challenge:** The children may need help with planting the seeds in the pots.
- **Increase the challenge:** The children could perform more systematic investigations. For example, investigating how much water is needed for plants to germinate by growing seeds in pots of soil with increasing amounts of water.

USEFUL QUESTIONS TO ASK THE CHILDREN:

- Which condition produced the healthiest looking plant? Why do you think this was?
- Which condition produced the weakest looking plant? Why do you think this was?
- What are the best conditions for growing plants in?

FURTHER WORK:

This investigation could lead on to children growing plants in the garden. Now that they know what plants need in order to grow, they can be challenged to, for example, grow the tallest sunflower.

EXPERIMENT 13

What's growing where?

LEARNING OBJECTIVES:
Investigate what plants are growing around our school.

INTRODUCTION:
The children investigate the dispersal of different plants around the school grounds using quadrats.

USEFUL PRIOR WORK:
The children do not need to have any particular prior knowledge before completing this investigation.

 BACKGROUND SCIENCE:
Quadrats are basic squares that can be thrown easily and used for sampling (if quadrats are not available then plastic hoops will do just as well). Scientists carry out sampling because it would be impractical to measure every living organism in a particular area. For example, they may wish to know about the different types of trees growing in a rainforest. Instead of counting every tree in the rainforest, which would take a long time and a lot of resources, they will just count the trees in a number of randomly selected places. These places will usually represent about 10 per cent of the area being studied. The scientists will then infer that whatever is growing in the random places they chose will also be growing (in the same ratios) in the rest of the forest. They can then extrapolate their results to work out (approximately) how many different trees are growing in the rainforest and in what quantities.

NATIONAL CURRICULUM LINKS:
- **Year 2 programme of study**: Living things and their habitats
  - Identify that most living things live in habitats to which they are suited and describe how different habitats provide for the basic needs of different kinds of animals and plants, and how they depend on each other.
  - Identify and name a variety of plants and animals in their habitats, including microhabitats.
- **Year 4 programme of study**: Living things and their habitats
  - Explore and use classification keys to help group, identify and name a variety of living things in their local and wider environment.
- **Year 6 programme of study**: Evolution and inheritance
  - Identify how animals and plants are adapted to suit their environment in different ways and that adaptation may lead to evolution.

MATERIALS NEEDED:
- Quadrats or plastic hoops
- Plant identification key
- Digital camera (optional)
- Data-loggers (optional)

 SAFETY AND TECHNICAL NOTES:
- Children should not remove any plants or animals from the habitat they are investigating.
- Tell the children not to throw the quadrats or plastic hoops up in the air to avoid the risk of injury.
- It is worth doing a 'sample' quadrat with the children so that they understand the process of throwing the quadrat and how to count the plants inside the quadrat.

- For areas covered by large amounts of one material, for example grass or soil, tell the children to estimate how much of the quadrat is covered by that material as fraction or a percentage and use that as the result. For example, 30%, etc.

METHOD:

TO BE DONE IN ADVANCE BY THE TEACHER:

Have some suitable plant identification keys or books available. Choose suitable places for the sampling.

 CHILDREN:

1 Choose the area you want to sample then throw your quadrat (not too high!) so that it lands on the ground.
2 If you are using a digital camera, take a photo of the area inside your quadrat.
3 Now count how many different types of plant are in your quadrat. Write this down in your results table.
4 If using a data-logger, you can record the light levels and temperature inside your quadrat.

✎ DATA COLLECTION IDEAS:

The children could use a digital camera to take a photo of each of their quadrats, or alternatively they could draw what they see.

Temperature: _____   Light levels: _____

Quadrat 1	
Type of plant or material	Number or % present

DIFFERENTIATION:

- **Decrease the challenge:** The children may find it easier to have their quadrats placed in random areas for them that are likely to produce a pattern of results, for example under a tree, in a sunny spot, etc.
- **Increase the challenge:** The children could take more measurements for each quadrat, for example soil moisture level, soil pH, wind speed, etc.

USEFUL QUESTIONS TO ASK THE CHILDREN:

- Which plant did you see the most often in your quadrats?
- Why do you think there were different plants growing in different places?
- Was there any pattern between the light levels/temperature and the type or amount of plants growing in your quadrat?

FURTHER WORK:

This investigation could be linked to the children studying different habitats – for example desert, rainforest, arctic – and the type of plants that grow there.

EXPERIMENT 14

Brushing our teeth

LEARNING OBJECTIVES:
Investigate the best way to brush our teeth.

INTRODUCTION:
The children investigate how to brush their teeth properly by using disclosing tablets to show the plaque that is present on their teeth.

USEFUL PRIOR WORK:
The children should know that they have to brush their teeth regularly to keep them clean, otherwise they may decay.

 BACKGROUND SCIENCE:
Dental plaque is a film that forms over our teeth. It contains millions of bacteria that live on our teeth. Those bacteria feed on the sugars from the food we eat. As they feed, they produce an acid that breaks down the enamel on our teeth, causing tooth decay. The best way to remove this film of bacteria is by brushing and flossing our teeth. Generally, plaque is easiest to remove from the front surfaces of the teeth as the toothbrush can easily reach those parts. Between the teeth and along the gum-line are harder to reach, particularly for children, as the brush needs to be angled a certain way. Disclosing tablets can help with tooth brushing as they stain the plaque, making it easy to see. When the stain has been removed, it means the plaque has been removed.

NATIONAL CURRICULUM LINKS:
- **Year 2 programme of study**: Animals, including humans
  - Describe the importance for humans of exercise, eating the right amounts of different types of food and hygiene.
- **Year 4 programme of study**: Animals, including humans
  - Identify the different types of teeth in humans and their simple functions.
- **Year 6 programme of study**: Animals, including humans
  - Recognise the impact of diet, exercise, drugs and lifestyle on the way their bodies function.

MATERIALS NEEDED:
- Dental disclosing tablets
- Toothbrushes
- Toothpaste
- Water
- Mirrors
- Beakers – ideally disposable plastic beakers
- Print-outs of an open mouth showing the teeth that the children can draw on

 SAFETY AND TECHNICAL NOTES:
- If doing this investigation with very young children, use a low fluoride toothpaste.
- Use plastic mirrors if possible.
- Ideally, do this investigation after lunch when the children are likely to have eaten something and therefore increased the amount of plaque on their teeth.

- Pour the contents of the beakers down the sink immediately after the investigation. Dispose of the beakers or, if that is not possible, ensure they washed at a high temperature with plenty of soapy water.
- Ensure children do not share toothbrushes and dispose of toothbrushes after the experiment.
- Ensure parental permission has been given for this experiment.

METHOD:

TO BE DONE IN ADVANCE BY THE TEACHER:
Read the instructions on how to use the disclosing tablets. Print out the mouth and teeth picture, one per student.

 CHILDREN:

1 Use the disclosing tablet to stain the plaque in your mouth. Your teacher will tell you how to use it.
2 Use the mirror to look in your mouth. Where can you see the plaque? Where on your teeth is there the most plaque? The darker the stain, the more plaque there is.
3 On your picture of a mouth, colour in wherever you can see plaque in your own mouth. Make the colour darker for where there is lots of plaque and lighter for where there is less plaque.
4 Fill a beaker with water. Use this beaker to dip your toothbrush into as you brush your teeth. Have one empty beaker to spit into. Use the toothbrush and toothpaste to brush the plaque off your teeth. When the stain is gone you have removed the plaque.
5 Think about how you need to hold and move the toothbrush. Do you have to move it in different ways in different parts of your mouth? Are some areas of plaque easier or harder to remove?

 DATA COLLECTION IDEAS:
The children can colour in a print out of a mouth showing where the plaque was located on their teeth. Alternatively 'before and after' photos can be taken.

DIFFERENTIATION:
- **Decrease the challenge:** The children may need help with using a proper brushing technique.
- **Increase the challenge:** The children could carry out a more systematic investigation, for example by comparing their plaque levels at different times of the day.

USEFUL QUESTIONS TO ASK THE CHILDREN:
- Where on your teeth did you have the most/least plaque? Why do you think this was?
- Which areas of your mouth were the hardest/easiest to brush?
- What was the best way to brush your teeth?

FURTHER WORK:
The children could investigate all the ways of helping to keep your teeth healthy – for example, brushing, flossing, using mouthwash, not eating too many sugary foods – and produce a health leaflet designed for children.

EXPERIMENT 15

Design a seed!

LEARNING OBJECTIVES:
Design a plant seed that can be easily dispersed.

INTRODUCTION:
The children design a seed that can be dispersed via either wind, animal or water dispersal.

USEFUL PRIOR WORK:
The children should know that plants grow from seeds and that plants compete for water, light and space to grow.

 BACKGROUND SCIENCE:
Seed dispersal is the name given to the process whereby seeds are transported away from the parent plant. Plants disperse their seeds away from themselves for different reasons. First, the parent plant will not have to compete for light, water, space, etc. with the offspring if the seeds are dispersed away from the parent plant. The plant will also be able to colonise a larger area if the seeds are spread around, thus helping to ensure its survival. Seed dispersal may also lower the problems caused by risk of pests or predators, which tend to favour areas with high densities of a particular plant.

Seeds can be dispersed in different ways. The most common are via the wind, via explosion from the parent plant, by animal transportation – either externally by becoming stuck onto their bodies or internally be being ingested and then the seeds being excreted – and via water transportation.

NATIONAL CURRICULUM LINKS:
* **Year 1 programme of study**: Plants
   – Identify and describe the basic structure of a variety of common flowering plants, including trees.
* **Year 2 programme of study**: Plants
   – Observe and describe how seeds and bulbs grow into mature plants.
* **Year 3 programme of study**: Plants
   – Explore the part that flowers play in the life cycle of flowering plants, including pollination, seed formation and seed dispersal.
   – Describe the life processes of reproduction in some plants and animals.
* **Year 4 programme of study**: Living things and their habitats
   – Recognise that living things can be grouped in a variety of ways.
* **Year 6 programme of study**: Plants
   – Give reasons for classifying plants and animals based on specific characteristics.

MATERIALS NEEDED:
* Selection of materials from which the children can make their seeds, for example plastic bottles, paper bags, straws, plasticine, paperclips, balloons, pipe-cleaners, kitchen roll tubes, etc.
* Photographs of seeds that are dispersed by wind, water and animals

 SAFETY AND TECHNICAL NOTES:
* Make sure any containers that used to contain food have been thoroughly cleaned.

METHOD:

TO BE DONE IN ADVANCE BY THE TEACHER:

Have a selection of materials ready for the children to choose from. Either divide the children into equal numbers – designing a seed for wind dispersal, water dispersal and animal dispersal – or have the children choose which one they would like to do.

 ### CHILDREN:

1   You are going to design a seed that will be good at being dispersed by either wind, animals or water.
2   Look at the photos you have been given with examples for your type of seed. What do they have in common? What makes them good at being dispersed by that method?
3   Look at the materials you can choose from and draw some possible designs for your seed. When you are happy with your final design, you can begin making your seed. Remember, your seed will be a lot bigger than real seeds!
4   When you have finished, test your seed to see how well it can disperse.

 ### DATA COLLECTION IDEAS:

The children can draw or take photographs of their seeds. Additionally the seeds can be 'tested' to see how well they disperse. For example, the wind dispersal seeds can be thrown or dropped, the water dispersal seeds can be placed on water to see how they float and the animal dispersal seeds can be attached to a rough fabric, for example a woolly jumper, to see if they 'stick' to it like they would on a passing animal.

DIFFERENTIATION:

- **Decrease the challenge:** The children could work in small groups for this investigation.
- **Increase the challenge:** The children could make more than one seed and test them to see which one is the best design for dispersing by that method.

USEFUL QUESTIONS TO ASK THE CHILDREN:

- What features did your seed need to have in order to be dispersed?
- Why do you think plants try to disperse their seeds as far away as they can?
- What would happen to plant seeds if they could not be dispersed?

FURTHER WORK:

The children could investigate other methods of seed dispersal – for example exploding, like in pea pods, or via internal animal dispersal through fruits such as tomatoes.

Find the stomata

LEARNING OBJECTIVES:

Observing the stomata on leaves.

INTRODUCTION:

The children investigate the stomata found on different leaves by painting them with clear nail varnish, peeling the nail varnish off the leaf and examining it with a magnifying glass.

USEFUL PRIOR WORK:

The children should know that plants make their own food by the process of photosynthesis.

 BACKGROUND SCIENCE:

Plants use the process of photosynthesis to make their own food. One of the requirements for photosynthesis is carbon dioxide, which plants take in as a gas from the atmosphere. The carbon dioxide enters the plant through small holes on the underside of their leaves called stoma (plural stomata). These holes are surrounded by guard cells, which open and close the stomata. Oxygen (a by-product of photosynthesis) is also released into the atmosphere through the stomata. The stomata are not open all the time as water can be lost through them by the process of transpiration. Instead, the stomata tend to be open during the day, when the plant can photosynthesise, and closed during the night when they are not photosynthesising. Different plants have different numbers and sizes of stomata.

NATIONAL CURRICULUM LINKS:

- **Year 2 programme of study**: Plants
  - Find out and describe how plants need water, light and a suitable temperature to grow and stay healthy.
- **Year 3 programme of study**: Plants
  - Identify and describe the functions of different parts of flowering plants: roots, stem/trunk, leaves and flowers.
  - Explore the requirements of plants for life and growth (air, light, water, nutrients from soil and room to grow) and how they vary from plant to plant.

MATERIALS NEEDED:

- A selection of leaves from different plants and tress (these can either be provided by the teacher or the children can collect their own from the school grounds)
- Clear nail varnish
- Microscopes or powerful magnifying glasses
- Hairdryer (optional)

 SAFETY AND TECHNICAL NOTES:

- Nail varnish can be flammable so should be kept away from any naked flames. A water-based varnish can be used instead if nail varnish is not allowed on site.
- Tell the children not to 'sniff' the nail varnish.
- The children should wash their hands after the investigation.
- Adults should operate the hairdryer or supervise children while they are using it.

METHOD:

TO BE DONE IN ADVANCE BY THE TEACHER:

If providing the children with the leaves, ensure you have a large selection of leaves available from different plants. Alternatively, have children collect the leaves they wish to test. If possible, wash the leaves the day before to remove dirt from them before the investigation. Make sure the leaves are dry before carrying out the investigation.

 CHILDREN:

1 Select the first leaf you wish to test.
2 Paint a thin layer of clear nail varnish over the bottom (not the shiny side) of the leaf. Allow it to dry or have the teacher dry it for you with a hairdryer.
3 When the polish is dry, carefully peel the nail varnish off the leaf. You may need an adult to help you do this.
4 Place the nail varnish you have peeled off under a microscope or look at it using a magnifying lens.
5 See if you can spot any stomata (they will look like small circles).
6 If you can see any stomata, count how many there are and write it on your results table.
7 Repeat the above on the top (shiny side) of your leaf.
8 Now do the same for your other leaves.

 DATA COLLECTION IDEAS:

Drawing of the leaf	Number of stomata on the bottom of the leaf	Number of stomata on the top of the leaf

DIFFERENTIATION:

• **Decrease the challenge:** Magnifying lenses or a visualiser can be used to observe the nail varnish.
• **Increase the challenge:** Microscopes can be used to observe the nail varnish, but the children may still need help with focusing them.

USEFUL QUESTIONS TO ASK THE CHILDREN:

• Where did you find most stomata, on the top or bottom of the leaves? Why do you think this was?
• Which leaf had the biggest number of stomata? Why do you think this was?
• Which leaf had the smallest number of stomata? Why do you think this was?

FURTHER WORK:

The teacher could carry out a demonstration of a water plant, such as pondweed, in a beaker of water. The water will allow the bubbles of gas (oxygen) given off by the plant to be seen, visually showing the role of the stomata.

EXPERIMENT 17

Chewing food

LEARNING OBJECTIVES:
Investigate the effect chewing has on food.

INTRODUCTION:
The children investigate the effect of chewing on different types of food by observing the food before it is chewed and then observing the changes as they chew it.

USEFUL PRIOR WORK:
The children should know that the role of the teeth is to chew our food.

 BACKGROUND SCIENCE:
Chewing is the first stage of the digestion process. It performs a number of functions. First, the teeth mechanically break up the food into smaller pieces, making it easier to swallow. Second, the salvia helps to moisten the food and form it into a 'ball', again making it easier to swallow. The saliva also contains enzymes, which break down starch into sugars. This is why if you chew on a piece of starchy food, for example bread, for a long time, it will eventually taste sweet. The process of chewing also alerts the stomach that food will be swallowed soon, which causes the stomach to become ready for the next stage of digestion. Humans have different types of teeth for different purposes. Incisors are designed for biting, canines are designed for tearing and molars are designed for grinding.

NATIONAL CURRICULUM LINKS:
- **Year 2 programme of study**: Animals, including humans
  - Find out about and describe the basic needs of animals, including humans, for survival (water, food and air).
- **Year 3 programme of study**: Animals, including humans
  - Identify that animals, including humans, need the right types and amount of nutrition, and that they cannot make their own food; they get nutrition from what they eat.
- **Year 4 programme of study**: Animals, including humans
  - Describe the simple functions of the basic parts of the digestive system in humans.
  - Identify the different types of teeth in humans and their simple functions.
- **Year 6 programme of study**: Animals, including humans
  - Describe the way in which nutrients and water are transported within animals, including humans.

MATERIALS NEEDED:
- A selection of foods for the children to chew, including dry bread, dry crackers, cut up pieces of raw fruit and vegetables and canned fruit
- Bowls or paper towels

 SAFETY AND TECHNICAL NOTES:
- Ensure the area where the children will be eating the food is clean.
- Children should wash their hands before and after the investigation.
- Be aware of any allergies.
- It may be helpful for the children to take a sip of water between each of their investigations.

METHOD:

TO BE DONE IN ADVANCE BY THE TEACHER:
Prepare the food by cutting them into small, bite-size chunks. Place them into bowls or on paper towels.

 CHILDREN:

1 Take a piece of dry bread. Observe it closely. What does it look like and feel like? Write your observations in your results table.
2 Chew the piece of bread slowly (do not swallow it!). What can you feel happen? What does the bread taste like? Hold the bread in your mouth for as long as possible. You may find it starts to taste sweet. This is because enzymes are breaking down the starch in the bread into sugars.
3 Now do the same with the dry cracker. Write down your observations in your results table.
4 Now try doing the same with the rest of the foods you have been given.

 DATA COLLECTION IDEAS:

Food	Observations before chewing the food	Observations while chewing the food

DIFFERENTIATION:
- **Decrease the challenge:** The children could be provided with a 'bank' of words that they can use to describe the foods before, during and after chewing.
- **Increase the challenge:** The children could carry out a more systematic investigation of starchy foods by chewing different types of starchy food – for example different types of bread, crackers, breadsticks, etc. – and seeing how long it takes for them to start tasting sweet.

USEFUL QUESTIONS TO ASK THE CHILDREN:
- What was similar about the foods when you chewed them?
- What was different about the foods when you chewed them?
- Why do you think it is useful for us to chew our food?

FURTHER WORK:
The children could study the jaws and teeth of different animals (for example herbivores and carnivores) and relate this to the type of food that they eat.

Green worms!

LEARNING OBJECTIVES:
Investigate how camouflage helps animals to survive.

INTRODUCTION:
The children investigate how camouflage can help species to survive by seeing how many 'worms' of different colours can be spotted on the ground.

USEFUL PRIOR WORK:
The children should know what camouflage is and that some animals are able to camouflage themselves.

BACKGROUND SCIENCE:
Camouflage is a type of adaptation that certain plants and animals exhibit. It enables organisms to either blend into their environment (for example, a lion in the savannah) or enables the organisms to blend into each other (for example a herd of zebras). This makes it harder for predators or prey to spot the animal, meaning that animal is more likely to survive. Camouflage is the result of evolution, whereby species adapt and evolve over millions of years and become better suited to their environment. As evolution is such a long process, any dramatic change in an environment can have devastating impacts on the organisms that live there, as they are not able to adapt quickly enough to their new habitat.

NATIONAL CURRICULUM LINKS:
- **Year 2 programme of study**: Living things and their habitats
  - Identify that most living things live in habitats to which they are suited and describe how different habitats provide for the basic needs of different kinds of animals and plants, and how they depend on each other.
- **Year 4 programme of study**: Living things and their habitats
  - Recognise that environments can change and that this can sometimes pose dangers to living things.
- **Year 6 programme of study**: Evolution and inheritance
  - Identify how animals and plants are adapted to suit their environment in different ways and that adaptation may lead to evolution.

MATERIALS NEEDED:
- Cocktails sticks painted in four different colours: green, brown, red and blue
- Timers
- Tweezers

 SAFETY AND TECHNICAL NOTES:
- The children should only pick up the 'worms' using the tweezers to avoid injury.
- The children should sit down while carrying out the investigation.
- The children should wash their hands after the investigation.

METHOD:

TO BE DONE IN ADVANCE BY THE TEACHER:

Prepare the cocktails sticks, which should be painted or dyed into the four different colours. Give each group of children twenty of each type of 'worm'. Put them all into one pot so that they are mixed up. Choose a suitable area for the investigation.

 CHILDREN:

1 Scatter the worms on the grass.
2 Sit down next to the 'worms'. Put the pot that contained the worms on the grass next to you.
3 When your partner tells you to start, begin collecting the worms you can see using the tweezers. Put the worms you collect into your pot.
4 Have your partner time you for 30 seconds. Stop when they tell you to.
5 Count up how many worms of the different colours you managed to pick up. Record this in your results table.
6 Repeat the investigation. This time scatter the worms on some bare soil.

 DATA COLLECTION IDEAS:

Colour of worm	Number picked up	
	On grass	On soil
Green		
Brown		
Red		
Blue		

DIFFERENTIATION:

- **Decrease the challenge:** Some children may find using the tweezers difficult. They could do the investigation using different coloured, thin straws that have been cut up into small pieces. They could then use their hands to pick them up.
- **Increase the challenge:** The children could investigate more surfaces from which to pick up the worms. For example, they could look at patterned surfaces and multi-coloured surfaces and see what effect this has.

USEFUL QUESTIONS TO ASK THE CHILDREN:

- Which colour worm was hardest/easiest to see on the grass? Why do you think this was?
- Which colour worm was hardest/easiest to see on the soil? Why do you think this was?
- What do you think would happen to the red and blue worms if they lived on the grass?

FURTHER WORK:

This investigation could have cross-curricular links with art. The children could design and paint an animal that is camouflaged to live in a particular area of the school.

EXPERIMENT 19

How varied are we?

LEARNING OBJECTIVES:

Investigate how much variation there is in our class.

INTRODUCTION:

The children investigate how much variation there is in the class by carrying out a whole class survey for characteristics such as height, shoe size, eye colour, etc.

USEFUL PRIOR WORK:

The children do not need to have any particular prior knowledge before completing this practical but should be able to use simple measuring devices, for example tape-measures.

 BACKGROUND SCIENCE:

All living organisms can be broken down into different categories and sub-categories. For example, humans belong to the animal kingdom and the sub-class mammals. The smallest category of classification is species. For humans, our species name is *Homo sapiens*. All members of the same species share similar characteristics and look similar. However, they are not identical. There will be variation within the species. This is due to both genetics and environmental factors. For example, humans inherit genes that influence our height and weight from our parents, but our diet as children may also affect our height and weight. Variation is good for species. In wild animals, it means there are more genes in the gene-pool, which means it is more likely that favourable genes will be passed on to the next generation.

NATIONAL CURRICULUM LINKS:

- **Year 1 programme of study**: Animals, including humans
  - Identify, name, draw and label the basic parts of the human body and say which part of the body is associated with each sense.
- **Year 5 programme of study**: Animals, including humans
  - Describe the changes as humans develop to old age.
- **Year 6 programme of study**: Evolution and inheritance
  - Recognise that living things produce offspring of the same kind, but normally offspring vary and are not identical to their parents.

MATERIALS NEEDED:

- A range of measuring equipment, for example tape-measures, string, rulers, callipers, etc.

 SAFETY AND TECHNICAL NOTES:

- Be sensitive to the emotional reactions of children. Do not, for example, weigh all the children in the class, and be aware of issues regarding genetics for children who are adopted.

METHOD:

TO BE DONE IN ADVANCE BY THE TEACHER:

Decide with the class what variation they will investigate. The children may all look at the same variation or different groups could investigate different types of variation and the results could be pooled together at the end. Good things to investigate include hair colour, eye colour, height, shoe size, hand span, length of stride, head circumference, length of index finger, ability to roll tongue, attached or non-attached ear lobes, right-handed or left-handed.

 CHILDREN:

1 Make a table that lists all the variation you will be investigating. Make sure it is big enough to include everyone in your class.
2 Decide what variation you wish to investigate.
3 Begin your investigation. You may need to use measuring equipment for some of the variations you are investigating.
4 Put your results in your results table as you collect them.

 DATA COLLECTION IDEAS:

The children can design their own basic table that lists the variation they will be investigating. Make sure the children's tables are correct before they begin their investigation.

DIFFERENTIATION:

- **Decrease the challenge:** The children could do the investigation on themselves – for example, drawing around their feet/hands, colouring in a picture of themselves, measuring their height with the help of an adult. These pictures and results could then be put onto a class display.
- **Increase the challenge:** The children could be encouraged to investigate a variation that is harder to measure – for example, width of index finger nail.

USEFUL QUESTIONS TO ASK THE CHILDREN:

- Which category had the most/least variation? Why do you think this was?
- Did any of your findings surprise you?
- Why do you think there was so much variation in our class?

FURTHER WORK:

The children could investigate variation for a different species, for example cats, dogs, or beetles. They could use photographs of different members of that species and complete a similar activity or they could move on to designing classification keys.

Colourful carnations

LEARNING OBJECTIVES:
Investigate how water travels in plants.

INTRODUCTION:
The children investigate how water travels in plants by using carnations and food colouring. The children place the carnation into water coloured with the food colouring and observe the effects.

USEFUL PRIOR WORK:
The children should know that plants need water in order to grow and stay alive.

 BACKGROUND SCIENCE:
Plants take in water via their roots. The water then travels up the stem in tubes called xylem. The reason the water travels up the stem (against the flow of gravity) is due to two processes called transpiration and capillary action. The leaves of a plant allow a small amount of water to leave the plant by evaporation (the water escapes through holes in the leaves called stomata). This process of water leaving the plant through the leaves is called transpiration. As it evaporates from the leaves water is 'pulled' up the stem from the roots. This is similar to the way a straw works. This is called capillary action. The water is easily pulled up the plant because the xylem tubes are very thin. Once the water has been taken up the stem it can then be transported around the rest of the plant, including to the leaves and flowers.

NATIONAL CURRICULUM LINKS:
- **Year 1 programme of study**: Plants
  - Identify and describe the basic structure of a variety of common flowering plants, including trees.
- **Year 2 programme of study**: Plants
  - Find out and describe how plants need water, light and a suitable temperature to grow and stay healthy.
- **Year 3 programme of study**: Plants
  - Investigate the way in which water is transported within plants.

MATERIALS NEEDED:
- White carnations
- Food colouring
- See-through beakers
- Water
- Knife
- Digital camera (optional)

SAFETY AND TECHNICAL NOTES:

- Trim the stems under water to create a fresh cut on each flower and to encourage longer blooming.
- Make sure the beakers are tall enough to stay upright when the carnations are in them.
- Only adults should cut the carnation stems in half.
- It takes about 24 hours for effect to be fully seen so it is best to start the investigation at the end of the day and observe the carnations again the following day.

METHOD:

TO BE DONE IN ADVANCE BY THE TEACHER:

For each group or child, cut one carnation stem in half lengthwise so that one half of the stem can be put into one beaker and the other half of the stem can be put into another beaker. Try to get the end of the cut as close to the flower as possible.

 CHILDREN:

1 You will need four beakers. Fill each of them with water.
2 Add about ten drops of food colouring to two of your beakers. Leave two of your beakers as plain water.
3 Put one carnation into a beaker with plain water and put one carnation into a beaker with food colouring.
4 Take the carnation that has been cut down the middle of the stem. Place one half of the stem into a beaker of plain water and place the other end into a beaker with food colouring. You will need to keep the beakers close together so you do not break the stem.
5 Predict what will happen in a few hours to your carnation. What do you think it will look like?

 DATA COLLECTION IDEAS:

The children could draw and colour in their carnations or they could take before and after photographs of them.

DIFFERENTIATION:

- **Decrease the challenge:** The children can be helped to set up their split carnation.
- **Increase the challenge:** The children could create a range of coloured water, from very strong to very dilute, and observe the effects.

USEFUL QUESTIONS TO ASK THE CHILDREN:

- What do you think will happen to the carnations? Why do you think this?
- What has happened to our carnations? Why do you think this is?
- What does this show about how water travels in plants?

FURTHER WORK:

The children could investigate how harmful pollution can be taken up by plants in water (like the food colouring in the investigation) and how this can be prevented, for example by not using pesticides.

Moving water

LEARNING OBJECTIVES:
Investigate how water can 'move' in and out of vegetables.

INTRODUCTION:
The children investigate what happens when pieces of carrot and celery are placed into water and salt water solutions.

USEFUL PRIOR WORK:
The children do not need to have any particular prior knowledge before completing this investigation.

 BACKGROUND SCIENCE:
The science behind this investigation is the effect of osmosis. Osmosis is the movement of water molecules from a solution with a low concentration of solute to a solution with a high concentration of solute through a partially permeable membrane. For osmosis to occur there needs to be two solutions of different concentrations, separated by a membrane. For example, if salt is added to water, that water will have a 'low concentration' of water molecules compared to water without any salt. In this investigation, pieces of carrot and celery are added to salt water and normal water. The membrane is the skin of the carrot and celery. The water will move according to whether the water inside the carrot or celery is more or less concentrated than the water in the beaker. If the water in the beaker contains more solute than the water in the carrot/celery, then the water will move from the carrot/celery into the beaker, leaving the carrot/celery shrivelled. If the water in the carrot/celery contains more solute than the water in the beaker, then the water will move from the beaker into the carrot/celery, leaving the carrot/celery swollen. Osmosis is the process by which plants take up water from the soil. The water in the roots of the plant is at a higher concentration than the water in the soil, causing the water to move from the soil into the root of the plant.

NATIONAL CURRICULUM LINKS:
- **Year 1 programme of study**: Plants
  - Identify and describe the basic structure of a variety of common flowering plants, including trees.
- **Year 2 programme of study**: Plants
  - Find out how plants need water, light and a suitable temperature to grow and stay healthy.
- **Year 3 programme of study**: Plants
  - Identify and describe the functions of different parts of flowering plants: roots, stem/trunk, leaves and flowers.
  - Investigate the way in which water is transported within plants.

MATERIALS NEEDED:
- Carrot
- Celery
- Beakers
- Warm water
- Salt
- Teaspoons
- Balance
- Knife
- Labels

 SAFETY AND TECHNICAL NOTES:
- Children should be told not to eat the carrot or celery.
- The water does not have to be boiling for this activity. Water from the hot tap will be sufficient.
- This investigation takes a few days so is best started on a Monday and finished on a Friday.

METHOD:

TO BE DONE IN ADVANCE BY THE TEACHER:
Cut up the carrot and celery into small chunks (about 2cm) if the children are not doing this themselves.

 CHILDREN:

1 You will need two pieces of carrot, two pieces of celery and four beakers.
2 Fill the beakers with water from the hot tap.
3 Add a few teaspoons of salt to two of the beakers. Stir the salt so that it dissolves. Label these two beakers 'salt water'. Label the other two beakers 'water'.
4 Weigh your pieces of carrot and celery using the balance. Record the mass on your results table. Draw a picture of what your carrot and celery look like and write a few words to describe them.
5 Put one piece of carrot into a beaker with the salt water and one piece of carrot into a beaker with just water.
6 Put one piece of celery into a beaker with the salt water and one piece of celery into the beaker with just water.
7 Put your beakers somewhere safe. Observe them each day. On the final day weigh your pieces of carrot and celery again and record this on your results table. Draw a picture of what your carrot and celery look like and write a few words to describe them.

 DATA COLLECTION IDEAS:

Vegetable	Before	Observations	
		After	
		Water	Salt water
Carrot	Mass	Mass	Mass
Celery	Mass	Mass	Mass

DIFFERENTIATION:
- **Decrease the challenge:** The children may need help with weighing the carrot/celery.
- **Increase the challenge:** The children can put the pieces of carrot/celery into the opposite beaker at the end of the investigation to see if they can reverse the effect. The salt should be washed of the carrot/celery first.

USEFUL QUESTIONS TO ASK THE CHILDREN:
- Why do you think the carrot/celery has shrivelled up?
- Why do you think the carrot/celery has swollen?
- How might the fact that water can 'move' be helpful to plants?

FURTHER WORK:
This investigation could be linked to plants and how plant roots take up water from the soil.

Bird beaks

LEARNING OBJECTIVES:
Investigate how birds' beaks are adapted to eat their food.

INTRODUCTION:
The children investigate adaptation by finding the best beak shape for eating different types of seeds.

USEFUL PRIOR WORK:
The children do not need to have any particular prior knowledge before completing this investigation.

 BACKGROUND SCIENCE:
All organisms are adapted to survive in the environment in which they live. This is the result of millions of years of evolution. For birds, this adaptation also includes having a beak that is best adapted for eating the type of food that they live on. Birds can eat a variety of different foods including worms, other insects, seeds, nuts and fruits. Most birds only eat a small range of foods due to the shape of their beaks. A bird that is adapted to eating the seeds from a sunflower, for example, would most likely have a small, pointed beak that is good at pecking away individual seeds. A bird that eats nuts, however, would need to have a much larger and more rounded beak.

NATIONAL CURRICULUM LINKS:
- **Year 1 programme of study**: Animals, including humans
  - Describe and compare the structure of a variety of common animals (fish, amphibians, reptiles, birds and mammals, including pets).
- **Year 2 programme of study**: Living things and their habitats
  - Identify that most living things live in habitats to which they are suited and describe how different habitats provide for the basic needs of different kinds of animals and plants, and how they depend on each other.
  - Describe how animals obtain their food from plants and other animals, using the idea of a simple food chain, and identify and name different sources of food.
- **Year 3 programme of study**: Animals, including humans
  - Identify that animals, including humans, need the right types and amount of nutrition, and that they cannot make their own food; they get nutrition from what they eat.
- **Year 4 programme of study**: Living things and their habitats
  - Recognise that environments can change and that this can sometimes pose dangers to living things.
- **Year 6 programme of study**: Evolution and inheritance
  - Identify how animals and plants are adapted to suit their environment in different ways and that adaptation may lead to evolution.

MATERIALS NEEDED:
* A selection of 'bird beaks', for example teaspoons, drinking straws, tweezers, large clothes pegs, chopsticks (ideally children's chopsticks that are held together at the top) and lolly sticks with sticky tape wrapped around them (sticky side outwards)
* A selection of 'bird food', for example chopped-up cooked spaghetti, chopped-up dry spaghetti, bird seed, nuts – large and small, raisins, uncooked rice, uncooked pasta

 SAFETY AND TECHNICAL NOTES:
* Remind the children not to eat any of the food.

METHOD:

TO BE DONE IN ADVANCE BY THE TEACHER:
Prepare the bird beaks and bird food. Place a mixture of the different bird food onto the centre of each table. Give each child on the table a different type of bird beak. Demonstrate how to use the different bird beaks so that the children know how to use them.

 CHILDREN:

1 Make sure you know how to use your bird beak.
2 When the teacher tells you to begin, try to collect as much bird food as you can. You may find some types of bird food easier to pick up than other types.
3 Stop when the teacher tells you to.
4 Count up how much of each type of bird food you managed to collect using your bird beak.

 DATA COLLECTION IDEAS:

Type of bird food	How much I collected

DIFFERENTIATION:
* **Decrease the challenge:** The children may find it hard to use the chopsticks and tweezers so these could be left out or an adult could take on the role of that 'bird'.
* **Increase the challenge:** The bird food could be placed in different containers that add to the challenge, for example the seeds could be placed into a small, plastic bottle so only small beaks can get to them.

USEFUL QUESTIONS TO ASK THE CHILDREN:
* Which food was the easiest/hardest for you to pick up using your beak? Why do you think this was?
* Why do you think that birds have different shaped beaks?
* What other factors might affect what kind of food a bird can eat?

FURTHER WORK:
The children could investigate specific examples of birds that have different beak shapes. They could find out what food that bird eats and why its beak is well adapted for the job.

Mouldy bread!

LEARNING OBJECTIVES:
Investigate the best conditions for growing mould on bread.

INTRODUCTION:
The children investigate the conditions needed for bread to develop mould by leaving bread in wet, dry, cold and warm conditions.

USEFUL PRIOR WORK:
The children should know that food can 'go bad' if left in the wrong conditions, and should not be eaten if it has gone bad.

 BACKGROUND SCIENCE:
Mould is an example of a fungus. Fungi belong to a separate kingdom of life (i.e. they are not plants or animals) and they fall into two categories – single-celled fungi (for example, yeast) and multi-cellular fungi (for example, mushrooms). Fungi do not contain chlorophyll and are therefore unable to make their own food via photosynthesis. Instead, they obtain their nutrition by breaking down organic matter. As fungi are living organisms, they require certain conditions in order to live. Fungi require water, a suitable temperature (generally warm but not too hot) and a supply of oxygen. If these conditions are not present then the fungi will not be able to live and reproduce. Not all moulds are harmful. For example, a mould produces the drug penicillin.

NATIONAL CURRICULUM LINKS:
- **Year 2 programme of study**: Living things and their habitats
  - Explore and compare the differences between things that are living, dead and things that have never been alive.
- **Year 2 programme of study**: Animals, including humans
  - Describe the importance for humans of exercise, eating the right amounts of different types of food and hygiene.
- **Year 4 programme of study**: Living things and their habitats
  - Recognise that living things can be grouped in a variety of ways.
- **Year 6 programme of study**: Living things and their habitats
  - Describe how living things are classified into broad groups according to common observable characteristics and based on similarities and differences, including micro-organisms, plants and animals.

MATERIALS NEEDED:
- Slices of white bread
- Zip-lock bags
- Sellotape
- Labels
- Water
- Acetate sheets printed with 1cm squares (optional)

 SAFETY AND TECHNICAL NOTES:
- Dispose of the mouldy bread as soon as it is no longer needed. Do not open the zip-lock bags at any point.
- It is best to begin this experiment at the start of the week so that the children can observe the bread every day for a week.

METHOD:

TO BE DONE IN ADVANCE BY THE TEACHER:
Have a suitable place to store the bread for the cold conditions investigation – a fridge or a cool box would be sufficient. If using a fridge that is used for storing food, place all the zip-lock bags into a large, plastic bag that is clearly labelled as 'not for consumption'.

 CHILDREN:

1 You need four slices of bread and four zip-lock bags. Place one slice of bread into a zip-lock bag. Close the bag and then seal the opening with Sellotape so that it is extra secure.
2 Label the bag 'dry bread, warm environment'.
3 Place another slice of bread into a zip-lock bag. Close the bag and then seal the opening with Sellotape again.
4 Label the bag and call it 'dry bread, cold conditions'.
5 Now, sprinkle a few drops of water onto the last two slices of bread. Do not make them wet, they should just be moist.
6 Place one of the slices into a zip-lock bag, close the bag and Sellotape the opening.
7 Label this bag and call it 'moist bread, cold environment'.
8 Place the last slice of bread into a zip-lock bag, close the bag and Sellotape the opening.
9 Label this bag and call it 'moist bread, warm environment'.
10 Place the bags labelled 'warm environment' somewhere warm, for example near a radiator (do not place them onto the radiator though).
11 Place the bags labelled 'cold environment' somewhere cold, for example a fridge or cool-bag.
12 Observe your bread slices everyday to see what happens.

 DATA COLLECTION IDEAS:
The children could take photographs of their bread slices everyday, draw the bread slices, or make detailed notes based on their observations. The children can examine their bread slices closely using a magnifying lens but they should not open the bags. The amount of mould growth can be measured using acetate printed with 1cm squares.

DIFFERENTIATION:
- **Decrease the challenge:** The children could simply rate the bread slices in the order of how much mould has grown on them rather than measuring the amount of mould.
- **Increase the challenge:** The children could carry out a more systematic investigation, for example comparing mould growth when different amounts of water are added to the bread.

USEFUL QUESTIONS TO ASK THE CHILDREN:
- Which conditions caused the most/least mould growth? Why do you think this was?
- What does the mould on your bread look like?
- What could we do to stop food going bad because of mould?

FURTHER WORK:
The children could investigate the uses of fungi – for example, looking at fungi used to make certain types of cheese and dried sausages.

Germinating seeds

LEARNING OBJECTIVES:
Investigate what different surfaces seeds will germinate on.

INTRODUCTION:
The children investigate whether seeds will germinate when planted on different substances.

USEFUL PRIOR WORK:
The children should know that plants grow from seeds and need to be planted on something in order to grow.

 BACKGROUND SCIENCE:
Germination is the first stage of plant growth. It lasts from when the plant first begins to emerge from the seed up until it has used up the food store in the seed and needs to start making its own food via photosynthesis. Seeds are usually capable of germinating on many different surfaces, not just compost or soil. This is because at this stage of its life, most of its needs are being met by what is stored in the seed. The plant does not need to take in any minerals and is too small to need 'anchoring' by roots into something to prevent it from falling over. The seed does, however, need water. This means that seeds will germinate on most surfaces as long as they are damp so that they have access to water.

NATIONAL CURRICULUM LINKS:
- **Year 1 programme of study:** Plants
  – Identify and describe the basic structure of a variety of common flowering plants, including trees.
- **Year 2 programme of study:** Plants
  – Observe and describe how seeds and bulbs grow into mature plants.
- **Year 3 programme of study:** Plants
  – Explore the requirements of plants for life and growth (air, light, water, nutrients from soil and room to grow) and how they vary from plant to plant.

MATERIALS NEEDED:
- Easy-to-grow plants seeds such as cress or mustard
- A variety of different mediums to grow the seeds on – for example, compost, paper towels, cotton wool, wood chips, sawdust, newspaper, used tea bag and gravel
- Petri dishes or lids from margarine tubs
- Water

 SAFETY AND TECHNICAL NOTES:
- The children should wash their hands after the investigation.

METHOD:

TO BE DONE IN ADVANCE BY THE TEACHER:
Have the growing mediums ready for the children to use. Dampen any of the growing mediums that are absorbent, for example the cotton wool. You may wish to let the children do this as part of their investigation. Select suitable places for the seeds to be left.

 CHILDREN:

1 Fill a Petri dish or margarine lid with each growing medium you are going to test.
2 Sprinkle some seeds over the growing medium. For any growing medium that is dry, gently pour over some water as well.
3 Leave your seeds somewhere safe. Come back and check on them everyday to see what happens. You may need to add some more water to your seeds.

 DATA COLLECTION IDEAS:
The children could take photographs of the seeds as they grow and use this a record of the seeds' growth. Emphasise to the children that they are not looking at how many seeds grew (as this was not a controlled variable in the investigation) but how well they grew, i.e. how quickly and how tall.

DIFFERENTIATION:
- **Decrease the challenge:** This could be carried out as a whole class investigation with each group investigating one growing medium.
- **Increase the challenge:** The children could plan a more detailed, fair test-style investigation and control more variables – for example the number of seeds, the amount of water, etc.

USEFUL QUESTIONS TO ASK THE CHILDREN:
- Which growing mediums did the plants grow well on? Why do you think this was?
- Which growing mediums did the plants not grow well on? Why do you think this was?
- Why do you think we usually plant seeds in compost/soil?

FURTHER WORK:
The children could carry on growing their seeds to see if the initial growing medium has any effect on the final plant.

EXPERIMENT 25

Fertilisers

LEARNING OBJECTIVES:
Investigate the effect of using fertilisers on plants.

INTRODUCTION:
The children investigate how fertilisers affect plant growth by growing plants with and without the use of common, household fertilisers.

USEFUL PRIOR WORK:
The children should know the basic requirements of plants.

 BACKGROUND SCIENCE:
Plants are living organisms and as such require certain conditions in order to live and grow. They require water, carbon dioxide, a suitable temperature and some kind of growing medium. However, they also need certain minerals in order to have healthy growth, and in some cases to be able to survive. These minerals are usually found in the soil and are 'recycled' back into the soil when a plant dies. The most common minerals needed are nitrogen, phosphorus, potassium and magnesium. Commercial 'plant food' is available that will usually contain some or all of these minerals. It is important to emphasise to the children that this is not really 'plant food', because plants make their own food via photosynthesis. Rather, it is extra nutrients that they need in order to stay healthy. If plants are lacking in minerals, their growth will often be stunted and they may have discoloured or yellowed leaves.

NATIONAL CURRICULUM LINKS:
- **Year 1 programme of study**: Plants
  - Identify and describe the basic structure of a variety of common flowering plants, including trees.
- **Year 2 programme of study**: Plants
  - Observe and describe how seeds and bulbs grow into mature plants.
  - Find out and describe how plants need water, light and a suitable temperature to grow and stay healthy.
- **Year 3 programme of study**: Plants
  - Explore the requirements of plants for life and growth (air, light, water, nutrients from soil and room to grow) and how they vary from plant to plant.

MATERIALS NEEDED:
- Quick-growing plants – radishes are particularly good for this
- Pots for growing the plants in
- Compost
- Water
- Commercial liquid plant food, for example Baby Bio

 SAFETY AND TECHNICAL NOTES:
- Supervise the children when they are using the fertilisers.
- Use liquid, household plant fertilisers, for example Baby Bio.
- The children should wash their hands after the investigation.

METHOD:

TO BE DONE IN ADVANCE BY THE TEACHER:
Make up the plant food according to the instructions. You should make up one batch that is the recommended amount of fertiliser and one batch that has half the recommended amount of fertiliser.

 CHILDREN:

1 You are going to grow three sets of plants. One without any fertiliser, one with half the recommended amount of fertiliser and one with the recommended amount of fertiliser.
2 Plant your seeds. Remember to keep it a fair test so think about how much compost and water to use.
3 Label one as 'no fertiliser'. Do not add any fertiliser to this pot.
4 Label one as 'half of the fertiliser'. Your teacher will give you the fertiliser you need to add to this pot.
5 Label one 'fertiliser'. Your teacher will give you the fertiliser you need to add to this pot.
6 Place all your pots in the same location to grow and examine them regularly as they grow.

 DATA COLLECTION IDEAS:
The children can examine their plants regularly and take photographs or draw what they can see. They can decide what factors mean the plant is growing 'well' – for example height, colour of leaves, number of leaves – and examine these in detail. If growing a root crop like radishes they could also examine the radishes produced in terms of size or mass.

DIFFERENTIATION:
• **Decrease the challenge:** This investigation could be carried out with house plants that are already grown. The children can compare what happens when one is given fertiliser and the other is not in terms of, for example, number of flowers produced. This investigation would need to be carried out over a longer period of time.
• **Increase the challenge:** The children could also investigate the effect of having too much fertiliser by growing a plant using more than the recommended amount of fertiliser. This typically causes very fast, but sometimes poor, growth and can affect crop production for example the size of the radishes produced.

USEFUL QUESTIONS TO ASK THE CHILDREN:
• What did our plant look like that was grown with: no fertiliser/half the recommended amount of fertiliser/the recommended amount of fertiliser? Why do you think this was?
• Why do you think farmers use fertilisers?
• Can you think of any bad things about using fertilisers when growing plants?

FURTHER WORK:
The children could investigate the commercial use of fertilisers in farms, including why they are used and the potential negative effects of using them. They could also compare fruit and vegetables grown organically with those grown using fertilisers.

Making an indicator

LEARNING OBJECTIVES:
Make an indicator from red cabbage.

INTRODUCTION:
The children make an indicator from red cabbage and use this to test whether some common household substances are acids, alkalis or neutral.

USEFUL PRIOR WORK:
The children do not need to have any particular prior knowledge before completing this investigation.

 BACKGROUND SCIENCE:
The word acid and alkali refer to the concentration of hydrogen ions in a substance. Acids have a high concentration of hydrogen ions while alkalis have a low concentration. The strength of an acid or alkali is measured using the pH scale. The pH scale runs from 1–14. Acids have a pH from 1–6. Alkalis have a pH from 8–14. Neutral substances have a pH of 7. Indicators are substances that change colour depending on whether an acid or an alkali is present. Red cabbage contains a substance called anthocyanin that can act as the indicator (this is also found in other purple vegetables, for example beetroot). When soaked in hot water the anthocyanin will be released. It turns pink in an acid, remains purple for a neutral substance and turns blue for an alkali.

NATIONAL CURRICULUM LINKS:
- **Year 5 programme of study**: Properties and changes of materials
  - Compare and group together everyday materials on the basis of their physical properties including their hardness, solubility, transparency, conductivity (electrical and thermal) and response to magnets.

MATERIALS NEEDED:
- A large red cabbage
- Knife (teacher only)
- Chopping board (or any suitable chopping surface)
- Large bowl
- Clear plastic cups or beakers
- Teaspoons
- A selection of common household substances. Examples could include: toothpaste, liquid soap, lemon juice, vinegar, orange juice, lemonade, cola, milk, baking soda, water, indigestion tablets, mild kitchen cleaner and cooking oil

 SAFETY AND TECHNICAL NOTES:
- The boiled water must be left to cool before being handled by the children.
- Tell the children not to eat any of the food items.
- The red cabbage can stain clothes and skin.

METHOD:

TO BE DONE IN ADVANCE BY THE TEACHER:
Chop up the red cabbage roughly and place it in the bowl. Boil a kettle then add the water to the bowl – just enough to cover the cabbage. Allow the red cabbage to steep in the water to allow the anthocyanin to be released (the water should go a deep purple colour). Leave the water to cool down.

 CHILDREN:

1 Set up a row of beakers or clear plastic cups.
2 Add one substance to be tested to each cup or beaker.
3 Add a few drops of the 'indicator' (the purple liquid) to one of these plastic cups or beakers. Swirl it around for a few seconds. If the substance you are testing is quite thick (for example toothpaste) it can be helpful to stir it using a teaspoon.
4 Record the colour change of the indicator in a table.
5 Repeat until all the substances have been tested (if you are stirring any substances then you must wash the spoon between the different substances).

 DATA COLLECTION IDEAS:

Substance	Colour seen	Acid, alkali or neutral?

DIFFERENTIATION:
- **Decrease the challenge:** The children could group photographs of the substances into 'acids', 'alkalis' and 'neutrals'.
- **Increase the challenge:** The children could try to make a neutral substance by mixing a known acid and known alkali together (make sure their choices are safe). They may need a few attempts in order to get the ratios correct.

USEFUL QUESTIONS TO ASK THE CHILDREN:
- What similarities are there between the substances that are acids?
- What similarities are there between the substances that are alkalis?
- How do you think we could make a neutral substance?

FURTHER WORK:
This activity could lead on to work on universal indicators that provide a range of colours that show how strong an acid or alkali is. Ask students if it is helpful to just know whether something is an acid or alkali or if it is better to know how strong it is. You can demonstrate this using the red cabbage indicator. Testing a strong acid such as limescale remover will turn the indicator red. Testing a strong alkali such as oven cleaner will turn the indicator green. NOTE: These should only be demonstrated by the teacher and not conducted by the students. Both substances are corrosive and will burn if they come into contact with the skin.

M&M chromatography

LEARNING OBJECTIVES:
Find out what coloured dyes are used in M&Ms.

INTRODUCTION:
The children will perform a basic chromatography on sweets, for example M&Ms in order to see what coloured dyes are used in the different coloured sweets.

USEFUL PRIOR WORK:
The children should know that mixtures can be separated.

 BACKGROUND SCIENCE:
Chromatography is a separation technique used to separate out different coloured compounds. Dots of the dye are placed at the bottom of a strip of paper, which is then placed upright into a solvent that the dyes will dissolve in. As the solvent travels up the paper, it carries the dissolved dyes with it. The dyes will be carried different distances along the chromatography paper according to how heavy the dye is. 'Heavier' dyes are not carried as far by the solvent, so are deposited first. 'Lighter' dyes are able to be carried further so are deposited later. Chromatography is usually carried out using chromatography paper, but coffee filter paper achieves similar results.

NATIONAL CURRICULUM LINKS:
• **Year 5 programme of study**: Properties and changes of materials
  – Use knowledge of solids, liquids and gases to decide how mixtures might be separated through filtering, sieving and evaporating.

MATERIALS NEEDED:
• M&Ms of different colours
• Coffee filter paper
• Clean paintbrushes
• Small beakers
• Pencils
• Paper towels
• Water

 SAFETY AND TECHNICAL NOTES:
• The children should be told not to eat the M&Ms unless they have been given permission to do so.
• Be aware that not all brands of M&Ms are suitable for vegetarians. Check the packaging.
• Smarties do not generally produce good results as they are now made from natural dyes that tend not to contain mixtures of colours.

METHOD:

TO BE DONE IN ADVANCE BY THE TEACHER:
Separate the M&Ms into their different colours and place them into separate containers.

 CHILDREN:

1 Choose the first M&M you want to test.
2 Write the colour of the M&M on the top of the coffee filter paper in pencil.
3 Put the M&M onto a paper towel and use a paintbrush and a small beaker of water to wet the M&M and transfer the dye onto the middle of the coffee filter paper.
4 Repeat until the M&M has gone white.
5 Add a couple of drops of water onto the coloured spot you have made on the filter paper.
6 Wait until the coloured dyes have separated out then fill in the results table.
7 Repeat the experiment with a different coloured M&M. Remember to clean your paintbrush and replace your water between each test.

 DATA COLLECTION IDEAS:

Colour of the M&M	Colours that we saw

DIFFERENTIATION:
- **Decrease the challenge:** The children could simply dry out the filter paper and use those for their results.
- **Increase the challenge:** The children could try the traditional chromatography technique. Wrap the top-end of a strip of coffee filter paper around a pencil. Place the dots of dye along the bottom-end of the strip, make sure they are not touching. Put enough water in a small beaker to just come up to the dots of dye. Place the strip into the beaker so that it is held in place by the pencil. The water will travel up the strip, separating out the dyes.

USEFUL QUESTIONS TO ASK THE CHILDREN:
- What colours did you find in the M&M?
- Which colours travelled the furthest/least distance? Why do you think this was?
- What other dyes could we separate using chromatography?

FURTHER WORK:
This investigation could be linked with cross-curricular work in art. The children could use the same technique to make pictures using water-based pens and water.

EXPERIMENT 28

Time to separate!

LEARNING OBJECTIVES:
Explore how to separate different mixtures.

INTRODUCTION:
The children investigate the best ways to separate different mixtures. They are provided with mixtures and a selection of different pieces of equipment to allow them to decide how best to separate the mixtures.

USEFUL PRIOR WORK:
Children should know what a mixture is.

 BACKGROUND SCIENCE:

A mixture is two or more substances that are physically mixed together, without any chemical bonds between the different substances. This is different from a compound where the substances are chemically joined together. This means that mixtures can be separated by physical processes such as filtering, sieving or using magnets. If a substance is dissolved in water it can be separated via distillation or evaporation. Separating mixtures is usually easier than separating compounds as the bonds holding the substances together in a compound would need to be broken. The method used to separate a mixture will depend on the properties of the substances in the mixture and the size of the particles in the mixture.

NATIONAL CURRICULUM LINKS:
- **Year 3 programme of study**: Forces and magnets
  - Observe how magnets attract or repel each other, and attract some materials and not others.
- **Year 4 programme of study**: States of matter
  - Compare and group materials together according to whether they are solids, liquids or gases.
- **Year 5 programme of study**: Properties and changes of materials
  - Use knowledge of solids, liquids and gases to decide how mixtures might be separated through filtering, sieving and evaporating.

MATERIALS NEEDED:
- A selection of different mixtures to separate – for example, marbles, sand and iron filings; water and dried rice; paperclips, sand and dried pasta; water and sand
- Equipment for separating mixtures – for example funnels, filter paper, sieves, magnets, beakers, cardboard

 SAFETY AND TECHNICAL NOTES:
- Supervise the children when they are using the iron filings.
- Use bar magnets wrapped in cling film, which will make it easier to remove the iron filings from the magnets.

METHOD:

TO BE DONE IN ADVANCE BY THE TEACHER:

Prepare a selection of mixtures that need to be separated. Have mixtures that contain two, three and more substances and mixtures that require different techniques to separate them.

 CHILDREN:

1 You will be given a selection of different mixtures to separate.
2 In your results table, write down what is in your first mixture. Decide how you will separate the different substances.
3 Try to separate the mixture into the different substances. Were you successful? Write down how you separated the mixture in your results table.
4 Now do the same with the rest of the mixtures.

 DATA COLLECTION IDEAS:

What is in the mixture?	Equipment we used to separate the mixture	How we separated the mixture	Were we successful in separating the mixture?

DIFFERENTIATION:

- **Decrease the challenge:** The children can be given mixtures that are simpler to separate.
- **Increase the challenge:** The children can be given mixtures that are harder to separate or be challenged to make their own separation devices, for example making a sieve from cardboard.

USEFUL QUESTIONS TO ASK THE CHILDREN:

- Which mixture was the easiest/hardest to separate? Why was this?
- What different separation techniques did you use?
- Were you able to successfully separate all of the mixtures? Would you do anything differently?

FURTHER WORK:

The children could learn about other separation techniques, for example chromatography.

EXPERIMENT 29

Dissolving sugars

LEARNING OBJECTIVES:
Investigating which type of sugar dissolves the fastest.

INTRODUCTION:
The children investigate which type of sugar dissolves the fastest by comparing granulated, icing, caster and brown sugar.

USEFUL PRIOR WORK:
The children should know what dissolving is and that sugar can dissolve in water.

 BACKGROUND SCIENCE:
A substance that can dissolve is called soluble. The liquid that it will dissolve in is called the solvent. Different substances may dissolve in different solvents. For example, nail varnish will not dissolve in water but will dissolve in acetone. Water is an example of a solvent that many substances will dissolve in. When a substance dissolves its particles become separated and spread out throughout the solvent. That is why they seem to 'disappear'. When a mixture is dissolved in a solvent we call the resulting mixture a solution. The solvent however can only 'hold' so much of the substance being dissolved. When no more of the substance can be dissolved in the solvent we say that it has become saturated. There are factors that can help speed up how fast a substance dissolves in a solvent. These include breaking up the substance into smaller pieces to increase its surface area, increasing the temperature of the water and stirring the mixture.

NATIONAL CURRICULUM LINKS:
- **Year 5 programme of study**: Properties and changes of materials
  - Know that some materials will dissolve in a liquid to form a solution, and describe how to recover a substance from a solution.
  - Use knowledge of solids, liquids and gases to decide how mixtures might be separated through filtering, sieving and evaporating.

MATERIALS NEEDED:
- Beakers
- Stirrers
- Measuring cylinders
- Timers
- Water
- Different types of sugar, for example granulated, caster, icing, brown

 SAFETY AND TECHNICAL NOTES:
- Boiling water is not needed for this experiment. Water from the hot tap will be sufficient.
- Remind the children not to eat the sugar.
- Remind the children that this is a fair test investigation so they will need to think about the variables they need to control.
- Encourage the children to use small amounts of sugar and stir the solution at some point in their investigations otherwise the sugar will take a very long time to dissolve.

METHOD:

TO BE DONE IN ADVANCE BY THE TEACHER:
Separate the different types of sugar into separate bowls. Label the bowls.

 CHILDREN:

1 Plan out your investigation, including the variables you need to control.
2 Choose which sugar you want to test first.
3 Measure out your sugar. Make sure you remember which sugar it is.
4 Measure out your water and add this to a beaker.
5 Add your sugar to the beaker and start the timer. Stir your sugar for as long as you decided to stir it in your plan.
6 Stop the timer when you can no longer see any sugar. Write the time in your results table. Repeat the investigation with this sugar two more times.
7 Repeat the investigation with the other sugars.

 DATA COLLECTION IDEAS:

Trial	Time taken to dissolve (s)			
	Granulated sugar	Icing sugar	Brown sugar	Caster sugar
I				
2				
3				
Average				

DIFFERENTIATION:
• **Decrease the challenge:** The children could have the water, temperature and amount of sugar prepared for them so they only have to concentrate on timing the sugar as it dissolves.
• **Increase the challenge:** The children could also investigate another factor, such as the effect of stirring.

USEFUL QUESTIONS TO ASK THE CHILDREN:
• Which sugar was the quickest/slowest to dissolve? Why do you think this was?
• What do you think would happen if we used boiling water instead?
• What effect do you think stirring the sugar had?

FURTHER WORK:
The teacher could carry out a demonstration using boiling water to show the children how much faster the sugar dissolves. A demonstration could also be set up with very cold water showing how long it will take the sugar to dissolve.

EXPERIMENT 30

Find the solvent!

LEARNING OBJECTIVES:
Find the right solvent for the right solute!

INTRODUCTION:
The children investigate which substance will dissolve in which solvent.

USEFUL PRIOR WORK:
The children should know what solvents and solutes are.

 BACKGROUND SCIENCE:
A solvent is a liquid that will dissolve a solid (solute). Solvents are usually compounds (two or more different types of atom chemically joined together). Different solvents will dissolve different solutes. Whether a solvent will dissolve a solute depends on the polarity of both the solvent and the solute. Solvents and solutes can be either polar or non-polar. This polarity is due to how the elements are bonded together in the solvent and solute. A polar solvent will only dissolve polar solutes and non-polar solvents will only dissolve non-polar solutes. Water is an example of a polar solvent and is often called the 'universal solvent' as it can dissolve a wide range of solutes. Vegetable oil and acetone are examples of non-polar solvents. Sugar is an example of a polar solute because it will dissolve in water but not vegetable oil or acetone. Lipstick is non-polar and will therefore dissolve in acetone. Wax is another non-polar solute and will dissolve in vegetable oil. Sand is an example of a solute that does not dissolve in any naturally occurring solvent.

NATIONAL CURRICULUM LINKS:
- **Year 5 programme of study**: Properties and changes of materials
  - Know that some materials will dissolve in a liquid to form a solution, and describe how to recover a substance from a solution.

MATERIALS NEEDED:
- Beakers
- Water
- Vegetable oil
- Nail polish remover
- Sugar
- Wax
- Sand
- Nail polish
- Cotton wool buds
- Measuring cylinders
- Teaspoons

 SAFETY AND TECHNICAL NOTES:
- Use warm water from the hot tap for this investigation.
- Ensure that the nail polish remover is the kind that contains acetone.
- Acetone (found in nail polish remover) is highly flammable, so keep the nail polish remover away from all naked flames. Supervise the children while using. Hand-sanitiser can be used instead if nail polish remover is not allowed on site.
- For the nail polish test, dip one end of a cotton wool bud in nail polish and leave it to dry. These can be prepared off site if nail polish is not allowed on site.
- For the wax test, grating small pieces of wax from a candle will produce suitable sized pieces of wax.
- Remind the children not to eat the sugar.
- The children should wash their hands after the investigation.

METHOD:

TO BE DONE IN ADVANCE BY THE TEACHER:
Prepare the nail polish and the wax tests (see technical notes).

 CHILDREN:

1 You will need three beakers.
2 Beaker 1: Use the measuring cylinder to measure 100ml of water. Add this to the beaker and label it 'water'.
3 Beaker 2: Use the measuring cylinder to measure 100ml of vegetable oil. Add this to the beaker and label it 'vegetable oil'.
4 Beaker 3: Use the measuring cylinder to measure 100ml of nail polish remover. Add this to the beaker and label it 'nail polish remover'.
5 Add 1 teaspoon of sugar to each beaker and stir. Does the sugar dissolve? Write the result in your results table.
6 Add 1 teaspoon of sand to each beaker and stir. Does the sand dissolve? Write the result in your results table.
7 Add 1 teaspoon of wax to each beaker and stir. Does the wax dissolve? Write the result in your results table.
8 Dip a cotton wool bud into each beaker. Make sure the painted end goes into the solvent. Does the nail polish dissolve? Write the results in your results table.

 DATA COLLECTION IDEAS:

Solvent	Solute			
	Sugar	Sand	Wax	Nail polish
Water				
Vegetable oil				
Nail polish remover				

DIFFERENTIATION:
- **Decrease the challenge:** The children could have the beakers pre-filled with the solvents.
- **Increase the challenge:** The children could predict and test whether other solutes will dissolve in the solvents. Check that all their choices are safe to carry out.

USEFUL QUESTIONS TO ASK THE CHILDREN:
- Which solutes dissolved in which solvents?
- Why do you think some solutes did not dissolve in some solvents?
- What other solutes dissolve/do not dissolve in water?

FURTHER WORK:
The children could carry out an investigation on how fast sugar will dissolve in water at different temperatures.

EXPERIMENT 31

Let's get saturated!

LEARNING OBJECTIVES:
Investigating the saturation point of water for three different types of sugar.

INTRODUCTION:
The children investigate how much sugar can be added to water before it becomes saturated. They do this with three different types of sugar: granulated sugar, caster sugar and icing sugar.

USEFUL PRIOR WORK:
The children should know that sugar can dissolve in water and that when sugar has dissolved, it is still present in the water.

 BACKGROUND SCIENCE:
A substance that can dissolve is called soluble. The liquid in which it can dissolve is called a solvent. The resulting mixture (when a soluble substance is dissolved in a solvent) is called a solution. All solvents, however, have a saturation point. This is the point at which no more of the soluble substance can be dissolved in the solvent. The saturation point varies depending on what substance is being dissolved. The larger the particles of the substance being dissolved, the less of the substance that can be dissolved in the solvent. In terms of sugar, granulated sugar has the largest particle size, followed by caster sugar, followed by icing sugar, therefore the water will reach saturation point faster for granulated sugar, followed by caster sugar, followed by icing sugar.

NATIONAL CURRICULUM LINKS:
- **Year 5 programme of study**: Properties and changes of materials
  - Know that some materials will dissolve in a liquid to form a solution, and describe how to recover a substance from a solution.

MATERIALS NEEDED:
- Beakers or plastic pots
- Granulated sugar
- Caster sugar
- Icing sugar
- Measuring cylinders
- Teaspoons
- Warm water

 SAFETY AND TECHNICAL NOTES:
- Remind the children not to eat the sugar.
- Doing this investigation with warm water from the hot tap will allow the sugar to dissolve much faster than if cold water is used.
- Encourage the children to use smaller volumes of water to reduce the amount of sugar needed to reach saturation point.

METHOD:

TO BE DONE IN ADVANCE BY THE TEACHER:
Separate out the different types of sugar into bowls for the children.

 CHILDREN:

1 You will need three beakers. Fill each beaker with the same amount of water.
2 Choose the sugar you would like to investigate first. Add a teaspoon of this sugar to one of your beakers and stir until you can no longer see the sugar.
3 Keep adding a teaspoon of sugar and stirring until the sugar stops dissolving into the water.
4 Record on your results table how many teaspoons of the sugar were able to dissolve in the water.
5 Repeat the investigation with the other types of sugar.

 DATA COLLECTION IDEAS:

Type of sugar	Number of teaspoons of sugar that dissolved in the water
Granulated	
Caster	
Icing	

DIFFERENTIATION:
- **Decrease the challenge:** The children may need help making sure that they use approximately the same amount of sugar each time they add a teaspoonful to the water.
- **Increase the challenge:** The children could measure out the sugar more accurately, for example by using an electronic balance.

USEFUL QUESTIONS TO ASK THE CHILDREN:
- Which type of sugar were you able to add the most of to the water before it stopped dissolving? Why do you think this was?
- Which type of sugar were you able to add the least of to the water before it stopped dissolving? Why do you think this was?
- Why do you think the sugars eventually stopped dissolving in the water?

FURTHER WORK:
A demonstration can be done by the teacher using three larger beakers of water in order to show that the more water there is, the more sugar can be dissolved. However, the order for reaching the saturation point – granulated sugar, caster sugar and icing sugar – remains the same.

EXPERIMENT 32

Cleaning water

LEARNING OBJECTIVES:
Clean some dirty water!

INTRODUCTION:
The children investigate the best way to clean dirty water using different separation techniques.

USEFUL PRIOR WORK:
The children should be familiar with carrying out basic separation techniques, such as sieving and filtering.

 BACKGROUND SCIENCE:
Dirty water is an example of a mixture. A mixture is two or more substances that are physically mixed together without any chemical bonds between the different substances. This is different from a compound where the substances are chemically joined together. This means that mixtures can be separated by physical processes such as filtering, sieving or evaporating. The dirty water can be initially cleaned using physical processes, which will remove any solid particles in the water. However, even though the water looks clean, it could still contain microscopic organisms such as bacteria that would make the water unsafe for drinking. These organisms would need to be removed by using chemicals (for example chlorine) or by boiling the water in order to kill the organisms and then condensing the steam back into liquid water.

NATIONAL CURRICULUM LINKS:
- **Year 5 programme of study**: Properties and changes of materials
  - Use knowledge of solids, liquids and gases to decide how mixtures might be separated through filtering, sieving and evaporating.
  - Demonstrate that dissolving, mixing and changes of state are reversible changes.

MATERIALS NEEDED:
- Dirty water, for example from a pond – alternatively tap water mixed with soil from the garden
- Beakers
- Measuring cylinders
- Funnels
- Filter paper
- Charcoal
- Sand
- Small pebbles

 SAFETY AND TECHNICAL NOTES:
- The children should wash their hands after carrying out the investigation.
- Remind the children not to drink the water even after they have 'cleaned' it.

METHOD:

TO BE DONE IN ADVANCE BY THE TEACHER:
Prepare the 'dirty water'. Make sure there is enough for each group.

 CHILDREN:

1 You have been given some dirty water. Your task is to clean the water as much as possible.
2 Look at the selection of equipment you can choose from. Decide how you will start to clean your water.
3 You can use more than one method for cleaning your water and you can clean your water as many times as you choose.

 DATA COLLECTION IDEAS:
The children could take 'before' and 'after' photographs of the water to show what the water looked like before and after 'cleaning'.

DIFFERENTIATION:
• **Decrease the challenge:** The children could follow instructions on how to carry out different separation techniques.
• **Increase the challenge:** The children could investigate how to separate salt from the water by evaporating and condensing the water.

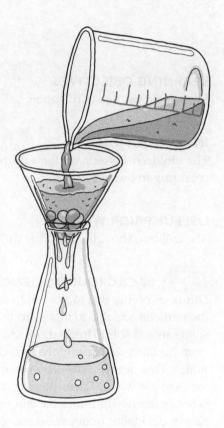

USEFUL QUESTIONS TO ASK THE CHILDREN:
• Which method produced the cleanest/dirtiest water? Why do you think this was?
• Do you think our water is now clean enough to drink? Why do you think this?
• Do you know any other ways that water is cleaned? Think about when you go swimming and our taps at home.

FURTHER WORK:
This investigation could be linked with cross-curricular work in geography. The children could study countries where people do not always have access to clean water and the consequences of this.

Diffusion rates

LEARNING OBJECTIVES:
Investigate the rate of diffusion.

INTRODUCTION:
The children investigate the rate of diffusion in water of different temperatures by adding food colouring to beakers of water.

USEFUL PRIOR WORK:
The children should know what diffusion is and that diffusion can happen in liquids.

 BACKGROUND SCIENCE:
Diffusion occurs due to the random movement of particles. It can occur in both liquids and gases as the particles are able to move around each other (diffusion does not occur in solids as the particles in solids are not able to freely move around). When you add, for example, liquid A to liquid B, the particles from liquid A will randomly spread out and eventually will be evenly spread throughout the 'new' liquid. This can be easily seen when a coloured liquid, for example squash, is added to a clear liquid, for example water. There are factors that will affect how quickly the diffusion happens. One of these is temperature. The hotter the temperature, the faster the rate of diffusion. This is because the particles have more kinetic (movement) energy, and so they are moving around more quickly. Stirring the liquid would also increase the rate of diffusion by physically moving the particles around.

NATIONAL CURRICULUM LINKS:
• **Year 4 programme of study**: States of matter
  – Observe that some materials change state when they are heated or cooled and measure or research the temperature at which this happens in degrees Celsius (°C).
• **Year 5 programme of study**: Properties and changes of materials
  – Know that some materials will dissolve in a liquid to form a solution, and describe how to recover a substance from a solution.

MATERIALS NEEDED:
• See-through beakers
• Labels
• Water
• Food colouring
• Measuring cylinders
• Timers
• Teaspoons or stirrers
• Kettle (optional)

 SAFETY AND TECHNICAL NOTES:
• Use plastic beakers if possible.
• Boiling water can be used as a demonstration by the teacher but should not be handled by the children. Water from the hot tap will be sufficient for this investigation.
• The food colouring will diffuse in the cold water but it will take a long time. It is best to conduct this investigation in the morning so that the beakers of cold water can be observed throughout the day.

METHOD:

TO BE DONE IN ADVANCE BY THE TEACHER:
Prepare the cold water for the children by placing some beakers of water into a fridge or use ice to create very cold water.

 CHILDREN:

1 You need three beakers. Label your beakers, 'cold water', 'warm water' and 'hot water'.
2 Use the measuring cylinder to measure 150ml of water from the cold tap. Pour this into the beaker labelled 'warm water'. Now use the measuring cylinder to measure out 150ml of water from the hot tap. Pour this into the same beaker (the one labelled 'warm water'). Stir the water a few times using a spoon or a stirring rod. Leave the water to settle.
3 Use the measuring cylinder to measure out 300ml of the cold water that your teacher will provide for you. Pour this water into the beaker labelled 'cold water'.
4 Use the measuring cylinder to measure out 300ml of water from the hot tap. Pour this into the beaker labelled 'hot water'.
5 Add three drops of food colouring to each beaker and then start your timer.
6 Record how long it takes for the food colouring to completely diffuse throughout the water. Write this in your results table. It may take a long time for some of the beakers!

 DATA COLLECTION IDEAS:

Water temperature	Time taken to diffuse (m, s)
Cold	
Warm	
Hot	
Boiling (if doing a demonstration)	

DIFFERENTIATION:
• **Decrease the challenge:** The water could be pre-prepared for the children. They could be given help to decide when the food colouring has completely 'diffused' throughout the water.
• **Increase the challenge:** The children could carry out a more systematic investigation over a range of temperatures and use a thermometer to record the exact temperatures of the water.

USEFUL QUESTIONS TO ASK THE CHILDREN:
• In which temperature of water did the food colouring diffuse the fastest/slowest? Why do you think this was?
• What else might speed up or slow down the diffusion of the food colouring in the water?
• Do you think we would find similar results if we used something else in the water, for example orange squash? Why do you think that?

FURTHER WORK:
The children could look at the rate of diffusion in gases. A simple demonstration could be set up whereby the children line up in the classroom and the teacher sprays a strong-smelling substance, for example perfume or air freshener (be aware of any allergies), at the front of the line and the children raise their hands when they can smell the substance.

The best straw

LEARNING OBJECTIVES:
Find the best drinking straw!

INTRODUCTION:
The children investigate capillary action by seeing how well drinking straws of different diameters are able to 'pick up' water.

USEFUL PRIOR WORK:
The children do not need to have any particular prior knowledge before completing this investigation.

 BACKGROUND SCIENCE:
Capillary action is the result of two different processes, cohesion and adhesion. Cohesion is the force that holds the molecules in a substance together. Water has very strong cohesion so the molecules 'stick together' with some force. Adhesion occurs when two different substances 'stick together'. Water is attracted to the plastic in a straw and so adheres to the plastic surface inside the straw. For capillary action (water being drawn up the straw) to occur, the force of adhesion needs to be greater than the force of gravity. In the case of a straw, the narrower the straw, the further up the straw the water will travel. This is because there is less water inside the straw, meaning the force of adhesion does not have to act on as many particles of water. Capillary action is the way water travels up the stems of plants from the roots.

NATIONAL CURRICULUM LINKS:
• **Year 3 programme of study**: Plants
  – Investigate the way in which water is transported within plants.

MATERIALS NEEDED:
• Drinking straws of different diameters
• Beakers
• Food colouring
• Water
• Ruler
• Scissors

 SAFETY AND TECHNICAL NOTES:
• Cold water is sufficient for this investigation.
• The children may want to practise 'lifting' the water out of the beaker a few times before performing the investigation. It would be helpful to demonstrate how to do this.
• Remind the children not to drink the water.

METHOD:

TO BE DONE IN ADVANCE BY THE TEACHER:

You may want to cut the different straws to the same length or have the children do this. Make sure any bendy parts of straws are removed. Measure the diameter of the straws using a tape-measure or string or have the children do this.

 CHILDREN:

1 Fill a beaker with water and then add a few drops of food colouring. Make sure it is quite dark so that you can see it easily when it is in the straw.
2 Make sure all your straws are the same length. Your teacher may have done this part for you.
3 Place your first straw into the beaker. It should not touch the bottom of the beaker. Wait for 10 seconds then place your finger over the top of the straw and slowly lift the straw out of the beaker. What can you see? Use the ruler to measure how high up the water is in the straw. Write the result in your results table.
4 Place the straw over the beaker and lift your finger off the straw. What happened?
5 Repeat step 3 and step 4 with the rest of your straws.

✎ DATA COLLECTION IDEAS:

Straw diameter (mm)	Height of water in straw (cm)

DIFFERENTIATION:

- **Decrease the challenge:** If the children find it hard to measure the water in the straw using a ruler, photographs could be taken instead that can then be compared later.
- **Increase the challenge:** The children could investigate whether the type of liquid has any effect on the capillary action of the straws by using different liquids, for example milk, vegetable oil and washing-up liquid.

USEFUL QUESTIONS TO ASK THE CHILDREN:

- Which straw did the water travel up the furthest/least? Why do you think this was?
- Why do you think the water travelled up the straws?
- Why do you think the water stayed in the straw until you took your finger off the top?

FURTHER WORK:

The children could research how plants use capillary action to transport water from the roots up the stem.

Let's make an emulsion

LEARNING OBJECTIVES:
Making our own emulsion.

INTRODUCTION:
The children make an emulsion using egg yolks, vinegar and vegetable oil.

USEFUL PRIOR WORK:
The children should know what mixtures are.

 BACKGROUND SCIENCE:
An emulsion occurs when a solid or liquid is mixed with another liquid, but does not dissolve in that liquid. Droplets of the liquid or particles of the solid become dispersed throughout the liquid. An example of this process would be vegetable oil and water. Oil does not dissolve in water and so droplets of oil become suspended in the water. As the particles in an emulsion are not chemically joined together, they have a tendency to 'separate out' into layers. This is why, for example, emulsion paint needs to be stirred before it is used. In order to help prevent this separation from happening, a substance called an emulsifier can be added to the mixture. This helps to keep the particles together. Mayonnaise is an example of an everyday emulsion. The egg yolks act as an emulsifier, keeping the vinegar and oil together. This is because egg yolks contain lecithin, a substance that has one end that is attracted to oil and one end that is attracted to vinegar, therefore helping to keep the oil and vinegar together.

NATIONAL CURRICULUM LINKS:
- **Year 4 programme of study**: States of matter
  - Compare and group materials together according to whether they are solids, liquids or gases.
- **Year 5 programme of study**: Properties and changes of materials
  - Know that some materials will dissolve in a liquid to form a solution, and describe how to recover a substance from a solution.
  - Use knowledge of solids, liquids and gases to decide how mixtures might be separated through filtering, sieving and evaporating.

MATERIALS NEEDED:
- Plastic bowls
- Vegetable oil
- Vinegar
- Water
- Egg yolks
- Whisks
- Measuring cylinders

 SAFETY AND TECHNICAL NOTES:
- The oil must be added very slowly while the mixture is being whisked. It is a good idea to demonstrate this to the children. They may find it easier for one person to pour the oil and one person to do the whisking.

- The resulting 'mayonnaise' should not be consumed and should just be used to demonstrate the properties of emulsions.
- The children should wash their hands after completing the investigation.
- Be aware of any allergies.

METHOD:

TO BE DONE IN ADVANCE BY THE TEACHER:
You may wish to prepare the separated egg yolks in advance. This investigation works best if no egg white is present.

 CHILDREN:

1 Use a measuring cylinder to measure out 10ml of vinegar. Pour this into a bowl.
2 Use a measuring cylinder to measure out 100ml of oil.
3 Pour this oil **very slowly** (a small amount at a time) into the bowl. Whisk the mixture constantly.
4 Observe your mixture. What does it look like? Write down your observations in your results table.
5 Using a clean bowl, measure out 10ml of vinegar and pour this into the bowl. Add the egg yolk to the bowl.
6 Whisk the mixture until it starts to become thicker.
7 Use a measuring cylinder to measure out 100ml of oil.
8 Pour this oil **very slowly** (a small amount at a time) into the bowl. Whisk the mixture constantly.
9 Observe your mixture. What does it look like? Write down your observations in your results table.

 DATA COLLECTION IDEAS:

Observations of the emulsion	
Without the emulsifier (egg yolk)	With the emulsifier (egg yolk)

DIFFERENTIATION:
- **Decrease the challenge:** The children may find it easier to carry out this investigation in a kitchen setting as a group activity.
- **Increase the challenge:** The children could investigate the effect of using different ratios of vegetable oil and vinegar on the resulting emulsion.

USEFUL QUESTIONS TO ASK THE CHILDREN:
- What observations did you make of the emulsion that did not contain egg yolk?
- What observations did you make of the emulsion that did contain egg yolk?
- Why do you think the emulsion was different when egg yolk was used?

FURTHER WORK:
This investigation could be linked with cross-curricular work in design and technology. The children could look at other food-based emulsions such as margarine and ice cream.

EXPERIMENT 36

Salty water

LEARNING OBJECTIVES:
Investigate how we can make objects float using salt.

INTRODUCTION:
The children investigate how much salt needs to be added to water in order to make different objects float. Salt is added to water in order to 'float' items that would normally sink.

USEFUL PRIOR WORK:
The children do not need to have any particular prior knowledge before completing this investigation.

 BACKGROUND SCIENCE:
Objects will float or sink in water according to their density (density = mass ÷ volume). If an object has a density greater than water, it will sink. This is because the upthrust provided by the water is not enough to keep the object afloat. The force of gravity pulling the object down is greater than the upthrust, so the object sinks. If the object has a density lower than the water, it will float as the upthrust of the water can keep the object afloat. By adding salt to water, you can increase the density of the water, therefore enabling objects to float that would previously have sunk. The amount of salt needed will vary according to the density of the object. The greater the object's density, the more salt will be needed for it to be able to float.

NATIONAL CURRICULUM LINKS:
• **Year 5 programme of study:** Forces
  – Explain that unsupported objects fall towards the Earth because of the force of gravity acting between the Earth and the falling object.

MATERIALS NEEDED:
• Large, see-through containers
• Water
• Salt
• A selection of objects to float – good choices are eggs (fresh, not boiled), tomatoes, cut-up chunks of apple, potatoes and kiwi

 SAFETY AND TECHNICAL NOTES:
• Keep water away from all electrical devices.
• The amount of salt needed may vary between the same type of object as individual variations in moisture content will affect how they float.
• Be aware of any allergies.

METHOD:

TO BE DONE IN ADVANCE BY THE TEACHER:
Fill the containers with water. Cut up any fruit and vegetables that are being used.

 ### CHILDREN:

1 Look at the items you have been given. Predict whether they will float or sink when you add them to the water. Draw where you think the item will be in your results table.
2 Add the item carefully to the water.
3 Draw where the items are in the container onto your results table.
4 When you have added all the items, start adding the salt slowly to the water.
5 Keep adding the salt until either 1) all your items are floating or 2) you run out of salt.
6 Record which item floated first, second, third, etc.

 ### DATA COLLECTION IDEAS:

Where I think the items will float/sink in the water	Where the items did float/sink in the water	Objects that sank floated in this order when we added salt to the water
		1.
		2.
		3.
		4.
		5.
		6.

DIFFERENTIATION:
- **Decrease the challenge:** The children may find it easier performing a simpler version of this investigation where each object is added to a separate beaker of water and they record how many teaspoons of salt were added before they floated.
- **Increase the challenge:** The children could measure the mass and volume of each object to calculate their density and see what effect this has on how much salt needs to be added to the water.

USEFUL QUESTIONS TO ASK THE CHILDREN:
- Which objects were the first/last to float? Why do you think this was?
- Why do you think adding salt to the water helped some of the objects to float?
- Where in nature would we find water that contains salt?

FURTHER WORK:
The children could research the Dead Sea in Jordan. The Dead Sea is a lake off the River Jordan with a very high level of salinity (almost ten times as much salt as the oceans). This makes it very easy to swim in as the salt water enables people to float.

EXPERIMENT 37

Observing melting

LEARNING OBJECTIVES:
Observe what happens when different substances are melted.

INTRODUCTION:
The children use a tea-light to melt different substances and observe what happens.

USEFUL PRIOR WORK:
The children should know the three states of matter: solids, liquids and gases.

 BACKGROUND SCIENCE:
Melting is an example of a change of state. When a substance changes from being a solid to a liquid, we say it has melted. Most melting occurs due to thermal energy (heat) being transferred to the substance. This thermal energy provides the particles in the solid with more kinetic (movement) energy, meaning they can break the bonds holding them together that keeps them as solids. Different substances will melt at different temperatures but the same substance will always melt at the same temperature (called its melting point). Different substances will also melt at different rates and in different manners; for example, as they melt, some solids (for example chocolate) soften first before becoming a liquid, whereas others (for example water) go straight from being a solid to a liquid.

NATIONAL CURRICULUM LINKS:
* **Year 1 programme of study**: Everyday materials
  – Describe the simple physical properties of a variety of everyday materials.
* **Year 4 programme of study**: States of matter
  – Compare and group materials together according to whether they are solids, liquids or gases.
  – Observe that some materials change states when they are heated or cooled, and measure or research the temperature at which this happens in degrees Celsius (°C).
* **Year 5 programme of study**: Properties and changes of materials
  – Compare and group together everyday materials on the basis of their physical properties including their hardness, solubility, transparency, conductivity (electrical and thermal) and response to magnets.
  – Demonstrate that dissolving, mixing and changes of state are reversible changes.

MATERIALS NEEDED:
* A selection of items to melt – good choices are chocolate, cheese, ice, butter and wax
* Tea-light candles
* Small foil containers for the melting activities
* Long wooden pegs

 SAFETY AND TECHNICAL NOTES:
* Use a tea-light candle in a sand tray for all the melting activities.
* Have children tie back long hair and roll up any loose clothing, for example sleeves.
* Make sure the room is well ventilated.
* Adults should light the candles.
* The children should place the substance to be melted in a small foil tray that they can then hold over the tea-light flame using the wooden peg. They should avoid placing the foil tray directly into the flame but rather hold the tray just above it.

METHOD:

TO BE DONE IN ADVANCE BY THE TEACHER:
Prepare all the items that will be melted. Only small amounts of each will be needed. When the investigation is ready to begin, light the candles for the children.

CHILDREN:
1 Choose your first item to melt.
2 Observe it closely. Write down your observations. What does it look like, feel like, smell like? Place it in the foil tray.
3 Carefully pick up the foil tray with the wooden peg and hold it above the flame of the candle until it starts to melt.
4 Observe it as it is melting. What can you see? What can you smell? What can you hear? Do not touch it though as it will be hot!
5 Put the foil tray in the sand and write down your observations. What does the item look like now you have stopped melting it? Does it look the same as it did at the start of the investigation?
6 Repeat with the other items you are melting.

 DATA COLLECTION IDEAS:

Item we are melting	Observations		
	What it was like before melting	What it was like during melting	What it was like after melting

DIFFERENTIATION:
- **Decrease the challenge:** The children could take photographs of the substances before, during and after melting to use as their results.
- **Increase the challenge:** The children could examine the substances more closely – for example with a magnifying lens – in order to make more detailed observations.

USEFUL QUESTIONS TO ASK THE CHILDREN:
- What were the substances like before you melted them?
- What did you observe when you were melting the substances?
- What were the substances like after you melted them?

FURTHER WORK:
The children could investigate the melting and freezing points of different substances and create a 'thermometer chart', showing which substances melt and freeze at which temperatures.

Observing burning

LEARNING OBJECTIVES:
Observe what happens when different substances are burned.

INTRODUCTION:
The children use a tea-light to burn different substances and observe what happens.

USEFUL PRIOR WORK:
The children do not need to have any particular prior knowledge before completing this investigation.

 BACKGROUND SCIENCE:
Burning is a chemical reaction and an example of an irreversible change (unlike melting, which *is* a reversible change). For something to burn, there needs to be a source of fire, a supply of oxygen and a flammable substance. A flammable substance is one that can easily ignite when it comes into contact with a flame. The heat from the flame provides the substance with enough energy to undergo the process of combustion. As this combustion takes place, the bonds between the particles in the substance are broken down. Usually, combustion results in the formation of new products, including carbon dioxide and water. These new products form when the particles in the substance react with the oxygen in the atmosphere. Sometimes, solid carbon is left behind at the end of combustion in the form of ash. This carbon did not react with the oxygen and so did not form carbon dioxide. If combustion results in this left-over carbon, it is called 'incomplete combustion'. If all the carbon has managed to react with oxygen then it is called complete combustion.

NATIONAL CURRICULUM LINKS:
- **Year 4 programme of study**: States of matter
  - Observe that some materials change state when they are heated or cooled and measure or research the temperature at which this happens in degrees Celsius (°C).
- **Year 5 programme of study**: Properties and changes of materials
  - Demonstrate that dissolving, mixing and changes of state are reversible changes.
  - Give reasons, based on evidence from comparative and fair tests, for the particular uses of everyday materials, including metals, wood and plastic.
  - Explain that some changes result in the formation of new materials (and that this kind of change is not usually reversible) including changes associated with burning and the action of acid on bicarbonate of soda.

MATERIALS NEEDED:
- A selection of items to burn – good choices are bread, cotton wool, synthetic fabric and paper
- Tea-light candles
- Long wooden pegs

 SAFETY AND TECHNICAL NOTES:
- Use a tea-light candle in a sand tray for all the burning activities.
- Have children tie back long hair and roll up any loose clothing, for example sleeves.
- Make sure the room is well ventilated.
- Adults should light the candles.
- The children should hold the substance to be burned using the wooden peg. They should hold the substance at the tip of the flame. To extinguish the substance they should place it into the sand.

METHOD:

TO BE DONE IN ADVANCE BY THE TEACHER:

Prepare all the items that will be burned. Only small amounts of each will be needed. When the investigation is ready to begin, light the candles for the children.

 CHILDREN:

1 Choose your first item to burn.
2 Observe it closely. Write down your observations. What does it look like, feel like, smell like?
3 Carefully pick up the item using the wooden tongs and hold it in the flame until it starts to burn.
4 Observe it as it is burning. What can you see? What can you smell? What can you hear? Do not touch though as it will be hot!
5 Put the item in the sand tray and write down your observations. What does the item look now you have stopped melting it? Does it look the same as it did at the start of the investigation?
6 Repeat with the other items you are burning.

 DATA COLLECTION IDEAS:

Item we are burning	Observations		
	What it was like before burning	What it was like during burning	What it was like after burning

DIFFERENTIATION:

- **Decrease the challenge:** The children could take photographs of the substances before, during and after melting to use as their results.
- **Increase the challenge:** The children could examine the substances more closely – for example with a magnifying lens – in order to make more detailed observations.

USEFUL QUESTIONS TO ASK THE CHILDREN:

- What were the substances like before you burned them?
- What did you observe when you were burning the substances?
- What were the substances like after you burned them?

FURTHER WORK:

The children could investigate non-flammable fabric and why it is used in household furniture.

EXPERIMENT 39

A rusty problem

LEARNING OBJECTIVES:

Investigate the conditions needed for rusting to happen.

INTRODUCTION:

The children investigate the conditions that are needed for iron to rust. To do this, iron nails are placed under different conditions to see which ones result in rusting.

USEFUL PRIOR WORK:

The children do not need to have any particular prior knowledge before completing this investigation, but it will be useful for them to know what rust is and that rust is generally considered to be a problem.

 BACKGROUND SCIENCE:

Rusting is a type of corrosion that affects iron and steel. The actual 'rust' (the reddish deposits on the surface of the metal) is iron oxide. Iron and steel will rust if they come into contact with both oxygen and water. The iron metal chemically combines with oxygen in the air in the presence of water, forming the iron oxide. Rusting in as an example of a non-reversible change. If rust is left it can 'eat away' at the metal, causing considerable damage to the affected structure. There are ways to prevent rusting from occurring. They usually involve a physical barrier that prevents either oxygen or water from coming into contact with the iron. Examples of these physical barriers include paint and grease.

NATIONAL CURRICULUM LINKS:

- **Year 2 programme of study**: Uses of everyday materials
  - Identify and compare the suitability of a variety of everyday materials – including wood, metal, plastic, glass, brick, rock, paper and cardboard – for particular uses.
- **Year 5 programme of study**: Properties and changes of materials
  - Give reasons, based on evidence from comparative and fair tests, for the particular uses of everyday materials including metals, wood and plastic.
  - Explain that some changes result in the formation of new materials (and that this kind of change is not usually reversible) including changes associated with burning and the action of acid on bicarbonate of soda.

MATERIALS NEEDED:

- A selection of iron nails (or other objects if nails are not available)
- A selection of beakers or plastic pots
- Paint
- Cooking oil
- A grease (for example, petroleum jelly)
- Water
- Labels

 SAFETY AND TECHNICAL NOTES:

- Supervise the children when they are handling the nails.
- Boiling water removes the oxygen from the water, allowing the children to see the effect of water but no oxygen.
- Allow the boiled water to cool before beginning the investigation.

- For the investigation with boiled water and cooking oil, the water should be added to the beaker first and then a thin layer of cooking oil should be poured on top of the water. This excludes oxygen from entering the boiled water.
- The nails should ideally be left for a week.

METHOD:

TO BE DONE IN ADVANCE BY THE TEACHER:
Cover the required number of nails in paint and in grease. You may want to let the children cover the nails in the grease themselves. Ensure that they cover all the surface of the nail.
Place the nails into pots labelled iron nail, painted iron nail and greased iron nail.

 ### CHILDREN:

1 Set up nine testing pots. Label the pots with the following labels: 'nail in air', 'nail in water', 'nail in boiled water', 'painted nail in air', 'painted nail in water', 'painted nail in boiled water', 'greased nail in air', 'greased nail in water', 'greased nail in boiled water'.
2 Put a normal nail into each pot labelled 'nail'.
3 Put a painted nail into each pot labelled 'painted nail'.
4 Put a greased nail into each pot labelled 'greased nail'.
5 For each pot labelled 'water', half fill the beaker with water so the nail is almost (but not completely) covered.
6 For each beaker labelled 'boiled water', completely cover the nail in the beaker with the water. Then carefully pour a thin layer of cooking oil on top of the water.
7 Put your beakers somewhere safe. You will examine them again in a week to see what has happened.

 ## DATA COLLECTION IDEAS:

Type of nail	Condition		
	Air	Water	Boiled water and cooking oil
Iron			
Iron – painted			
Iron – greased			

DIFFERENTIATION:
- **Decrease the challenge:** The children could take photographs of the nails at the end of the investigation and use these as their results.
- **Increase the challenge:** The children could also investigate different types of water – for example tap water, bottled water, rain water, filtered water – to see if this has any effect on how the iron rusts.

USEFUL QUESTIONS TO ASK THE CHILDREN:
- Which conditions resulted in rusting? Why do you think this was?
- What has happened to the nails that have rusted?
- Why do you think painting and greasing the nails stopped them from rusting?

FURTHER WORK:
The children could investigate the problems associated with rust, for example in commercial machinery or in cars and bikes.

Conductor or insulator?

LEARNING OBJECTIVES:
Test materials to see if they conduct electricity.

INTRODUCTION:
The children investigate which materials conduct electricity by testing them in a simple circuit.

USEFUL PRIOR WORK:
The children should be able to build a simple series circuit.

 BACKGROUND SCIENCE:
An electric current is the flow of electrons. Electrons are one of the three sub-particles that make up atoms (the other two are protons and neutrons). Some materials allow electrons to flow through them easily. These materials are therefore able to 'conduct' electricity. Metals are an example of a conductor. On the other hand, an insulator does not allow these electrons to flow through them, therefore they are not able to conduct electricity. As a circuit needs to be complete in order to work, if an insulator is placed in the circuit, this will 'break' the circuit (even though there is no visible 'gap') as the current cannot flow through the insulator. If a conductor is placed in the circuit then the current will still be able to flow through the circuit, therefore the circuit will still work.

NATIONAL CURRICULUM LINKS:
* **Year 4 programme of study**: Electricity
  - Construct a simple series circuit, identifying and naming its basic parts, including cells, wires, bulbs, switches and buzzers.
  - Identify whether or not a lamp will light in a simple series circuit based in whether or not the lamp is part of a complete loop with a battery.
  - Recognise some common conductors and insulators, and associate metals with being good conductors.
* **Year 5 programme of study**: Properties and changes of materials
  - Compare and group together everyday materials on the basis of their physical properties including their hardness, solubility, transparency, conductivity (electrical and thermal) and response to magnets.
* **Year 6 programme of study**: Electricity
  - Use recognised symbols when representing a simple circuit in a diagram.

MATERIALS NEEDED:
* Equipment for building a simple series circuit
* Materials to test in the circuit including conductors and insulators – for example teaspoons, wooden spoon, plastic spoon, paperclips, rubbers, graphite pencils, metal springs, cardboard tubes, metal nails, etc.

 SAFETY AND TECHNICAL NOTES:
* Remind children about working safely with electricity.
* Tell children not to touch the bulbs when they are being used as they can become hot.
* Circuits should be disconnected when not in use.

METHOD:

TO BE DONE IN ADVANCE BY THE TEACHER:
Prepare the materials that the children will be testing in their circuits.

 CHILDREN:

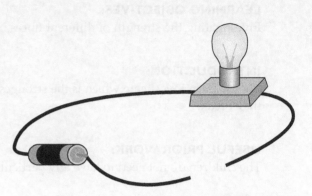

1 Build a simple series circuit that includes one lamp. Check your circuit works.
2 Make a gap in your circuit to test the objects you have been given. Think about how you will connect the objects to your circuit.
3 Test your first object. Does the bulb light up? Record the results in your results table.
4 Test the rest of your objects. Complete the results table and divide your objects into two groups: conductors (those that allowed the lamp to light up) and insulators (those that did not allow the lamp to light up).

 DATA COLLECTION IDEAS:

Object tested	Material the object is made from	Conductor or insulator?

DIFFERENTIATION:
- **Decrease the challenge:** The children may find it easier to have the circuit pre-made on a piece of board so that they only have to attach the material they are testing.
- **Increase the challenge:** The children can predict which materials they think will be conductors and insulators before the investigation, or could choose their own objects to test.

USEFUL QUESTIONS TO ASK THE CHILDREN:
- What objects were conductors? What did they have in common?
- What objects were insulators? What did they have in common?
- Why do you think some objects are able to conduct electricity?

FURTHER WORK:
The children could look at how to use electricity safely and the role that insulators can play in this, for example using a wooden broom to push an electrical object away from someone who has suffered an electric shock.

EXPERIMENT 41

The strongest thread

LEARNING OBJECTIVES:
Investigating the strength of different fibres.

INTRODUCTION:
The children investigate which is the strongest fibre by suspending weights from different fibres until they break.

USEFUL PRIOR WORK:
The children do not need to have any particular prior knowledge before completing this investigation.

 BACKGROUND SCIENCE:
A fibre is a strand of material that is used to make other materials, usually by combining lots of the same type of fibre together. Textile fibres are one type of fibre and can be either natural – for example cotton – or synthetic (man-made) – for example nylon. Textile fibres can be divided into two groups: yarns, which are many strands spun together (for example, wool) and threads, which are long thin strands (for example, silk). Despite their size, textile fibres can be very strong. The strength of fibres is tested using a maximum tension test. This involves seeing how much weight the fibre is able to hold before breaking. Man-made fibres tend to be more consistent in their strength, whereas natural fibres can vary due to the lack of uniformity in different fibres.

NATIONAL CURRICULUM LINKS:
- **Year 1 programme of study**: Everyday materials
  - Describe the simple physical properties of a variety of everyday materials.
  - Compare and group together a variety of everyday materials on the basis of their simple physical properties.
- **Year 2 programme of study**: Uses of everyday materials
  - Identify and compare the suitability of a variety of everyday materials – including wood, metal, plastic, glass, brick, rock, paper and cardboard – for particular uses.
- **Year 3 programme of study**: Forces
  - Notice that some forces need contact between two objects, but magnetic forces can act at a distance.
- **Year 5 programme of study**: Properties and changes of materials
  - Compare and group together everyday materials on the basis of their physical properties including their hardness, solubility, transparency, conductivity (electrical and thermal) and response to magnets.
  - Give reasons, based on evidence from comparative and fair tests, for the particular uses of everyday materials, including metals, wood and plastic.
- **Year 5 programme of study**: Forces
  - Explain that unsupported objects fall towards the Earth because of the force of gravity acting between the Earth and the falling object.

MATERIALS NEEDED:
- A variety of different fibres to test, for example cotton, nylon, wool, silk, string
- Clamp stands
- Weights
- Plastic tubs with handles

SAFETY AND TECHNICAL NOTES:

- Set up your clamp stand on the floor to avoid any damage to tables.
- Have padding underneath the plastic tubs for when the fibres break and the weights fall down.
- Most of the fibres are quite strong and will hold a lot of weight. Tying a small plastic tub with handles to the end of the thread will allow larger amounts of weight to be added.

METHOD:

TO BE DONE IN ADVANCE BY THE TEACHER:
Prepare the fibres that the children will be using. Make them the same length, about 20cm is sufficient and will mean they won't fall too far when they break.

 CHILDREN:

1 Set up your clamp stand on the floor. Make sure you have plenty of space around you.
2 Choose the first fibre you want to test. Tie the handle of the plastic tub to one end of the fibre. Tie the other end of the fibre to the clamp stand.
3 Place the padding underneath the plastic tub to protect the floor when the fibre breaks.
4 Add a weight, one at a time, to the plastic tub. Wait a few seconds before adding another weight to see if the fibre will break.
5 When the fibre breaks, count how much weight was in the plastic tub and record this in your results table.
6 Repeat the investigation with the rest of the fibres.

 DATA COLLECTION IDEAS:

Type of fibre	Amount of weight when the thread broke (g)

DIFFERENTIATION:
- **Decrease the challenge:** The children could have the clamp stands and fibres set up for them so they only need to add the weights to the tub.
- **Increase the challenge:** The children could investigate other properties of the threads, for example if they are waterproof, how flexible they are, etc.

USEFUL QUESTIONS TO ASK THE CHILDREN:
- Which thread was able to hold the most weight? Why do you think this was?
- Which thread held the least amount of weight? Why do you think this was?
- As well as being strong, what other properties might we want threads to have?

FURTHER WORK:
This investigation could be linked with cross-curricular work in design and technology. The children could learn different techniques such as weaving with wool and sewing with cotton.

EXPERIMENT 42

Design a bag

LEARNING OBJECTIVES:
Find the best material for making a bag.

INTRODUCTION:
The children investigate which material is best for making a bag by testing the strength of different materials.

USEFUL PRIOR WORK:
The children should know that objects are made from different materials that are best suited to the job.

 BACKGROUND SCIENCE:
One physical property of a material is its tearing strength. This refers to how much force needs to be applied to the material before it tears. Different materials will have different tearing strengths depending on what the material is made from. Paper is made from fibres that have been compressed together. Generally, the thicker the paper, the stronger it will be, as there are more fibres holding the paper together. Most plastics have a higher tearing strength than paper. They are able to resist breaking by stretching slightly when a load is applied to them. Textile fibres typically have the highest tearing strength as the individual fibres themselves are very strong and there are many fibres joined together to make the material.

NATIONAL CURRICULUM LINKS:
- **Year 2 programme of study**: Uses of everyday materials
  - Identify and compare the suitability of a variety of everyday materials – including wood, metal, plastic, glass, brick, rock, paper and cardboard – for particular uses.
- **Year 5 programme of study**: Properties and changes of materials
  - Compare and group together everyday materials on the basis of their physical properties including their hardness, solubility, transparency, conductivity (electrical and thermal) and response to magnets.
  - Give reasons, based on evidence from comparative and fair tests, for the particular uses of everyday materials, including metals, wood and plastic.

MATERIALS NEEDED:
- A variety of different materials to test, for example normal paper, sugar paper, tracing paper, wrapping paper, sandwich bags, cotton
- Small weights
- Weight holder
- Clamp stand (or Sellotape to the edge of a table)

SAFETY AND TECHNICAL NOTES:

- Place padding underneath the weights so that when the material tears and the weights fall off they will land on something soft.

METHOD:

TO BE DONE IN ADVANCE BY THE TEACHER:

Have different materials available for the children to test. You may want to cut them into the same size or have the children decide what size to use.

 CHILDREN:

1 Attach the first material you wish to test onto the clamp stand. Make sure it is hanging downwards.
2 Attach the weight holder to the material by piecing it through the material. Think about where you will put the weight holder for each material (make it a fair test).
3 Now start adding weights one at a time to your weight holder. Wait for a few seconds after you add each weight to make sure the material is not about to tear.
4 When the material completely tears and the weight holder falls off, you can record how much weight you added before the material tore onto your results table. You may want to test the same material more than once so that you can take an average.
5 Now repeat the investigation with the other materials.

 DATA COLLECTION IDEAS:

Material tested	Amount of weight added before tearing (g)			
	Trial 1	Trial 2	Trial 3	Average

DIFFERENTIATION:

- **Decrease the challenge:** The children could do a simpler investigation by placing an A4-sized piece of paper between four books so that the paper is only a small distance off the table but is 'enclosed' within the books. Small heavy objects such as marbles can then be added to the paper until the paper rips. The marbles will be trapped between the book so will be easy to collect and count.
- **Increase the challenge:** The children could investigate more than the property of each of the materials, for example how many drops of water can be dripped onto the material before it breaks, (if at all).

USEFUL QUESTIONS TO ASK THE CHILDREN:

- Which would be the best/worst material for making a bag? How do you know this?
- What other properties of a material might be important when designing a bag?
- What other tests could we do to see which material would be best for making a bag?

FURTHER WORK:

The children could examine a selection of different bags, for example basic plastic carrier bags, plastic bag for life, fabric bag for life, etc. and make a list of the advantages and disadvantages of each one.

EXPERIMENT 43

Keep it dry!

LEARNING OBJECTIVES:
Investigate whether some materials are waterproof.

INTRODUCTION:
The children investigate which material is best for keeping cotton wool dry by wrapping the cotton wool in different materials before immersing it in water.

USEFUL PRIOR WORK:
The children do not need to have any particular prior knowledge before completing this investigation.

 BACKGROUND SCIENCE:
A waterproof material is one that is impervious to water. The particles are so close together in the material that there are no pores through which the water can pass. If an object is completely waterproof, then no water will pass through. Some waterproof materials, however, do not allow liquid water to pass through but will allow water vapour to pass through. An example is Gore-Tex. These materials tend to be more comfortable to wear than materials that do not allow water or water vapour to pass through. Nylon, for example, does not allow water or water vapour through. This means that sweat will not pass through the material, and so it will not make 'breathable' clothes. This is why we get very hot wearing nylon. As well as solid materials, certain liquids are also waterproof, for example oil. Oil will not allow water to pass through it.

NATIONAL CURRICULUM LINKS:
- **Year 1 programme of study**: Everyday materials
  - Describe the simple physical properties of a variety of everyday materials.
- **Year 2 programme of study**: Uses of everyday materials
  - Identify and compare the suitability of a variety of everyday materials – including wood, metal, plastic, glass, brick, rock, paper and cardboard – for particular uses.
- **Year 5 programme of study**: Properties and changes of materials
  - Give reasons, based on evidence from comparative and fair tests, for the particular uses of everyday materials, including metals, wood and plastic.

MATERIALS NEEDED:
- A selection of different materials to test for example, tin foil, newspaper, sandwich bags, tissue paper, baking parchment, cling film, sugar paper
- Cotton wool balls
- Measuring cylinders
- Beakers
- Water
- Timers
- Elastic bands
- Paper towels

 SAFETY AND TECHNICAL NOTES:
- This is a fair test investigation, so the children will need to consider what other factors they will need to keep the same.
- Remind the children that their hands should be dry when they unwrap the cotton wool.

METHOD:

TO BE DONE IN ADVANCE BY THE TEACHER:
Prepare the materials that the children will be testing. Try to make them similar sizes.

 CHILDREN:

1 Use the measuring cylinder to measure out your chosen amount of water. Add the water to each of your beakers.
2 Wrap the cotton wool balls in the different materials you are testing. You may need to use an elastic band to keep some of the materials in place.
3 Add the cotton wool balls to your beakers and start your timer. Leave the cotton wool balls in the water for your chosen amount of time.
4 When the time has finished, take the cotton wool balls out of the beakers and place them onto a paper towel.
5 Dry your hands then carefully unwrap each cotton wool ball. Is it wet or dry? Record the results in your results table.

 DATA COLLECTION IDEAS:

Material	Cotton wool ball was wet	Cotton wool ball was dry

DIFFERENTIATION:
- **Decrease the challenge:** The children could use cotton wool buds that are wrapped in the material and then dipped into the water.
- **Increase the challenge:** The children could choose their own materials to test, which could include liquids – for example Vaseline and paint. In these cases the cotton wool would need to be pulled apart to examine whether the inside is dry.

USEFUL QUESTIONS TO ASK THE CHILDREN:
- Which materials kept the cotton wool dry? Why do you think this was?
- Which materials allowed the cotton wool to become wet? Why do you think this was?
- What other properties might we want a material to have if we were making something waterproof?

FURTHER WORK:
The children could research wet suits and dry suits, including the similarities and differences, the materials they are made from and how they work.

EXPERIMENT 44

Drying the washing

LEARNING OBJECTIVES:
Investigate the best conditions for drying our washing outside.

INTRODUCTION:
The children investigate the factors that speed up how fast clothes will dry on a washing line, including wind, temperature and surface area.

USEFUL PRIOR WORK:
The children should know that water can evaporate into the air.

 BACKGROUND SCIENCE:
Wet clothes will eventually dry due to the process of evaporation. Evaporation is when a liquid changes into a gas. This is similar to what happens during boiling, however there are some key differences. Evaporation only happens at the surface of the liquid, whereas boiling takes place throughout the liquid. This is because the particles on the surface of water are only held in place by the particles below them. Evaporation can occur at any temperature; however, boiling will only occur at the boiling point of the liquid, for example water's boiling point is 100 degrees Celsius.

Evaporation will be faster at higher temperatures. This is because the particles will have more kinetic energy, which makes it easier for the particles to escape the liquid. Other factors can also affect how fast evaporation occurs. If there is wind present, the particles of water that have evaporated are 'blown away' by the wind, bringing new air into contact with the water (air can only hold so much water), therefore allowing evaporation to happen faster. Also, if the air is 'dry', i.e. not humid, evaporation will happen faster, (again, this is because air can only hold so much water).

NATIONAL CURRICULUM LINKS:
- **Year 1 programme of study**: Seasonal changes
  - Observe and describe weather associated with the seasons and how day length varies.
- **Year 4 programme of study**: States of matter
  - Identify the part played by evaporation and condensation in the water cycle and associate the rate of evaporation with temperature.
- **Year 5 programme of study**: Properties and changes of materials
  - Demonstrate that dissolving, mixing and changes of state are reversible changes.

MATERIALS NEEDED:
- Fabric – ideally a cotton-based fabric
- String for a washing line
- Pegs
- Bowls
- Water
- Electric fan or hairdryer with a cool setting
- Timers

SAFETY AND TECHNICAL NOTES:

• Adults should operate the fan and hairdryer unless the children can be closely supervised.

METHOD:

TO BE DONE IN ADVANCE BY THE TEACHER:

Cut the fabric up into squares measuring 5cm by 5cm. Cut up the string into the length needed for the washing line. This will depend on how many pieces of fabric are being used but approximately 30cm should be sufficient. Select a cold area and a warm area for the temperature test. Examples include a fridge or cool, dark cupboard and next to a radiator. You can divide the children into groups to investigate one of the factors or you can allow the children to choose which factor they would like to investigate.

 CHILDREN:

1 Remember this is a fair test investigation. Think about what you need to keep the same in the investigation, what you will measure and what you will be changing.
2 Set up your 'washing line' in your chosen locations. Keep the washing line taught so the fabric squares stay at the same height.
3 Wet the fabric squares you have been given by soaking them in a bowl of water. Squeeze out the excess water from the fabric squares.
4 Hang your fabric squares on the washing line using the pegs. If you are investigating the effect of wind you will want to use the fan/hairdryer now.
5 Set your timer and leave your fabric squares for the designated amount of time.
6 Check your fabric squares and see how much they have dried.

 DATA COLLECTION IDEAS:

The children can devise a qualitative rating scale for how dry the squares of fabric are, for example on a scale of 1–10. They could produce comparative squares for each of these numbers to compare with the squares of fabric from the investigation.

DIFFERENTIATION:

• **Decrease the challenge:** The children may find it easier to work in groups looking at one condition – for example warm, hot, cold, wind – and looking at the different results together.
• **Increase the challenge:** The children could carry out a more systematic investigation, for example looking at the effect of temperature on evaporation by investigating a set range of temperatures, or the effect of wind by looking at a set amount of time for the 'wind'.

USEFUL QUESTIONS TO ASK THE CHILDREN:

• In which conditions did the fabric squares dry the fastest? Why do you think this was?
• In which conditions did the fabric squares dry the slowest? Why do you think this was?
• What would be the best weather for drying clothes outside?

FURTHER WORK:

The children could research humidity in terms of what it is, the humidity of different countries and the effect it has.

EXPERIMENT 45

Comparing soils

LEARNING OBJECTIVES:
Investigate the characteristics of different soil samples.

INTRODUCTION:
The children investigate the characteristics of different types of soil by looking at their physical appearance, pH, and how much water can pass through the soil.

USEFUL PRIOR WORK:
The children should know that plants can grow in soil and that plants need water to live and grow.

 ## BACKGROUND SCIENCE:
Soil is formed from rocks broken down via weathering and decayed organic matter. Soil can vary in its composition due to the type and ratios of rocks and organic matter it has formed from. Generally soil is classed as either:

- **sandy**: soil with high levels of sandy particles, tending to be very dry with water draining quickly
- **clay**: soil with high levels of clay particles, tending to be quite thick, wet and clumped together, water does not drain well
- **loam**: with a mix of both sandy and clay soil, forming a soil that can hold water but also allow it to drain through the soil. Loam soil is generally considered to be the best type of soil.

Soil can also vary in its pH due to the concentration of minerals in the soil and also due to external factors such as the presence of acid rain. Some plants prefer growing in acidic soils (for example, foxgloves and heathers) whereas others prefer an alkaline soil (for example, cabbages and cauliflowers).

NATIONAL CURRICULUM LINKS:
- **Year 2 programme of study**: Plants
  - Find out how plants need water, light and a suitable temperature to grow and stay healthy.
- **Year 3 programme of study**: Plants
  - Explore the requirements of plants for life and growth (air, light, water, nutrients from soil and room to grow) and how they vary from plant to plant.
- **Year 3 programme of study**: Rocks
  - Recognise that soils are made from rocks and organic matter.

MATERIALS NEEDED:
- Sand and pottery clay for comparisons
- Samples of different types of soil – these can be taken from around the school or 'pre-made' if there is not much variety in the school; for example, by using standard compost and mixing with different quantities of sand and loam or clay
- Magnifying lenses
- Measuring cylinders
- Beakers
- Funnels
- Filter paper
- Water
- Timers
- Soil pH testing kit (available from garden centres)

 ## SAFETY AND TECHNICAL NOTES:
- Children should wash their hands after the investigation.
- If you want the children to collect their own soil samples to analyse, make sure they are supervised and have suitable equipment for collecting the soil, for example small trowels and beakers.
- The instructions for testing the soil pH will be included with the soil pH testing kit.

METHOD:

TO BE DONE IN ADVANCE BY THE TEACHER:

Collect or prepare the soil samples if the children are not collecting their own. Try to make the soil samples different from each other. This can be done by adding sand, loam or clay to the soil samples. Adding lemon juice will make the soil more acidic.

 CHILDREN:

1 Look at your first soil sample closely. Use the magnifying lens to help you. What can you see? What do the particles in the soil look like? What colours can you see? Write down your observations.
2 Take some of your soil sample and squeeze it in your hands. What does it feel like? Does it stick together or break up? Rub it between your fingers. Does it feel grainy or smooth?
3 Now use a measuring cylinder to measure out 100ml of your soil sample. Place a funnel over a beaker and line it with the filter paper. Your teacher will show you how to fold the filter paper.
4 Pour your soil carefully into the funnel. It doesn't matter if some of it falls through into the beaker.
5 Now use the measuring cylinder to measure 25ml of water. Pour this water slowly over your soil. As soon as all the water has been poured start your timer.
6 Watch the water drain through the soil into the beaker. When all the water has drained through stop your timer. Write the time it took for the water to drain through in your results table. If the water does not drain through the soil at all write 'did not drain' in your results table.
7 Now test the pH of the remaining soil in your sample. Your teacher will tell you how to test the pH. Write the result in your results table.
8 Repeat the investigation with the other soil samples.

 DATA COLLECTION IDEAS:

Characteristic	Sample 1	Sample 2	Sample 3
Appearance			
Texture			
Water drainage			
pH			

DIFFERENTIATION:

• **Decrease the challenge:** The children could work in groups, with each group investigating one soil sample. These results could then be pooled at the end of the session. This would give the children more time to make detailed observations.
• **Increase the challenge:** The children could investigate the particle size of the soil samples by shaking the soil in a clear, plastic bottles half-filled with water and seeing how the particles settle into layers with the largest particles at the bottom. Note that it can take up to an hour for the particles to settle.

USEFUL QUESTIONS TO ASK THE CHILDREN:

• How did our soils differ from each other?
• Why do you think the soils differed in how quickly the water drained through?
• Which soil would be best for growing plants in? Why do you think that?

FURTHER WORK:

The children could investigate in detail how soil is formed. They could also look at the effect of pH on soils and find out which plants prefer an acidic soil and which plants prefer an alkaline soil.

EXPERIMENT 46

Testing rocks

LEARNING OBJECTIVES:
Observe different rocks to find their similarities and differences.

INTRODUCTION:
Children investigate the characteristics of different rocks. They will compare the mass, appearance, texture and permeability of the rocks.

USEFUL PRIOR WORK:
The children do not need to have any particular prior knowledge before completing this investigation.

 BACKGROUND SCIENCE:
Rocks can be formed in one of there ways. Igneous rocks – for example granite – result from the lava from volcanic eruptions cooling and solidifying. These rocks often have crystals inside them. The sizes of these crystals vary depending on whether the rock cooled quickly or slowly. Sedimentary rocks – for example sandstone – are formed from layers of sediment that have been transported by, for example, rivers or glaciers. The sediments settle on top of each other and become compacted, squeezing out the water and cementing the layers together. Metamorphic rocks are formed when one type of rock is transformed into a different rock by extreme heat or pressure. An example is marble, which is formed from limestone. Rocks will have different properties depending on which type of rock they are.

NATIONAL CURRICULUM LINKS:
- **Year 1 programme of study**: Everyday materials
  - Identify and name a variety of everyday materials, including wood, plastic, glass, metal and rock.
  - Describe the simple physical properties of a variety of everyday materials.
- **Year 2 programme of study**: Uses of everyday materials
  - Identify and compare the suitability of a variety of everyday materials – including wood, metal, plastic, glass, brick, rock, paper and cardboard – for particular uses.
- **Year 3 programme of study**: Rocks
  - Compare and group together different kinds of rocks on the basis of their appearance and simple physical properties.
- **Year 5 programme of study**: Properties and changes of materials
  - Compare and group together everyday materials on the basis of their physical properties including their hardness, solubility, transparency, conductivity (electrical and thermal) and response to magnets.

MATERIALS NEEDED:
- A selection of different rocks to examine
- Hand-lenses or magnifying glasses
- Beakers or plastic pots
- Paper towels
- Droppers
- Water

 SAFETY AND TECHNICAL NOTES:
- Try to use named rocks if possible so that the children know exactly what they are looking at. Good ones to use are: sandstone, chalk, slate, obsidian, marble and granite.

METHOD:

TO BE DONE IN ADVANCE BY THE TEACHER:
Have a selection of different rocks ready for the children to observe.

 CHILDREN:

1 Look at your first rock closely. Use the magnifying lens to help you. What can you see? What does the surface look like? What colours can you see? Write down your observations in your results table.
2 Feel your rock. Is it hard or soft and crumbly? Is it smooth or rough? What happens when you rub your finger along the surface of the rock? Write down your observations in your results table.
3 Place your rock on a paper towel and put a few drops of water onto the rock. Watch the water. Does it sink into the rock (if it does then the rock is porous) or does it run off the rock (if it does then the rock is not porous)?
4 Predict whether you think your rock will float or sink. Now add it to a beaker of water and see if it floats or sinks. Write the result in your results table.

 DATA COLLECTION IDEAS:

Characteristic	Rock 1	Rock 2	Rock 3	Rock 4
Appearance				
Texture				
Permeable?				
Floats or sinks?				

DIFFERENTIATION:
- **Decrease the challenge:** The children could work in groups, with each group investigating one rock. These results could then be pooled at the end of the session. This would give the children more time to make detailed observations.
- **Increase the challenge:** The children could carry out a more systematic test of the permeability of the rocks by weighing the rocks, then placing them in a beaker of water for a set period of time and then weighing the rock again to see how much water has been absorbed.

USEFUL QUESTIONS TO ASK THE CHILDREN:
- How did our rocks differ from each other?
- Why do you think some rocks were permeable to water and some rocks were not?
- Which rock would be best for building a statue that would be outside? Why do you think this?

FURTHER WORK:
The children could consider what jobs the different types of rocks would be good for based on their properties. For example, granite is often used for kitchen worktops as it is strong and hard but also decorative. However, it is also very expensive.

EXPERIMENT 47

Acid rain!

LEARNING OBJECTIVES:
Investigate the effect of acid rain.

INTRODUCTION:
The children make their own acid rain and then test its effects on different rocks.

USEFUL PRIOR WORK:
The children should know that pollution could cause acid rain.

 BACKGROUND SCIENCE:
Acid rain is caused when certain gases in the atmosphere dissolve in the water in the atmosphere. The most common gases that cause acid rain are carbon dioxide, sulphur dioxide and nitrogen oxide. These gases are typically released when fossil fuels are burned (for example in power stations) or are released in car exhaust fumes. Rain is normally slightly acidic anyway; however, the gases increase the acidity to the level where it can do damage to materials and living organisms. Acid rain can contribute to chemical weathering of rocks. This is where rocks are broken down by the action of the acid. Certain rocks, such as chalk and limestone, are more affected by acid rain than rocks such as granite and marble. Acid rain can also impact living organisms by increasing soil acidity and the acidity of lakes, rivers and ponds.

NATIONAL CURRICULUM LINKS:
- **Year 1 programme of study**: Seasonal changes
  - Observe and describe weather associated with the seasons and how day length varies.
- **Year 3 programme of study**: Rocks
  - Compare and group together different kinds of rocks on the basis of their appearance and simple physical properties.
- **Year 5 programme of study**: Properties and changes of materials
  - Explain that some changes result in the formation of new materials (and that this kind of change is not usually reversible) including changes associated with burning and the action of acid on bicarbonate of soda.

MATERIALS NEEDED:
- Measuring cylinder
- White wine vinegar or lemon juice
- Small beakers or plastic pots
- Droppers
- A selection of different rocks including chalk, limestone, sandstone, slate, granite and marble
- Magnifying glasses
- Paper towels or white tiles

 SAFETY AND TECHNICAL NOTES:
- Remind the children not to eat the vinegar or lemon juice.

METHOD:

TO BE DONE IN ADVANCE BY THE TEACHER:
If you prefer, you can make up the 'acid rain' yourself. You could make a highly concentrated version to act as a demonstration at the end of the investigation.

 CHILDREN:

1   Make up your 'acid rain'. Use the measuring cylinder to measure 5ml of water. Pour this into a beaker. Add five drops of the vinegar or lemon juice to the water. This is your acid rain.
2   Observe your first rock carefully. Use your magnifying glass to look at the rock closely. What does it look like? What does it feel like? Record your results in your results table.
3   Use the dropper to add a few drops of the acid rain to the rock. What can you see and hear happening? Record your results in your results table.
4   After you have added the acid rain, observe your rock again. What does it look like? What does it feel like? Record your results in your results table.
5   Repeat the investigation with the rest of the rocks.

 DATA COLLECTION IDEAS:

Type of rock	Observations		
	Before acid rain is added	While acid rain is being added	After acid rain has been added

DIFFERENTIATION:
- **Decrease the challenge:** The children could work in groups and investigate one rock, allowing them to make more detailed observations.
- **Increase the challenge:** The children could investigate the effect of acid rain of different concentrations by making their 'acid rain' with different amounts of vinegar or lemon juice.

USEFUL QUESTIONS TO ASK THE CHILDREN:
- What happened when you added the acid rain to the different rocks? Why do you think this happened?
- What do you think would happen if the acid rain was more or less concentrated?
- Apart from rocks, what else might acid rain damage?

FURTHER WORK:
The children could investigate the effect of acid rain on living organisms by, for example, planting runner bean seeds and growing them with 'acid rain' and normal water.

Ice cube challenge

LEARNING OBJECTIVES:
Investigate the best place to keep ice cubes in the classroom.

INTRODUCTION:
The children place ice cubes in different places around the classroom to see how fast they melt.

USEFUL PRIOR WORK:
The children should know that ice melts into liquid water.

BACKGROUND SCIENCE:
Water forms into ice at 0°C. As the temperature of the liquid water decreases, the amount of kinetic (movement) energy that the particles in the water has also decreases. As the particles are moving around less in the water, it becomes easier for them to form bonds between each other. These bonds are the reason why water expands as it freezes, rather than contracting like other substances. The bonds cause the ice to form a crystalline structure, which takes up more space than the liquid water. When ice is warmed, the particles begin to vibrate more and more. Eventually, these vibrations become strong enough to break the bonds holding the particles together, so the ice melts. Certain factors can increase or decrease the rate at which the ice melts. Surrounding the ice in an insulating material such as polystyrene helps to reduce the amount of thermal energy transferring to the ice, therefore slowing down the rate at which it melts.

NATIONAL CURRICULUM LINKS:
* **Year 1 programme of study**: Everyday materials
  – Describe the simple physical properties of a variety of everyday materials.
* **Year 4 programme of study**: States of matter
  – Compare and group materials together according to whether they are solids, liquids or gases.
  – Observe that some materials change state when they are heated or cooled and measure or research the temperature at which this happens in degrees Celsius (°C).
* **Year 5 programme of study**: Properties and changes of materials
  – Demonstrate that dissolving, mixing and changes of state are reversible changes.

MATERIALS NEEDED:
* Ice cubes
* Magnifying lenses
* Paper towels

 SAFETY AND TECHNICAL NOTES:
* Ensure that no ice cubes are placed near electrical objects.

METHOD:

TO BE DONE IN ADVANCE BY THE TEACHER:
Prepare enough ice cubes for the class.

 CHILDREN:

1 Observe an ice cube closely. What does it look like? What does it feel like? Record your observations.
2 Choose the places that you want to place your ice cubes. Choose some places that you think will be warm and some places that you think will be cold.
3 Put your ice cubes in your chosen places. Make sure you put your ice cube on a paper towel.
4 Come back and look at your ice cubes in 1 minute. Observe them closely. Record your observations.
5 Come back at regular times to observe your ice cubes. Observe them and record your observations. Which ice cube melted completely first?

 DATA COLLECTION IDEAS:

Where we placed the ice cube	Observations			
	After 1 minute	After 5 minutes	After 10 minutes	After 20 minutes

DIFFERENTIATION:
• **Decrease the challenge:** The children should be encouraged to think about places in the classroom that might be warmer or colder, for example having one window open and one window closed.
• **Increase the challenge:** The children could choose some locations outside to store their ice cubes, including covering them with soil or leaves.

USEFUL QUESTIONS TO ASK THE CHILDREN:
• Where did you put the ice cube(s) that melted the quickest? Why do you think they melted so quickly?
• Where did you put the ice cube(s) that melted the slowest? Why do you think they melted so slowly?
• What does this tell us about the temperature of our classroom?

FURTHER WORK:
The children could look at insulating their ice cubes, for example wrapping them in bubble wrap or placing them in polystyrene.

EXPERIMENT 49

Where did the water go?

LEARNING OBJECTIVES:
Investigate what happens to water when we leave it out in different places.

INTRODUCTION:
The children investigate evaporation by leaving beakers of water in different places and observing what happens.

USEFUL PRIOR WORK:
The children do not need to have any particular prior knowledge before completing this investigation.

 BACKGROUND SCIENCE:
Evaporation is when a liquid changes into a gas. This is similar to boiling, however there are some key differences. Evaporation only happens at the surface of the liquid whereas boiling takes place throughout the liquid. Evaporation of water can occur at any temperature, although it will be faster at higher temperatures. This is because the particles of water will have more kinetic energy, which makes it easier for the particles of water to escape the liquid. Other factors can also affect how fast evaporation occurs. The larger the surface area of the liquid, the faster the rate of evaporation will be. This is due to evaporation only occurring at the surface of a liquid. If air is blown past the water, for example wind or from a fan, the rate of evaporation will be faster as the particles of water that have evaporated are 'blown away', bringing new air into contact with the water (air can only hold so much water). Also, if the surrounding air is 'dry', i.e. not humid, evaporation will happen faster, (again, this is because air can only hold so much water).

NATIONAL CURRICULUM LINKS:
- **Year 4 programme of study**: States of matter
  - Identify the part played by evaporation and condensation in the water cycle and associate the rate of evaporation with temperature.
- **Year 5 programme of study**: Properties and changes of materials
  - Use knowledge of solids, liquids and gases to decide how mixtures might be separated through filtering, sieving and evaporating.

MATERIALS NEEDED:
- Plastic beakers
- Markers for writing on the beakers
- Measuring cylinders
- Paper towels
- Water

 SAFETY AND TECHNICAL NOTES:
- Use plastic beakers in case they are knocked over.
- Ensure that no beakers are placed near electrical devices.

METHOD:

TO BE DONE IN ADVANCE BY THE TEACHER:
Prepare a cold and a hot place for the some of the beakers to go. A fridge and underneath a radiator are good choices.

 ### CHILDREN:

1 Use a measuring cylinder to measure out your chosen amount of water. Pour this into each of your beakers.
2 Use the marker to put a line on your beaker to show where the water comes up to.
3 Choose where you want to place your beakers. Place one outside, one somewhere very cold and one somewhere very warm. Make sure you put your beaker onto a paper towel.
4 Come back and observe your beakers each day. Use the marker to mark where the water comes up to each time.

 ### DATA COLLECTION IDEAS:
The children can take photographs of the beakers each day and use these as a record for how quickly the water evaporated.

DIFFERENTIATION:
- **Decrease the challenge:** The children may need help choosing suitable places to put the beakers.
- **Increase the challenge:** The children could dissolve salt in the water at the start of the investigation and see if they can retrieve the same amount of salt from the beakers when the water has evaporated.

USEFUL QUESTIONS TO ASK THE CHILDREN:
- In which location did the water evaporate the fastest? Why do you think this was?
- In which location did the water evaporate the slowest? Why do you think this was?
- What other factors might affect how fast water evaporates?

FURTHER WORK:
The children could investigate if different liquids evaporate at the same rate by repeating the investigation with different liquids, for example tea, undiluted squash and diluted squash.

Make a fossil

LEARNING OBJECTIVES:
Make your own fossil.

INTRODUCTION:
The children make a model of a fossil using plasticine and plaster of Paris.

USEFUL PRIOR WORK:
The children should know what a fossil is.

 BACKGROUND SCIENCE:
A fossil is a previously living organism that has been preserved. Fossils can be found of both plants and animals and can be very small (for example, impressions of a leaf in a rock) or very large (for example, a dinosaur skeleton). Usually, it is the harder parts of the organism's body that survive as a fossil, for example bones or exoskeletons. The softer tissues are normally broken down over time or eaten by other organisms. Fossils can form in different ways including the organism being buried or mineralisation of the organism. The type of fossils found as an impression in rocks are called impression fossils. They are two-dimensional prints caused by an impression left from the dead organism or from an impression left by an organism when it was alive, for example footprints. Impression fossils do not actually contain any material from the organism, they are simply indentations. Fossils can tell us a lot about how life has evolved on Earth by studying the type of organisms that have lived on the Earth at different periods of time.

NATIONAL CURRICULUM LINKS:
- **Year 3 programme of study**: Rocks
  - Describe in simple terms how fossils are formed when things that have lived are trapped within rock.
- **Year 6 programme of study**: Evolution and inheritance
  - Recognise that living things have changed over time and that fossils provide information about living things that inhabited the Earth millions of years ago.

MATERIALS NEEDED:
- Plaster of Paris
- Small plastic cups
- Modelling tools or cocktail sticks
- Plasticine
- Picture of fossils
- Sea shells (optional)

 SAFETY AND TECHNICAL NOTES:
- Do not allow children to put their fingers into setting plaster of Paris while it is setting. It is an exothermic reaction (gives off heat) and can cause severe burns.
- Do not pour plaster of Paris down the sink. Allow it to set and then throw it away.
- It is best to leave the fossils to dry overnight.
- Supervise children if they are using cocktail sticks.

METHOD:

TO BE DONE IN ADVANCE BY THE TEACHER:
If using seashells, make sure they are clean and dry.

 ### CHILDREN:

1 Take a small piece of plasticine and flatten it out. Make sure the surface is smooth and that it can fit inside your plastic cup.
2 Use the modelling tools or cocktail stick to draw the design of your fossil into the plasticine. Make sure you do not go through the plasticine.
3 When your design is finished, place your fossil into your plastic cup with the design facing upwards.
4 Carefully pour some plaster of Paris into your cup until it covers your fossil.
5 Place your fossil somewhere safe and leave it overnight to dry.
6 When your fossil is dry, carefully pull away the plastic cup (you may need to use scissors to help you) and remove your fossil!
7 You can now paint your fossil.

 ### DATA COLLECTION IDEAS:
The children can take photographs of their fossils. They can also be used to make or decorate other items, for example necklaces or bag-charms.

DIFFERENTIATION:
- **Decrease the challenge:** The children could press a shell into the plasticine to make an impression.
- **Increase the challenge:** The children could be encouraged to make larger or more complicated fossils, for example an ammonite.

USEFUL QUESTIONS TO ASK THE CHILDREN:
- In what ways is the fossil you made similar to a real fossil?
- In what ways is the fossil you made different from a real fossil?
- Where in the world might we find real fossils?

FURTHER WORK:
If possible, the children could observe real fossils. This could be linked with cross-curricular work in art and the children could make art-work incorporating the fossils.

EXPERIMENT 51

How strong is your magnet?

LEARNING OBJECTIVES:
Investigating the strength of different magnets.

INTRODUCTION:
The children investigate the strength of different magnets by
seeing how many paperclips they can pick up.

USEFUL PRIOR WORK:
The children should know what magnets are and that they can
be used to pick up magnetic materials.

 BACKGROUND SCIENCE:
A magnet is something that is able to attract magnetic materials.
Magnets have different strengths depending on the material they
are made from and how much they have been magnetised. These
two factors influence the strength of the magnetic field that exists
around the magnet. This magnetic field is able to exert a force on
magnetic materials, pulling or 'attracting' the magnetic object
towards the magnet. If an object is magnetic, that means it is made
of a magnetic material, but it has not been magnetised. Examples
of magnetic materials are iron, cobalt, nickel and steel. A magnet
is made from a magnetic material that has also been magnetised.
Magnets can come in different shapes, including bar magnets,
horseshoe magnets and disk magnets.

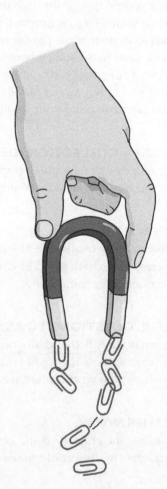

NATIONAL CURRICULUM LINKS:
• **Year 3 programme of study**: Forces and magnets
  – Observe how magnets attract or repel each other, and attract
    some materials and not others.

MATERIALS NEEDED:
• A selection of different magnets including bar and horseshoe
  magnets
• Paperclips

 SAFETY AND TECHNICAL NOTES:
• Avoid using very small, disk magnets as these can be
  swallowed by younger children.

METHOD:

TO BE DONE IN ADVANCE BY THE TEACHER:
Have a selection of different magnets ready for the children to test. Have small pots of paperclips for each group.

 CHILDREN:
1 Select the first magnet you want to test.
2 Predict how many paperclips you think the magnet will pick up. Write this in your results table.
3 Dip each pole of the magnet into the pot of paperclips and carefully lift it up again.
4 Count how many paperclips the magnet has picked up. Write this in your results table.
5 Repeat again with the other magnets.

 DATA COLLECTION IDEAS:

Magnet type and size	How many paperclips I predict the magnet will pick up	How many paperclips the magnet did pick up

DIFFERENTIATION:
• **Decrease the challenge:** The children could draw around the magnet in the results table.
• **Increase the challenge:** The children could conduct a more systematic investigation by adding paperclips one by one to each pole of the magnet until no more will attach.

USEFUL QUESTIONS TO ASK THE CHILDREN:
• Which magnet was the strongest/weakest? How do you know this?
• Were all bar magnets/horseshoe magnets the same strength? Why do you think this was?
• Were all big/small magnets the same strength? Why do you think this was?

FURTHER WORK:
This investigation could be linked to making a game involving magnets. The children can investigate the properties of the different magnets they have been given and then construct a game based on those magnets. For example, a fishing game where the role of a dice determines which magnet is used to collect the 'fish' (paperclips).

Making an electromagnet

LEARNING OBJECTIVES:
Making and testing an electromagnet.

INTRODUCTION:
The children make a simple electromagnet and investigate how strong the electromagnet is and how the strength can be increased.

USEFUL PRIOR WORK:
The children should know what magnets are and that they can be used to pick up magnetic materials. They should also be able to build simple electric circuits.

 BACKGROUND SCIENCE:
An electromagnet works on the principle that if an electric current is flowing in a wire than a magnetic field will form around the wire. This magnetic field in turn magnetises the metal in the electromagnet, temporarily turning the metal into a magnet. An electromagnet is a temporary magnet because once you switch off the electric current, the magnetic field no longer exists and the metal stops acting as a magnet. The strength of an electromagnet can be increased in three ways. These are: adding an iron core (in this case it is an iron nail), by adding more coils or by increasing the electric current.

NATIONAL CURRICULUM LINKS:
- **Year 3 programme of study**: Forces and magnets
  - Observe how magnets attract or repel each other, and attract some materials and not others.

MATERIALS NEEDED:
- Large iron nail
- Long length (about 30cm) of insulated wire
- Crocodile clips and wires
- Powerpack or batteries
- Paperclips

 SAFETY AND TECHNICAL NOTES:
- The nail can become hot while the electromagnet is in use. Instruct the children not to touch the actual nail.
- The electromagnet should be switched off when not in use.
- The electromagnet will generally be stronger if a powerpack is used rather than a battery.
- Resources can be purchased from Better Equipped (www.betterequipped.co.uk) and Hope Education (www.hope-education.co.uk).
- Circuit symbols are provided in Appendix 2.

METHOD:

TO BE DONE IN ADVANCE BY THE TEACHER:
Ensure that the insulated wires have a section of about 3cm of exposed wire at each end. Older or more experienced children may be able to do this themselves using wire cutters.

CHILDREN:

1 Leaving the exposed ends of the wire loose, wind the wire around the iron nail as many times as you can. Try not to let the coils sit on top of each other.
2 Connect the exposed ends of the wire to the powerpack or touch the ends of the wire against the terminals of the battery.
3 Place a paperclip onto the end of the nail and see if it is attracted.
4 Now turn off your magnet by either switching off the powerpack or removing the wires from the ends of the battery. What happened to the paperclip?
5 Repeat the investigation by wrapping the wire around the nail different numbers of times and counting the 'coils', then test how many paperclips your electromagnet will pick up. Remember to switch off your electromagnet whenever you are not using it.

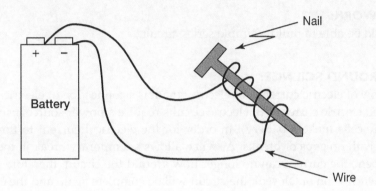

 DATA COLLECTION IDEAS:

Number of coils	Number of paperclips picked up

DIFFERENTIATION:
- **Decrease the challenge:** The children may need help wrapping the wire around the nail so that the coils do not sit on top of each other, which can make the electromagnet less effective.
- **Increase the challenge:** The children could also investigate the effect of current by comparing the electromagnet when used with a powerpack to the electromagnet when used with a battery.

USEFUL QUESTIONS TO ASK THE CHILDREN:
- What happened to the strength of your electromagnet when you had more coils? Did you see any pattern in your results?
- Why do you think we had to leave the ends of the wire exposed?
- Why did the magnet stop working when you switched off the electric current?

FURTHER WORK:
The children could investigate the everyday uses of electromagnets, which are found in, for example, motors, loudspeakers, scrapyards and maglev trains.

EXPERIMENT 53

Let's make a switch

LEARNING OBJECTIVES:
Design and make a switch for a circuit.

INTRODUCTION:
The children investigate the best design for a making a switch in a simple series circuit.

USEFUL PRIOR WORK:
The children should be able to build a simple series circuit.

 BACKGROUND SCIENCE:
Electricity is the flow of electric current. An electric circuit is a connection of electrical components that allow the flow of an electric current. All electric circuits require a power source, usually in the form of a cell (two or more cells make a battery). In order for the electrical current to flow there must be a 'complete' circuit, with no gaps or breaks. A switch allows a temporary break in the circuit. When the switch is off or 'open', the current can no longer flow around the circuit, therefore the circuit will not work. When the switch is on or 'closed', the circuit will be complete again and the electric current will be able to flow around the circuit. There are different types of switches depending on the use of the item. For example, push switches (found in lights) tilt switches (found in electric heaters) and foot switches (found in sewing machines).

NATIONAL CURRICULUM LINKS:
- **Year 4 programme of study**: Electricity
  - Construct a simple series electrical circuit, identifying and naming its basic parts, including cells, wires, bulbs, switches and buzzers.
- **Year 5 programme of study**: Properties and changes of materials
  - Compare and group together everyday materials on the basis of their physical properties including their hardness, solubility, transparency, conductivity (electrical and thermal) and response to magnets.
  - Give reasons, based on evidence from comparative and fair tests, for the particular uses of everyday materials, including metals, wood and plastic.
- **Year 6 programme of study**: Electricity
  - Compare and give reasons for variations in how components function, including the brightness of bulbs, the loudness of buzzers and the on/off position of switches.
  - Use recognised symbols when representing a simple circuit in a diagram.

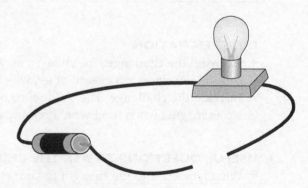

MATERIALS NEEDED:
- Batteries
- Connecting wires
- Bulbs or buzzers
- A selection of materials for making a switch, for example small squares of plastic sheet (about 3cm), paperclips, drawing pins, cardboard, rubber, graphite pencils, small plastic tubes, metal balls, etc.

SAFETY AND TECHNICAL NOTES:

- Remind children about working safely with electricity.
- Tell children not to touch the bulbs when they are being used as they can become hot.
- Circuits should be disconnected when not in use.
- Resources can be purchased from Better Equipped (www.betterequipped.co.uk) and Hope Education (www.hope-education.co.uk).
- Circuit symbols are provided in the back of the book.

METHOD:

TO BE DONE IN ADVANCE BY THE TEACHER:

You may wish to make some example switches for the children to look at before they make their own. A simple switch can be made from two squares of plastic that are Sellotaped together on one side. A paperclip or drawing pin can be stuck onto each piece of the plastic. When the two pieces of plastic are brought together and the paperclip/pins touch, the switch will be 'on'. Another type of switch is a tilt switch. This can be made using a small plastic tube (old film canisters are ideal) with a ball bearing inside and a drawing pin pushed through the lid. When the tub is tilted so that the ball touches the drawing pin the switch is 'on'.

 CHILDREN:

1 Build a simple series circuit and leave a gap for your switch.
2 Look at the materials you can choose from. Draw a design for your switch. When you are happy with your design, build your switch and test it in your circuit.
3 Decide if you want to change or improve anything about your switch and test it again.

 DATA COLLECTION IDEAS:

The children can draw circuit diagrams of their circuits using recognised symbols. They could also take a photograph of their circuits.

DIFFERENTIATION:

- **Decrease the challenge:** The children might find it easier to have a template to follow for making a switch.
- **Increase the challenge:** The children could be challenged to make different types of switches, for example a tilt switch and a push switch.

USEFUL QUESTIONS TO ASK THE CHILDREN:

- What design did you use for your switch? Why did you choose that design?
- How does your switch work?
- Are there any ways that you can improve your switch design?

FURTHER WORK:

This investigation could be linked with cross-curricular work in design and technology. The children could design and build a device that requires a switch, for example a battery-powered torch.

Fruit circuits!

LEARNING OBJECTIVES:
Make a battery using a fruit.

INTRODUCTION:
The children investigate how fruits can be used as a battery in a simple circuit and how the current in the circuit can be increased by adding more fruit or more electrodes.

USEFUL PRIOR WORK:
The children should know what an electrical circuit is and how to construct a basic circuit.

 BACKGROUND SCIENCE:
An ordinary battery consists of two different metals in an acidic solution. A fruit battery works on the same principle. The inside of the fruit is acidic (which is why this investigation works best with very acidic fruit such as lemons and limes) and the zinc-galvanised nail and the penny are the two different metals. These metals are called 'electrodes'. When the circuit is complete, the current flows from the penny, through the juice in the fruit (the 'electrolyte') and into the nail. The current is low but is enough to power a small electrical component such as an LED (light-emitting diode). More than one fruit battery can be used in a circuit, making the circuit more powerful.

NATIONAL CURRICULUM LINKS:
- **Year 4 programme of study:** Electricity
  - Construct a simple series electrical circuit, identifying and naming its basic parts, including cells, wires, bulbs, switches and buzzers.
- **Year 6 programme of study:** Electricity
  - Associate the brightness of a lamp or the volume of a buzzer with the number and voltage of cells used in a circuit.

MATERIALS NEEDED:
- Lemons or limes (or a combination) – enough for four per group
- Connecting wires
- Ammeter or low-level LEDs
- Pennies
- Zinc-galvanised nails
- Digital camera (optional)

 SAFETY AND TECHNICAL NOTES:
- Tell children not to eat the fruit.
- Do not allow the pennies and the zinc-galvanised nails to touch each other in the lemon.
- Adding more fruit or more electrodes (pennies and nails) will increase the strength of the current.
- The circuit can be tested by connecting it to a low-level LED, which should light up (although it may not be very bright) if four or more lemons or limes are used. If LEDs are not available an ammeter can be connected in series in the circuit to show that there is a current flowing.
- Resources can be purchased from Better Equipped (www.betterequipped.co.uk) and Hope Education (www.hope-education.co.uk).
- Circuit symbols are provided in the back of the book.

METHOD:

TO BE DONE IN ADVANCE BY THE TEACHER:
Cut slits into the lemons and limes that will fit the pennies. The pennies will eventually be pushed into the fruit halfway. The zinc-galvanised nails will also be pushed into the fruit opposite the pennies (make sure they do not touch). You may wish to do this for the children, depending on their age.

 CHILDREN:

1 Push the penny halfway into the slit that has been cut into your lemon/lime. Now push the nail halfway into the opposite side of the lemon (your teacher may have done this for you). Make sure the nail and the penny do not touch each other.
2 Do the same for all your other lemons/limes.

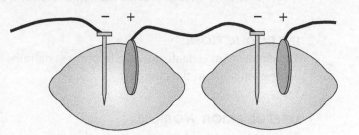

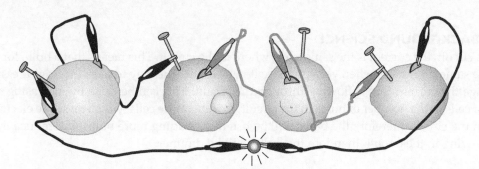

3 Connect up all your lemons/limes into a circuit using connecting wires. Each connecting wire should connect a penny to a nail.
4 Connect the final two ends of the last connecting wire to an ammeter or an LED. Observe what happens.

5 Try removing one lemon/lime at a time from your circuit and observe what happens to your LED/ammeter.

 DATA COLLECTION IDEAS:
Pupils can draw or take photographs of their circuits.

DIFFERENTIATION:
• **Decrease the challenge:** The children may need help with assembling the circuit, especially with making sure the connecting wires are attaching a nail to a penny each time.
• **Increase the challenge:** The children could investigate the effect of adding more electrodes to the fruit. This can be done by adding another nail and penny to each piece of fruit.

USEFUL QUESTIONS TO ASK THE CHILDREN:
• What happened to the LED/ammeter when we connected our circuits?
• What happened when you removed a lemon/lime from your circuit? Why do you think this was?
• Do you think that fruit batteries are a useful way of powering circuits?

FURTHER WORK:
The children could investigate whether other fruit, such as apples and bananas for example, produce the same results as lemons/limes. They could also experiment with potatoes, which work well as 'batteries' as they contain phosphoric acid.

Brighter bulbs

LEARNING OBJECTIVES:
Investigate how we can change the brightness of a bulb.

INTRODUCTION:
The children investigate how the brightness of bulbs in a series circuit changes depending on how many components are in the circuit.

USEFUL PRIOR WORK:
The children should know what an electrical circuit is and how to construct a simple series circuit.

 BACKGROUND SCIENCE:
In a series circuit, the current is the same everywhere in the circuit. This means that a bulb, for example, will be the same brightness wherever you place it in a circuit. The way to alter the brightness of a bulb is to change the current that is flowing through the circuit. This can be done by increasing either the number of cells or the number of bulbs in the circuit. Adding more cells will increase the electric current flowing in the circuit, therefore the bulbs will be brighter. Adding more bulbs will reduce the electric current flowing in the circuit, therefore the bulbs will be dimmer.

NATIONAL CURRICULUM LINKS:
- **Year 4 programme of study**: Electricity
  - Construct a simple series electrical circuit, identifying and naming its basic parts, including cells, wires, bulbs, switches and buzzers.
- **Year 6 programme of study**: Electricity
  - Associate the brightness of a lamp or the volume of a buzzer with the number and voltage of cells used in a circuit.

MATERIALS NEEDED:
- Cells
- Connecting wires and crocodile clips
- A selection of bulbs

 SAFETY AND TECHNICAL NOTES:
- Remind children about working safely with electricity.
- Tell children not to touch the bulbs when they are being used as they can become hot.
- Circuits should be disconnected when not in use.
- The children should use bulbs that are the same voltage to ensure that they glow with the same brightness.
- Resources can be purchased from Better Equipped (www.betterequipped.co.uk) and Hope Education (www.hope-education.co.uk).
- Circuit symbols are provided in the back of the book.

METHOD:

TO BE DONE IN ADVANCE BY THE TEACHER:
Test the electrical components to ensure that they are working.

CHILDREN:

1 Connect up a simple series circuit with one bulb and one cell. Check that the circuit works. This is your comparison circuit. You will compare how bright the bulbs glow in this circuit with the test circuits that you build. Switch off your comparison circuit.
2 Build a series circuit with one bulb and two cells. This is your test circuit.
3 Switch on your test circuit and your comparison circuit. Compare the brightness of the bulbs. Write down your results and switch off both circuits.
4 Add another cell to your test circuit. You should have one bulb and three cells in your test circuit.
5 Switch on your test circuit and your comparison circuit. Compare the brightness of the bulbs. Write down your results and switch off both circuits.
6 Take out two cells from your test circuit and add one more bulb. You should have two bulbs and one cell in your test circuit.
7 Switch on your test circuit and your comparison circuit. Compare the brightness of the bulbs. Write down your results and switch off both circuits.
8 Add one more bulb to your test circuit. You should have three bulbs and one cell in your circuit.
9 Switch on your test circuit and your comparison circuit. Compare the brightness of the bulbs. Write down your results and switch off both circuits.

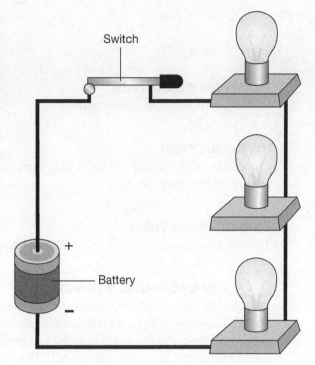

 DATA COLLECTION IDEAS:

Circuit	Bulb(s) were brighter in test circuit	Bulb(s) were brighter in comparison circuit
I bulb, 2 cells		
I bulb, 3 cells		
2 bulbs, I cell		
3 bulbs, I cell		

DIFFERENTIATION:

- **Decrease the challenge:** The children could have the circuits pre-made on boards so that they only have to test the circuits rather than build them. They could also take photographs of the circuits as a visual record for which circuits had the brightest bulbs.
- **Increase the challenge:** The children could test a greater range of combinations – for example two cells and two bulbs, two cells and three bulbs – and place the combinations in order of increasing brightness.

USEFUL QUESTIONS TO ASK THE CHILDREN:

- Which combination had the brightest/dimmest bulbs? Why do you think this was?
- Why do you think we had a comparison circuit in our investigation?
- What do you think would happen if we kept adding cells to a circuit with just one bulb?

FURTHER WORK:

The children could investigate the safety issues around electricity (especially the idea of having too much current flowing in a circuit) and produce safety posters, leaflets of videos.

Floating and sinking

LEARNING OBJECTIVES:
Investigate floating and sinking objects.

INTRODUCTION:
The children investigate which objects float and which objects sink, and how sinking objects can be altered so that they can float.

USEFUL PRIOR WORK:
The children should have a basic understanding of forces, including the concept of 'balanced forces'.

 ## BACKGROUND SCIENCE:
Objects will float or sink depending on their density. If their density is less than the density of the water, then the object will float. If their density is greater than the density of the water, then it will sink. This is because the force of gravity pulling the object down is greater than the force of the water pushing the object up (the forces are unbalanced). This 'pushing' force of the water is called *upthrust*. If the objects floats, this means that the force of gravity is balanced by the force of the upthrust. Some objects that normally sink can be altered so that they float. This can be done by changing their shape (therefore changing their density).

NATIONAL CURRICULUM LINKS:
- **Year 1 programme of study**: Everyday materials
  - Describe the simple physical properties of a variety of everyday materials.
- **Year 2 programme of study**: Uses of everyday materials
  - Identify and compare the suitability of a variety of everyday materials – including wood, metal, plastic, glass, brick, rock, paper and cardboard – for particular uses.
- **Year 5 programme of study**: Forces
  - Explain that unsupported objects fall towards the Earth because of the force of gravity acting between the Earth and the falling object.
  - Identify the effects of air resistance, water resistance and friction that act between moving surfaces.

MATERIALS NEEDED:
- Large, see-through bowls
- Water
- A selection of objects to float including: peeled orange, unpeeled orange, apple, pear, plasticine, paper, paperclips and straws
- Rolling pins (optional)

 ## SAFETY AND TECHNICAL NOTES:
- As water is being used make sure that there are no electrical devices nearby.
- An unpeeled orange typically floats and a peeled orange typically sinks. This is because there is a layer of trapped air between the peel and the orange. It is a good idea to have a peeled and an unpeeled orange that 'work' that can be used as a demonstration in case the children's oranges do not do what is expected.

METHOD:

TO BE DONE IN ADVANCE BY THE TEACHER:
Prepare all the objects to be floated and fill the water tanks.

 CHILDREN:

Investigation 1:
1 Choose the first object you want to test. Predict whether it will float or sink. Write this in your results table.
2 Put the object into the water. Record on your results table whether it floats or sinks.
3 Do this for the rest of the objects.

Investigation 2:
1 Take some plasticine and roll it into a ball.
2 Predict whether it will float or sink. Write this in your results table.
3 Put the plasticine into the water. Record on your results table whether it floats or sinks.
4 Now, flatten the plasticine as much as possible. You may be able to use a rolling pin.
5 Predict whether the plasticine will float or sink. Write this in your results table.
6 Put the plasticine into the water. Record on your results table whether it floats or sinks.
7 Make your plasticine into different shapes and test them to see whether they float or sink. Write your predictions and results in your results table.

 DATA COLLECTION IDEAS:

Object	My prediction: floats or sinks?	Results: floats or sinks?

Shape of the plasticine	My prediction: floats or sinks?	Results: floats or sinks?

DIFFERENTIATION:
- **Decrease the challenge:** The children can be provided with plasticine already made into different shapes so they just have to predict and test whether they will float.
- **Increase the challenge:** The children could investigate whether the volume of an object has any effect on whether it will float or sink. The volume can be found by placing the object in a measuring cylinder containing water and seeing how much water is displaced.

USEFUL QUESTIONS TO ASK THE CHILDREN:
- Which objects floated/sank? Why do you think this was?
- What shapes allowed the plasticine to float? Why do you think this was?
- Do the objects that floated/sank have anything in common?

FURTHER WORK:
The children could make boats from different materials and in different shapes and see which ones float the best.

EXPERIMENT 57

Density, density

LEARNING OBJECTIVES:
Investigate the density of different of liquids.

INTRODUCTION:
The children investigate density by layering different liquids of different densities into a beaker and seeing which objects float in which layer.

USEFUL PRIOR WORK:
The children should have a basic understanding of forces, including the concept of 'balanced forces' and floating and sinking.

 BACKGROUND SCIENCE:
Density refers to the mass of a substance divided by its volume. Liquids that have the same volume may have different densities because they have different masses. The higher the mass of a liquid, the higher its density will be. This generally means that thick, viscous liquids have higher densities. When an object is added to a liquid, it will sink due to the force of gravity unless the force exerted upwards by the liquid is equal to the force exerted by gravity. Typically a liquid with a higher density will exert a larger upwards force, meaning they are able to support heavier objects. Liquids of different densities will also be able to float on top of each other, with the liquid having the highest density forming a layer at the bottom. Sometimes the liquids will need time to 'settle' into layers, with the liquids that have lower densities gradually floating to the top.

NATIONAL CURRICULUM LINKS:
- **Year 1 programme of study**: Everyday materials
  - Describe the simple physical properties of a variety of everyday materials.
- **Year 5 programme of study**: Forces
  - Identify the effects of air resistance, water resistance and friction that act between moving surfaces.

MATERIALS NEEDED:
- Large, see-through beakers or measuring cylinders
- Washing-up liquid
- Honey
- Water
- Cooking oil
- A selection of objects to float, including marbles, small stones, paperclips, plasticine, ping pong balls and pennies

 SAFETY AND TECHNICAL NOTES:
- Make the density columns for the children. See the instructions below.

METHOD:

TO BE DONE IN ADVANCE BY THE TEACHER:

It is best to make the 'density columns' in advance for the children as they may struggle with adding the different liquids. Add the liquids slowly, starting with the honey, then the washing-up liquid, then the water and then the cooking oil. Use the same volume for each liquid. Pour the liquids down the side of the beaker. You may wish to demonstrate the making of a density column so that the children can see how the liquids sit on top of each other.

 CHILDREN:

1   Look carefully at your density column. What does it look like? Which liquid is on the bottom? Which liquid is on the top? Write down your observations.
2   Choose your first object. Predict where you think it will float in your density column.
3   Drop the object into your density column. Which layer did it float in? Record your result.
4   Repeat the investigation with all of the other objects.

 DATA COLLECTION IDEAS:

The children could draw their density column or take photographs to show where the different objects were floating.

DIFFERENTIATION:

- **Decrease the challenge:** A simpler density column of just oil and water could be used.
- **Increase the challenge:** The children could attempt to calculate the density of the liquids used by measuring the mass of a certain volume for each liquid.

USEFUL QUESTIONS TO ASK THE CHILDREN:

- Why do you think the liquids in the density column formed into layers?
- Which objects floated in the different layers? Why do you think this happened?
- Why did some objects sink to the bottom of the density column?

FURTHER WORK:

The density columns can be 'shaken up' (it is recommended that an adult does this) so that all the liquids mix together, then placed to the side to allow the liquids to re-settle into the layers.

Friction

LEARNING OBJECTIVES:
Investigating the friction of different surfaces.

INTRODUCTION:
The children investigate how far a toy car will travel along different surfaces that provide different amounts of friction.

USEFUL PRIOR WORK:
The children should know what friction is and that friction can slow objects down or stop them moving.

 ## BACKGROUND SCIENCE:
Friction is caused when two different surfaces move over each other. Friction is an example of a force and it will either slow an object down or prevent it from moving altogether. It acts in the opposite direction to the direction the object is moving. For example, if a book is pushed to the right across a table then friction would be acting to the left. The more friction there is, the slower an object will move. What causes friction is a combination of the roughness of the surface and the effect of adhesion. If a surface is rough, then any object moving along it will have to 'push through' any raised parts of the surface, slowing the object down. Adhesion occurs when materials are attracted to each other and electromagnetic bonds form. These bonds need to be broken for the objects to move against each other, resulting again in friction. Friction can be reduced by using smoother surfaces or by using lubricants, which can 'fill in' the gaps on a rough material, making the surface smoother.

NATIONAL CURRICULUM LINKS:
- **Year 2 programme of study**: Uses of everyday materials
  - Identify and compare the suitability of a variety of everyday materials – including wood, metal, plastic, glass, brick, rock, paper and cardboard – for particular uses.
- **Year 3 programme of study**: Forces and magnets
  - Compare how things move on different surfaces.
- **Year 5 programme of study**: Properties and changes of materials
  - Give reasons, based on evidence from comparative and fair tests, for the particular uses of everyday materials, including metals, wood and plastic.
- **Year 5 programme of study**: Forces
  - Identify the effect of air resistance, water resistance and friction that act between moving surfaces.

MATERIALS NEEDED:
- Toy car or similar
- Different surfaces, for example tile, carpet, wood, ice, sand, felt, linoleum, rulers

 ## SAFETY AND TECHNICAL NOTES:
- Make sure that all the surfaces are the same length. 30cm will be sufficient.

METHOD:

TO BE DONE IN ADVANCE BY THE TEACHER:

Prepare the different surfaces that will be tested.

 CHILDREN:

1 Choose the first surface you want to test. Place the surface flat on your table.
2 Place the toy car at the end of the surface.
3 Place one finger on the toy car and **gently** push the toy car along the surface. Do not take your finger off the car.
4 When the car stops, use your ruler to measure how far the car has travelled.
5 Repeat the investigation with the other surfaces.

 DATA COLLECTION IDEAS:

Material	Distance the car travelled (cm)

DIFFERENTIATION:

• **Decrease the challenge:** The children could simply rank how difficult it was to push the car along the surface on a scale of 1–10.
• **Increase the challenge:** The children could repeat the investigation with different objects being pushed along the surfaces to see if they get similar results.

USEFUL QUESTIONS TO ASK THE CHILDREN:

• Which surface did the car travel the furthest distance on? Why do you think this was?
• Which surface did the car travel the shortest distance on? Why do you think this was?
• What do you think happens when roads are wet or icy?

FURTHER WORK:

The children could look at stopping distances of cars including why they are important and the factors that can affect it.

EXPERIMENT 59

How much force?

LEARNING OBJECTIVES:
Investigate how much force is needed to lift or move different objects.

INTRODUCTION:
The children investigate how much force is needed to lift different objects using a force meter.

USEFUL PRIOR WORK:
The children should know what a force is and that forces are measured in newtons (N).

 BACKGROUND SCIENCE:
A force is something that changes the speed, shape or direction of an object. Forces are measured in newtons (N). To measure how much force it would take to lift or move something we can use a force meter. A force meter is basically a spring enclosed in a plastic case and attached to a hook. When a force is applied to the spring it will stretch. The force meter will have markings on the casing to enable you to read off how much force was needed to stretch the spring that far. As force meters work by stretching the spring, the zero is found at the top of the force meter and the numbers increase as they go down the casing. Children may need to be shown how to read force meters. Force meters come in different sizes for measuring different ranges of forces.

NATIONAL CURRICULUM LINKS:
- **Year 3 programme of study**: Forces
  - Notice that some forces need contact between two objects, but magnetic forces can act at a distance.

MATERIALS NEEDED:
- Force meter
- A selection of different objects to investigate, for example a book, ruler, door, soft toy, pencil case, balance (optional)

 SAFETY AND TECHNICAL NOTES:
- If the children are lifting objects with the force meter, ensure they do it over the table in case the object falls off.
- Make sure the children do not use the force meter on something that will be too heavy as the force meter may break.

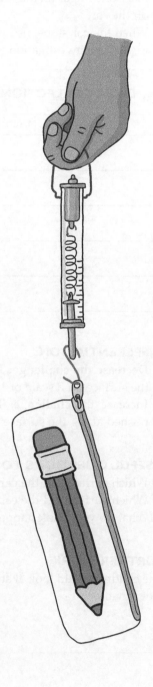

METHOD:

TO BE DONE IN ADVANCE BY THE TEACHER:
Have a selection of objects for the children to test.

 CHILDREN:

1 Choose the first object you want to measure.
2 If you can lift the object using the force meter then hook it onto the force meter, lift the object and then read off the result.
3 If you can not lift the object then hook the force meter over the object and pull it towards you along the table. When the object starts moving, read off the result.
4 Repeat the investigation using the rest of the objects.

✏ **DATA COLLECTION IDEAS:**

Object	Force needed to lift or move the object (N)

DIFFERENTIATION:
• **Decrease the challenge:** The children may need help attaching items to the force meter and reading the result.
• **Increase the challenge:** The children could investigate if there is a relationship between the mass of the object and how much force is needed to lift or pull it.

USEFUL QUESTIONS TO ASK THE CHILDREN:
• Which objects needed the most amount of force to lift or move them? Why do you think this was?
• Which objects needed the least amount of force to lift or move them? Why do you think this was?
• What other factors might affect have much force is needed to move an object?

FURTHER WORK:
The children could make their own force meters.

Bouncy balls!

LEARNING OBJECTIVES:
Investigating how bouncy different balls are.

INTRODUCTION:
The children investigate how well different balls bounce by looking at how many times they bounce when dropped from a set height.

USEFUL PRIOR WORK:
The children should know that objects fall to the Earth because of gravity.

 BACKGROUND SCIENCE:
When an object is dropped, it will fall towards the Earth because of the effect of gravity. Gravity acts equally on all objects, so heavier objects do not fall faster than lighter objects. When an object that is dropped comes into contact with a surface, such as the ground, it will experience a contact force. This force may stop the object moving altogether. However, if the object can be compressed slightly, the force will push the particles of the object closer together, converting some of its kinetic (movement) energy into potential energy (stored energy). This potential energy is what allows the object to 'bounce', as the particles that were squashed together now begin to move apart again. This is why objects that are elastic are more likely to bounce than solid objects. The more elastic the object is, the more it will be compressed when it first comes into contact with the surface, therefore the more potential energy will be stored in the object and the higher it will bounce, resulting in further potential energy being stored when it next hits the surface, resulting in more bounces overall.

NATIONAL CURRICULUM LINKS:
- **Year 1 programme of study**: Everyday materials
  - Describe the simple physical properties of a variety of everyday materials.
- **Year 2 programme of study**: Uses of everyday materials
  - Identify and compare the suitability of a variety of everyday materials – including wood, metal, plastic, glass, brick, rock, paper and cardboard – for particular uses.
- **Year 3 programme of study**: Forces
  - Compare how things move on different surfaces.
- **Year 5 programme of study**: Properties and changes of materials
  - Give reasons, based on evidence from comparative and fair tests, for the particular uses of everyday materials, including metals, wood and plastic.
- **Year 5 programme of study**: Forces
  - Explain that unsupported objects fall towards the Earth because of the force of gravity acting between the Earth and the falling object.

MATERIALS NEEDED:
- A selection of different balls, for example football, tennis ball, ping pong ball, sponge balls, rubber balls
- Metre rulers

SAFETY AND TECHNICAL NOTES:

- This investigation is best carried out in wide, empty space, such as a gym.
- Demonstrate to the children that they should just drop the ball, and not throw it, when carrying out the investigation.
- Remind children to be sensible with the balls and not to throw them around.

METHOD:

TO BE DONE IN ADVANCE BY THE TEACHER:
Have a selection of different balls for the children to test.

 CHILDREN:

1 Choose the first ball you want to test.
2 Hold the metre ruler straight up with one end on the floor.
3 Hold the ball next to the top of the metre ruler.
4 Let go of the ball.
5 Count how many times the ball bounces on the floor.
6 Record this in your results table.
7 Repeat the investigation with the rest of the balls.

 DATA COLLECTION IDEAS:

Type of ball	Number of times the ball bounced

DIFFERENTIATION:
- **Decrease the challenge:** The children may need help counting the number of times the ball bounced.
- **Increase the challenge:** The children could investigate what effect the surface has on how high or how many times the ball bounced by repeating the investigation on different surfaces such as a rubber mat, carpet, grass, etc.

USEFUL QUESTIONS TO ASK THE CHILDREN:
- Which ball bounced the most? Why do you think this was?
- Which ball bounced the least? Why do you think this was?
- What other factors might affect how high/how many times the ball bounced?

FURTHER WORK:
A demonstration could be done to show that gravity acts equally on all objects by dropping a ping pong ball and a tennis ball at the same, showing that they will hit the floor at the same time.

Speedy cars

LEARNING OBJECTIVES:
Investigate how to make a car go down a ramp faster.

INTRODUCTION:
The children investigate the different factors that affect the speed of a toy car travelling down a ramp.

USEFUL PRIOR WORK:
The children should know what friction is and that friction can slow objects down.

 BACKGROUND SCIENCE:
A toy car will roll down a ramp due to the force of gravity. As gravity acts the same on all objects regardless of their mass, changing the mass of the car would not make it travel any faster. However, factors such as the angle of the ramp and the surface of the ramp would affect how fast it travels. A ramp is an example of an inclined plane. Objects move faster down inclined planes as the forces acting on them are unbalanced. The steeper the ramp, the faster the object will travel. A car will also move faster down a ramp that has a smooth or lubricated surface compared to one with a rough surface due to the effect of friction. The less friction there is, the faster the car will travel down the ramp.

NATIONAL CURRICULUM LINKS:
- **Year 3 programme of study:** Forces and magnets
  - Compare how things move on different surfaces.
- **Year 5 programme of study:** Forces
  - Explain that unsupported objects fall towards the Earth because of the force of gravity acting between the Earth and the falling object.
  - Identify the effects of air resistance, water resistance and friction that act between moving surfaces.

MATERIALS NEEDED:
- Toy cars
- Adjustable ramps, or books/blocks that can be placed under the ramps to change the height/incline
- Different surfaces that can go on the ramps, for example carpet, rubber, linoleum, tiles
- Timers
- Rulers

 SAFETY AND TECHNICAL NOTES:
- Demonstrate how to set up and adjust the height of the ramp or change the surface of the ramp.
- Make sure the ramps are set up in a place where it will not be a hazard if the cars roll away from the experiment.

METHOD:

TO BE DONE IN ADVANCE BY THE TEACHER:

Have the different surfaces for the ramps available.

As this is a 'fair test' style investigation, talk with the children about what they will need to keep the same in their investigation, depending whether they investigate the height of the ramp or the surface of the ramp.

 CHILDREN:

1 Decide if you want to investigate the height of the ramp or the surface of the ramp.
2 Set up your ramp. Measure the height of your ramp if you are investigating the height. If you are investigating the surface of the ramp, choose which one you want to test first.
3 Roll your car down the ramp and record how long it takes to reach the end of the ramp. You might want to have a few practice goes before starting your investigation.
4 Record the time in your results table.
5 Choose a different height or surface for your ramp and repeat your investigation.

DATA COLLECTION IDEAS:

Height of ramp (mm) or surface of the ramp	Time taken to travel down the ramp (s)

DIFFERENTIATION:

- **Decrease the challenge:** The children could be provided with pre-made ramps of different heights or surfaces.
- **Increase the challenge:** The children could calculate the speed that the car is travelling using the equation speed = distance ÷ time, where distance is the length of the ramp and speed is the time taken to travel down the ramp.

USEFUL QUESTIONS TO ASK THE CHILDREN:

- What happened to the time taken for the car to travel down the ramp when the height of the ramp was changed? Why do you think this was?
- What happened to the time taken for the car to travel down the ramp when the surface of the ramp was changed? Why do you think this was?
- What other factors might affect how fast the car travels down the ramp?

FURTHER WORK:

The children could investigate the use of ramps in everyday life, for example ramps for disabled people, and look at how they need to be designed.

EXPERIMENT 62

Let's make a helicopter

LEARNING OBJECTIVES:
Investigate the rate at which paper helicopters fall to the ground

INTRODUCTION:
The children investigate the factors that affect how fast a paper helicopter will fall to the ground by altering either the length of the wings, the number of paperclips or type of paper used to make the helicopter.

USEFUL PRIOR WORK:
The children should have a basic understanding of forces and know that objects fall to the Earth because of gravity.

 BACKGROUND SCIENCE:
Objects fall to the ground due to the force of gravity. Theoretically, all objects fall at the same rate as gravity acts the same on all objects. This situation would always be found in a vacuum. However, one factor that causes objects to fall at different rates in the real world is air resistance. Air resistance slows falling objects down. The amount of air resistance acting on an object is due to that object's size and shape. Some shapes are more streamlined (an aeroplane for example) so have less air resistance acting on them. The less air resistance there is, the faster an object will fall. The mass of an object does not make a difference to the rate that the object falls, i.e. heavier objects do not necessarily fall faster than lighter objects.

NATIONAL CURRICULUM LINKS:
- **Year 5 programme of study**: Forces
  - Explain that unsupported objects fall towards the Earth because of the force of gravity acting between the Earth and the falling object.
  - Identify the effects of air resistance, water resistance and friction that act between moving surfaces.

MATERIALS NEEDED:
- Paper helicopter template
- Scissors
- Timers
- Paperclips
- Different types of paper
- Sycamore seed (optional)

 SAFETY AND TECHNICAL NOTES:
- Do not let children stand on chairs or tables when dropping their helicopters.
- For the investigation involving adding more paperclips to the helicopter, make sure that the children understand that it is not the added mass of the paperclips that is making the helicopter fall faster, but the fact that the extra paperclips affect how fast the blades of the helicopter spin, therefore affecting the amount of air resistance.

METHOD:

TO BE DONE IN ADVANCE BY THE TEACHER:
Have templates for the paper helicopters ready. You may wish to have templates with different-sized blades in case the children decide to investigate this factor.

CHILDREN:
1 Cut out the paper helicopter and fold it as shown on the instructions
2 Add a paperclip to the bottom of your paper helicopter. This helps make your helicopter more stable.
3 Drop the helicopter and observe how it falls. Use a timer and see how long it takes to fall. Do this a few times.
4 Decide what you would like to investigate. You could choose to make the helicopter out of different types of paper, add more paperclips to the bottom, drop the helicopter from different heights, change the length of the helicopter blades or choose something of your own.
5 Make the helicopters you need for your investigation.
6 Think about what other variables you need to control in your investigation.
7 When you are ready, drop your helicopters and use the timer to record how long it takes them to fall to the ground.

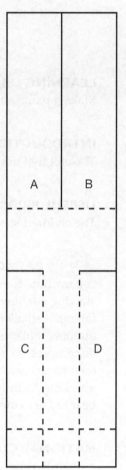

 DATA COLLECTION IDEAS:
The children can design their own results table based on whichever investigation they are carrying out. Older children should be encouraged to calculate an average for each of their trials. The children could also video their helicopters falling.

DIFFERENTIATION:
- **Decrease the challenge:** The children may need help with cutting out and folding the paper helicopters.
- **Increase the challenge:** The children could investigate more than one factor.

USEFUL QUESTIONS TO ASK THE CHILDREN:
- What effect did your factor have on how fast your helicopter fell? Why do you think this was?
- Are there any other factors that may speed up or slow down our paper helicopters?
- What do our paper helicopters have in common with sycamore seeds?

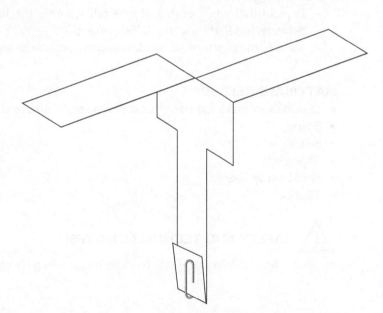

FURTHER WORK:
This investigation could be linked to seed dispersal, for example sycamore seeds work in a similar way to the paper helicopters.

EXPERIMENT 63

Let's make a parachute

LEARNING OBJECTIVES:
Make a parachute for a teddy bear.

INTRODUCTION:
The children design and test their own parachute.

USEFUL PRIOR WORK:
The children should know what friction is and that friction can slow objects down.

 BACKGROUND SCIENCE:
A parachute is a large piece of material that is designed to trap air, therefore creating air resistance and slowing a falling object down. The size of the parachute is determined by the size of the object that is falling. A smaller object will only need a smaller parachute. Parachutes that are used by people jumping out of aeroplanes are made from nylon, which is a very strong but also light material. It is also able to be compressed into a smaller space until it is needed. In this investigation the children can design their own parachute to protect a small teddy bear. When the parachutes are made, they can be tested by attaching them to the teddy bear, dropping the bear from a height and timing how long it takes the bear to fall to the ground. The best parachute is the one that lets the bear fall the slowest to the ground.

NATIONAL CURRICULUM LINKS:
• **Year 5 programme of study**: Forces
 – Explain that unsupported objects fall towards the Earth because of the force of gravity acting between the Earth and the falling object.
 – Identify the effects of air resistance, water resistance and friction that act between moving surfaces.

MATERIALS NEEDED:
• Materials to make the parachutes, for example different types of paper, plastic bags, bin liners
• String
• Sellotape
• Paperclips
• Small teddy bear
• Timers

 SAFETY AND TECHNICAL NOTES:
• Do not let children stand on chairs or tables when dropping testing their parachutes.

METHOD:

TO BE DONE IN ADVANCE BY THE TEACHER:

Prepare the materials that the children can use to make their parachutes. Show the children some photographs of parachutes and discuss the basic design of them.

 ### CHILDREN:

1 Draw some ideas for the design of your parachute. When you have chosen your final design, choose the materials you would like to build your parachute.
2 Build your parachute.
3 When your parachute is finished, you can test it on the teddy bear. When it is your turn, attach your parachute to the bear and drop the bear from the chosen height. Your teacher or partner will time how long the bear takes to reach the ground.

 ### DATA COLLECTION IDEAS:

The time taken for each parachute to fall to the ground can be recorded and a class table can be created. Photographs or videos can also be taken of each parachute dropping.

DIFFERENTIATION:

- **Decrease the challenge:** The children could have a template to use when making their parachute.
- **Increase the challenge:** The children could calculate the speed that the parachute is travelling using the equation speed = distance ÷ time, where distance is the height the parachute was dropped from and time is the time taken to reach the ground.

USEFUL QUESTIONS TO ASK THE CHILDREN:

- What was the best design for the parachute? Why do you think this was?
- Why does a parachute help to slow objects down?
- What other useful properties should a parachute have?

FURTHER WORK:

The children could investigate how their parachutes work under different conditions, for example outside or with a fan to simulate wind.

EXPERIMENT 64

Taking the heat

LEARNING OBJECTIVES:
Investigate which material is best at conducting heat.

INTRODUCTION:
The children investigate whether wood or metal is best at conducting heat by heating spoons in hot water.

USEFUL PRIOR WORK:
The children should know that heat can travel via conduction.

 BACKGROUND SCIENCE:
Conduction is one type of heat transfer. All matter is made up of particles (atoms). When a substance is heated, these particles gain energy (kinetic energy), which causes them to vibrate more. As they vibrate, they bump into the particles near to them. This causes the energy to pass to these particles, which in turn vibrate more and bump into the particles near to them. This process allows heat to travel from one end of the substance to the other. The rate at which this transfer happens is the substance's 'conductivity'. The better a conductor a substance is, the faster the heat will transfer through the substance. Substances that allow heat to conduct through them are called conductors. Substances that do not allow heat to conduct through them or slow down the transfer of heat are called insulators. Metals are an example of a good conductor. Wood is an example of a good insulator.

NATIONAL CURRICULUM LINKS:
• **Year 1 programme of study**: Everyday materials
  – Describe the simple physical properties of a variety of everyday materials.
• **Year 2 programme of study**: Uses of everyday materials
  – Identify and compare the suitability of a variety of everyday materials – including wood, metal, plastic, glass, brick, rock, paper and cardboard – for particular uses.
• **Year 4 programme of study**: States of matter
  – Observe that some materials change state when they are heated or cooled and measure or research the temperature at which this happens in degrees Celsius (°C).
• **Year 5 programme of study**: Properties and changes of materials
  – Compare and group together everyday materials on the basis of their physical properties including their hardness, solubility, transparency, conductivity (electrical and thermal) and response to magnets.
  – Give reasons, based on evidence from comparative and fair tests, for the particular uses of everyday materials, including metals, wood and plastic.

MATERIALS NEEDED:
• Metal and wooden spoons, ideally the same size
• Beakers
• Cardboard
• Vaseline
• Paperclips
• Timers
• Water

SAFETY AND TECHNICAL NOTES:

- The water in this investigation does not have to be boiling, water from the hot tap will be sufficient.
- Place the paperclips near the end of the spoon. Use plenty of Vaseline to hold them in place.
- To prevent the Vaseline from being melted by the steam rising from the water, it is best to have a cover over the top of the beaker. This can be made from cardboard with slots cut in for the spoons to be pushed through.
- Put the spoons into the beaker with the bowl of the spoon in the water.

METHOD:

TO BE DONE IN ADVANCE BY THE TEACHER:

Prepare the covers for the beaker if the children are not making them themselves.

 CHILDREN:

1 Use the Vaseline to stick a paperclip to the end of the metal spoon and wooden spoon. Make sure it does not fall off when you lift up the spoon.
2 Fill your beaker with the hot water and place the cover over the top.
3 Push the spoons through the slots in the cover, the bowl of the spoon should be in the water and the handle of the spoon should be sticking out.
4 Start the timer. Time how long it takes for the paperclip to fall off the end of the spoon.
5 Repeat your investigation two more times and take an average of your results.

 DATA COLLECTION IDEAS:

| Trial | Time taken for the paperclip to fall off the spoon (s) | |
	Metal	Wood
1		
2		
3		
Average		

DIFFERENTIATION:

- **Decrease the challenge:** The children could have the 'spoons' pre-made for them.
- **Increase the challenge:** The children could investigate different types of metal to see if there is any difference in their conductivity.

USEFUL QUESTIONS TO ASK THE CHILDREN:

- Which paperclip fell off first? Why do you think this was?
- What happened to make the paperclip fall off?
- Why do you think we put a cover over the beaker?

FURTHER WORK:

This investigation could be linked to the materials that cooking implements are made from. The children could look at why wooden spoons are used for stirring and why copper pans are better for cooking than aluminium pans.

Swinging time!

LEARNING OBJECTIVES:
Investigate how the length of a pendulum affects how long the pendulum takes to swing.

INTRODUCTION:
The children investigate how altering the length of a pendulum affects how long the pendulum takes to swing.

USEFUL PRIOR WORK:
The children do not need to have any particular prior knowledge before completing this investigation.

BACKGROUND SCIENCE:
A pendulum is a fixed device that can swing freely if a force is applied to it. Playground swings and grandfather clocks are examples of pendulums. A pendulum can swing if a force is directly applied to it, for example if it is pushed or pulled (like a playground swing) or it can swing due to the force of gravity. This happens if the pendulum is lifted and then dropped. The force of gravity will pull it back down. The time it takes a pendulum to swing and then return to its original starting position is called its period. The length of the pendulum (length of string) affects the length of the period. Also, the longer the string of the pendulum, the longer the period of the pendulum swing. This is because the pendulum has further to travel. The mass of the pendulum will not have an effect on the period as gravity acts on all objects equally.

NATIONAL CURRICULUM LINKS:
- **Year 5 programme of study**: Forces
  - Recognise that some mechanisms, including levers, pulleys and gears, allow a smaller force to have a greater effect.

MATERIALS NEEDED:
- Pendulum (a ball of plasticine or a ping pong ball on the end of some thick string will be sufficient)
- Clamp stand or the end of a table
- Timers
- Rulers
- Scissors

 SAFETY AND TECHNICAL NOTES:
- Use 30cm as the maximum length of the pendulum.
- If using the end of a table instead of a clamp stand, attach the string securely using Sellotape and ensure that the pendulum can swing freely without obstructions.
- Demonstrate that the swing the children are measuring is the time taken for the pendulum to swing to the other side then return back to its starting position.
- The pendulum should be released from a 90° angle so that the pendulum swings 180° in total.
- Remind the children that they should just let go of the pendulum, not apply any force.
- Remind the children not to stand too close to the pendulum so the pendulum does not hit them while it is swinging.

METHOD:

TO BE DONE IN ADVANCE BY THE TEACHER:

Prepare the pendulums, unless you want to have the children do this themselves. If the children are making their own pendulums, instruct them to make the string 30cm to begin with.

 CHILDREN:

1 If you are using a clamp stand, set this up and Sellotape the end of the string to it. If you are using a table, Sellotape the string to the edge of the table so that is hangs downward and can swing freely.
2 Raise your pendulum to the starting point (your teacher will show you how to do this). Let go of the pendulum and have your partner start the timer. You may want to practise this a few times to make sure the timer is started when you let go of the pendulum.
3 When the pendulum swings back to the starting point, stop the timer. Record the result in your results table.
4 Repeat two more times and record the results in your results table.
5 Remove the pendulum from the clamp stand or table and use a ruler to measure the next length you will be testing. Cut off the excess string and reattach your pendulum.
6 Repeat the investigation with all the lengths that you are testing.

 DATA COLLECTION IDEAS:

Length of pendulum (cm)	Time taken for one swing of the pendulum			
	Trial 1 (s)	Trial 2 (s)	Trial 3 (s)	Average (s)

DIFFERENTIATION:

• **Decrease the challenge:** The children may find this investigation easier as a whole class demonstration. A large pendulum could be made up using a ball on the end of a length of rope or a skipping rope. The investigation could be carried out in the playground (though only on a non-windy day) or the gym.
• **Increase the challenge:** The children could investigate other factors, such as the height from which the pendulum is swung.

USEFUL QUESTIONS TO ASK THE CHILDREN:

• What happened to the length of time taken for one swing when you shortened the length of the pendulum? Did you see any pattern in your results?
• Why do you think this happened?
• Where in everyday life do we find pendulums?

FURTHER WORK:

The children could investigate swings in the playground or a local park to see if they achieve the same results. The starting point would need to be a lower angle for this investigation.

Stretching springs

LEARNING OBJECTIVES:
Investigate what happens when we stretch a spring.

INTRODUCTION:
The children investigate the effect of adding weight to a spring by measuring how far the spring stretches each time.

USEFUL PRIOR WORK:
The children should know that some materials are able to stretch and that objects are pulled towards the Earth due to the effect of gravity.

 BACKGROUND SCIENCE:
Some objects have the property of elasticity. If a property is elastic it means that it can be pulled, stretched or otherwise distorted, but then will return to its original shape when the forces acting on it are removed. Examples of elastic objects include elastic bands and springs. Elastic objects may also follow Hooke's law (named after the scientist who discovered it, Robert Hooke). Hooke's law states that the amount of stretch exhibited by the elastic object will be proportional to the amount of force that is applied to the object. So if you double the amount of weight added to the object, for example, you will double the amount of stretch shown by the object. Some elastic objects have what is called an 'elastic limit'. This is the point at which too much weight has been added so that it will no longer return to its original shape. Springs are examples of objects with an elastic limit. Some elastic objects, on the other hand, will just break if too much weight is added to them – for example elastic bands.

NATIONAL CURRICULUM LINKS:
- **Year 2 programme of study:** Uses of everyday materials
  - Find out how the shapes of solid objects made from some materials can be changed by squashing, bending, twisting and stretching.
- **Year 5 programme of study:** Properties and changes of materials
  - Give reasons, based on evidence from comparative and fair tests, for the particular uses of everyday materials, including metals, wood and plastic.

MATERIALS NEEDED:
- Springs
- Clamp stands
- Small weights or objects with equal mass, for example marbles
- Plastic bags for example sandwich bags
- Rulers
- Sellotape

 SAFETY AND TECHNICAL NOTES:
- Test the springs first to find their elastic limit and do not give the children enough weights to reach this point.
- The springs can be hung from a clamp stand. If these are not available the spring can be Sellotaped to the end of a table as long as it is allowed to stretch freely.

METHOD:

TO BE DONE IN ADVANCE BY THE TEACHER:
Test the springs to find their elastic limit.

CHILDREN:

1 Attach your spring to the clamp stand or the end of the table. Make sure it is secure.
2 Attach the plastic bag to the end of the spring. You should be able to open the bag and put things inside. Make sure it is securely attached to the spring.
3 Measure the length of the spring. Write this into your results table.
4 Now add one weight to the plastic bag. Measure the length of the spring. Write this into your results table.
5 Keep adding one weight at a time, measuring the length of the spring and writing this result into your results table.

DATA COLLECTION IDEAS:

Number of weights	Length of spring (cm)

DIFFERENTIATION:
- **Decrease the challenge:** The children may find measuring the length of the spring difficult. If possible, use springs that give a large amount of stretch each time to make the measuring easier.
- **Increase the challenge:** The children could also investigate elastic bands and compare the results to those of the spring.

USEFUL QUESTIONS TO ASK THE CHILDREN:
- Did you notice any pattern in how much the spring was stretching each time you added a weight?
- What happened to the spring when you took all of the weights off?
- What do you think would happen if we kept adding weights to the spring?

FURTHER WORK:
The teacher could demonstrate how, if too much weight is added, the spring will reach its elastic limit point and no longer return to its original shape.

Making a rainbow

LEARNING OBJECTIVES:
Investigate how to separate white light into the colours of the spectrum.

INTRODUCTION:
The children investigate how to separate white light into the colours of the spectrum by using a prism.

USEFUL PRIOR WORK:
The children should know that white light is made up of the seven colours of the spectrum (rainbow).

 ## BACKGROUND SCIENCE:
White light is made up of the seven colours of the spectrum: red, orange, yellow, green, blue, indigo and violet. These different colours of light have different wavelengths. Red has the longest wavelength and violet has the shortest. The process by which white light is split into these seven colours is called dispersion. As the white light enters the prism from the air, the speed at which it is moving changes. This change in speed happens again as the light leaves the prism and enters the air again. These changes of speed cause the light to be refracted (bent) as it enters and leaves the prism. The degree to which the light bends depends on the wavelength of the light; therefore, the different colours of the spectrum bend at different angles. This causes the different colours of light to leave the prism at different angles, effectively separating them. This process is usually achieved in a classroom by the use of a ray-box and a prism. The ray-box needs to have a cover with a single slit in it so that an individual ray of light can be seen coming from it. This ray of light can then be directed through a triangular prism. As the light emerges from the other side of the prism it should be split into the colours of the spectrum.

NATIONAL CURRICULUM LINKS:
- **Year 3 programme of study**: Light
  - Recognise that we need light in order to see things and that dark is the absence of light.
- **Year 6 programme of study**: Light
  - Recognise that light appears to travel in straight lines.

MATERIALS NEEDED:
- Prisms
- Ray-boxes with slits (you can make you own by cutting a 1mm slit into a piece of black card that will fit over the end of the light box)
- Large pieces of white card

 ## SAFETY AND TECHNICAL NOTES:
- Remind the children not to touch the bulb in the ray-box as it will become hot.
- Resources can be purchased from Better Equipped (www.betterequipped.co.uk) and Hope Education (www.hope-education.co.uk).
- Circuit symbols are provided in the back of the book.

METHOD:

TO BE DONE IN ADVANCE BY THE TEACHER:
Ensure that each ray-box has a one-slit opening through which an individual ray of light can come out.

 CHILDREN:
1 Put your ray-box and prism onto the white card. The card will help you to see your spectrum.
2 Switch on the ray-box. You should be able to see a beam of light coming out from it.
3 Move your ray-box and prism around until the beam of light is entering the prism. Do not let the ray-box touch the prism.
4 Keep adjusting your ray-box until you can see the spectrum of colours on the other side of your prism.

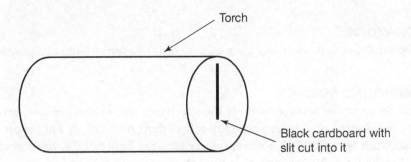

Torch

Black cardboard with slit cut into it

 DATA COLLECTION IDEAS:
The children could draw how their ray-box and prism are set up and the spectrum that they can see.

DIFFERENTIATION:
- **Decrease the challenge:** The children may need help adjusting the ray-box and prism so that the spectrum can be seen.
- **Increase the challenge:** The children could attempt to use another prism after the first prism in order to put the spectrum 'back together' again to make white light.

USEFUL QUESTIONS TO ASK THE CHILDREN:
- Which colours were you able to see in your spectrum?
- Which colour looked like it was bent the most/least?
- Where else have you seen rainbows and rainbow colours in everyday life?

FURTHER WORK:
The children could make colour wheels – a round piece of card divided into seven equal segments, with each segment coloured with one of the spectrum colours. This can then be placed onto a thin pencil or pen through a hole in the middle of the colour wheel. When it is spun fast, the colours appear to merge together, giving the impression that the card is white. This helps to demonstrate that the colours of the spectrum can be put back together to make white light.

Colourful light

LEARNING OBJECTIVES:
Investigate the effect of coloured filters.

INTRODUCTION:
The children investigate the effect of using different coloured filters when looking at different coloured objects.

USEFUL PRIOR WORK:
The children should know that white light is made up of the seven colours of the spectrum.

 BACKGROUND SCIENCE:
White light is made up of the seven colours of the spectrum, red, orange, yellow, green, blue, indigo and violet. We see coloured objects because they reflect their own colour but absorb all of the other colours of the spectrum. So a red book, for example, reflects red light but absorbs orange, yellow, green, blue, indigo and violet light. A black object absorbs all the colours of light and white objects reflect all the colours of light. A coloured filter acts in a similar way. It only allows its own colour to pass through. So a red filter only allows red light to pass through it and blocks all the other colours. This means if you hold a red filter over a red object, the object will still appear red. This is because it is allowing the red light the object is reflecting to pass through it. However, if you hold a red filter over a green object, the object will appear black. This is because the filter will not allow the green light the object is reflecting to pass through it.

NATIONAL CURRICULUM LINKS:
- **Year 6 programme of study**: Light
  - Explain that we see things because light travels from light sources to our eyes or from light sources to objects and then to our eyes.

MATERIALS NEEDED:
- A selection of objects in different colours including red, blue and green
- Filters including red, blue and green

 SAFETY AND TECHNICAL NOTES:
- The filters can be made from squares of coloured acetate. To increase their longevity, place a black cardboard or sugar paper frame around them.

METHOD:

TO BE DONE IN ADVANCE BY THE TEACHER:
Have a selection of different-coloured objects that the children can look at through the filters. Coloured plastic bottles work well. Make sure these are clean and dry if they contained food or drink.

CHILDREN:

1 Choose your first object. Record its colour in your results table.
2 Predict what colour you think the object will look like through the different filters. Write these predictions in your results table.
3 Use each filter to look at your object. Record what colour it looks like through the filter on your results table. Were your predictions correct?
4 Repeat the investigation with different objects.

 DATA COLLECTION IDEAS:

Object	Colour	Prediction: what colour I think the object will look through the filter			Colour the object looked through the filter		
		Red	Green	Blue	Red	Green	Blue

DIFFERENTIATION:

- **Decrease the challenge:** The children may find this investigation easier as a whole class demonstration. An overhead projector can be used to shine a light onto a white board and A4-sized filters can be used.
- **Increase the challenge:** The children could use filters of secondary colours of light, yellow, cyan and magenta, and investigate what happens. The filters will allow the primary colours of light that make them up through the filter. So yellow will allow red and green light to pass through the filter. Yellow objects would look yellow, but red and green objects will look red and green as well.

USEFUL QUESTIONS TO ASK THE CHILDREN:

- Which objects looked red/blue/green through the red/blue/green filter? Why do you think this was?
- Why do you think some objects looked black when you looked at them through a filter?
- Can you think of anywhere that we use coloured filters in everyday life?

FURTHER WORK:

The children could research colour blindness and how this is caused and the effect it has. PIP colour vision test plates could be used to illustrate this. (Be sensitive to any children who may be colour-blind in the class.)

Designing curtains

LEARNING OBJECTIVES:
Investigate the best material for making curtains.

INTRODUCTION:
The children investigate which material makes the best curtains by seeing which one blocks the most light.

USEFUL PRIOR WORK:
The children should know that light can travel through some materials and be blocked by other materials.

 BACKGROUND SCIENCE:
Light, unlike sound, does not need a material to travel through (it can travel through a vacuum). However, certain materials can block the transmission of light. Materials can be classified into one of three groups. Transparent materials allow all, or almost all, light through so that objects can be seen clearly through them. Translucent materials allow some light through but objects cannot be seen as clearly through them. Opaque materials do not allow light to pass through them. How much light passes through a material can be judged visually or measured more accurately using a data-logger with a light sensor or probe.

NATIONAL CURRICULUM LINKS:
- **Year 1 programme of study**: Everyday materials
  - Compare and group together a variety of everyday materials on the basis of their simple physical properties.
- **Year 2 programme of study**: Uses of everyday materials
  - Identify and compare the suitability of a variety of everyday materials – including wood, metal, plastic, glass, brick, rock, paper and cardboard – for particular uses.
- **Year 3 programme of study**: Light
  - Recognise that we need light in order to see things and that dark is the absence of light.
- **Year 5 programme of study**: Properties and changes of materials
  - Compare and group together everyday materials on the basis of their properties, including their hardness, solubility, transparency, conductivity (electrical and thermal) and response to magnets.
- **Year 6 programme of study**: Light
  - Explain that we see things because light travels from light sources to our eyes or from light sources to objects and then to our eyes.

MATERIALS NEEDED:
- A selection of different fabrics or materials cut to the same size
- Shoebox with a hole cut in one end
- Torch
- Data-logger with light sensor (optional)

SAFETY AND TECHNICAL NOTES:

- Remind the children not to shine the light into anyone's eyes (including their own).
- The shoe box will need to have a hole cut into one end that is as large as the end of the torch.
- The materials should be cut into a size that allows them to cover the hole that is cut into the shoe box.
- It is best if this investigation is carried out in a darkened room.

METHOD:

TO BE DONE IN ADVANCE BY THE TEACHER:
Prepare the shoeboxes and the materials to be tested.

 CHILDREN:

1 Place the shoebox and torch onto the table. Line up the torch so that the light shines through the hole in the shoe box. Put the torch as close to the shoe box as you can.
2 Pick the first material you want to test. Hang it over the end of the shoe box so that it covers the hole. You may need to use some Sellotape to hold it in place.
3 Switch on the torch and see how much light is able to pass through the material onto the other end of the shoe box.
4 Repeat the investigation with the other materials.

 DATA COLLECTION IDEAS:
The children can visually decide how much light has passed through the material. They could do this on a scale, for example 1–10. Alternatively they could rank the materials in order of how much light they let through.

DIFFERENTIATION:

- **Decrease the challenge:** The children could simply group the materials into categories such as 'allows a lot of light through', 'allows some light through', 'allows no light through'.
- **Increase the challenge:** The children could use a data-logger with a light probe in order to measure the amount of light passing through the material. For this investigation to be most effective, the room should be as dark as possible.

USEFUL QUESTIONS TO ASK THE CHILDREN:

- Which material would make the best curtains? How do you know this?
- Which material would make the worst curtains? How do you know this?
- What did the materials that made bad curtains have in common?

FURTHER WORK:
This investigation could be linked with cross-curricular work in history. The children could look at why black-out curtains were used during the war and the material these were made from.

Mirror, mirror on the wall

LEARNING OBJECTIVES:
Investigate how light is reflected from mirrors.

INTRODUCTION:
The children investigate how light is reflected from a mirror, including the relationship between the angle of incidence and the angle of reflection.

USEFUL PRIOR WORK:
The children should know that light can be reflected from some surfaces.

 BACKGROUND SCIENCE:
All objects can be seen because they reflect light from a light source into our eyes. However, very smooth, shiny surfaces (such as glass) enable us to see a 'reflection'. This is because the surface is so smooth that very little, if any, light is scattered off the surface, allowing us to see a clear image. Plane (flat) mirrors are the most common type of mirror and the one type that children would have most experience with in their everyday lives. These provide a 'mirror image' of the object, which means that everything is switched around in the image. The angle at which light hits a mirror is called the angle of incidence. The angle at which the light is reflected off a mirror is called the angle of reflection. The angle of incidence and the angle of reflection are always the same in a plane mirror. So, if the light hits the mirror at an angle of 45°, it will be reflected off the mirror at an angle of 45°.

NATIONAL CURRICULUM LINKS:
- **Year 3 programme of study**: Light
  - Note that light is reflected from surfaces.
- **Year 6 programme of study**: Light
  - Recognise that light appears to travel in straight lines.

MATERIALS NEEDED:
- Plane mirrors
- Mirror holder (or anything that will allow the mirror to stand upright)
- Ray-box with a 1mm-slit cover (or make your own: see diagram in 'Making a rainbow')
- White card
- Different coloured pens or pencils
- Protractors (optional)

 SAFETY AND TECHNICAL NOTES:
- Use plastic plane mirrors if possible.
- Remind the children not to shine the light into anyone's eyes (including their own).
- Remind the children not to touch the bulb in the ray-box as it will become hot.

METHOD:

TO BE DONE IN ADVANCE BY THE TEACHER:
This investigation works better in a darkened room, so if possible draw the curtains and lower the lights.

CHILDREN:

1 Place your mirror upright on the white card.
2 Use your ray-box to shine a beam of light onto the mirror. Use a coloured pencil or pen to draw over the path that the light takes to the mirror.
3 Use the same coloured pencil or pen to draw over the path that the light takes as it is reflected off the mirror.
4 Move your ray-box so that it is at a different angle to the mirror.
5 Use a different-coloured pencil or pen to draw over the path that the light takes to the mirror.
6 Use the same coloured pencil or pen to draw over the path that the light takes as it is reflected off the mirror.
7 Keep moving your ray-box to different angles and drawing over the path of the light, using a different colour each time.

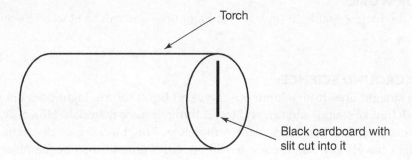

Torch

Black cardboard with slit cut into it

 DATA COLLECTION IDEAS:

The children can draw over the paths of light in different colours. When the investigation is finished they can look at the light paths they have drawn and see if they can spot a pattern between the light hitting the mirror and the light being reflected off the mirror.

DIFFERENTIATION:

• **Decrease the challenge:** The children may need help with adjusting the angle of the ray-box and drawing the light paths. Also, a large print-out of a protractor could be used as well. The children could place this onto their card and shine the light beam along a particular angle. The protractor would then show them that the light is reflected along the same angle.
• **Increase the challenge:** The children could use a normal protractor to measure the angles of incidence and the angles of reflection more accurately.

USEFUL QUESTIONS TO ASK THE CHILDREN:

• What happens to the light when it hits the mirror? Why do you think this is?
• Did you notice anything about the angle the light hits the mirror at and the angle the light is reflected off the mirror?
• Where would you find mirrors being used in everyday life?

FURTHER WORK:

The children could investigate the use of different types of mirror in everyday life, for example in periscopes, rear-view mirrors in cars, dental mirrors, etc.

In the shadows

LEARNING OBJECTIVES:
Investigating how to change the size of a shadow.

INTRODUCTION:
The children investigate how to change the size of a shadow by changing the distance of an opaque object from a light source.

USEFUL PRIOR WORK:
The children should know that light travels in straight lines and can be blocked by an object, causing a shadow.

 BACKGROUND SCIENCE:
Light travels in straight lines from a luminous (gives off light) source. Light does not need a medium to travel through (unlike sound) and can also travel through some materials. However, some materials – called opaque materials – can block light completely. This blocking of the light is what causes shadows. As light travels in straight lines, it will not bend around the opaque object; therefore, the shape of the shadow will match the shape of the object causing the shadow. The size of a shadow is affected by how close the object causing the shadow is to the light source. The closer the object is to the light source, the bigger the shadow will be. This is because the closer the object is to the light source, the more light it is able to block.

NATIONAL CURRICULUM LINKS:
- **Year 3 programme of study**: Light
  - Recognise that shadows are formed when the light from a light source is blocked by a solid object.
  - Find patterns in the way that the size of shadows changes.
- **Year 6 programme of study**: Light
  - Recognise that light appears to travel in straight lines.
  - Use the idea that light travels in straight lines to explain why shadows have the same shape as the objects that cast them.

MATERIALS NEEDED:
- Torches
- Screen or wall
- Opaque object
- Rulers

 SAFETY AND TECHNICAL NOTES:
- Remind the children not to shine the light into anyone's eyes (including their own).
- This investigation works better in a darkened room.

METHOD:

TO BE DONE IN ADVANCE BY THE TEACHER:
This investigation works better in a darkened room, so if possible draw the curtains and dim the lights.

 CHILDREN:

1 Set up your torch and opaque object so that the light shines on the object and a shadow is cast on the screen or wall. Have your torch 1 metre away from the opaque object.
2 Measure how high the shadow is using the 30cm ruler.
3 Now move the light source so that is 10cm closer to the object. Measure the height of the shadow again.
4 Keep moving the light source closer to the object and measuring the height of the shadow.

 DATA COLLECTION IDEAS:

Distance of light source to object (cm)	Height of shadow
100	
90	
80	
70	
60	
50	

DIFFERENTIATION:
- **Decrease the challenge:** The children could draw around the shadow onto a piece of card instead and use these as their results.
- **Increase the challenge:** The children could investigate objects of different shapes to see if they find a similar pattern of results.

USEFUL QUESTIONS TO ASK THE CHILDREN:
- What was causing the shadow?
- What happened to the size of the shadow as the object moved closer to the light source? Why do you think this was?
- Why do you think our shadows are smaller at midday when the sun is high in the sky?

FURTHER WORK:
This investigation could be linked with cross-curricular work in design and technology. The children could design and make a sundial that could be used in the playground.

Musical water

LEARNING OBJECTIVES:
Investigate how to make music from bottles of water.

INTRODUCTION:
The children investigate how the sound made by a glass bottle of water changes according to how much water is inside and how it is 'played'.

USEFUL PRIOR WORK:
The children should have a basic knowledge of sound and understand what is meant by pitch.

 BACKGROUND SCIENCE:
All sounds are caused by vibrations. When an object is vibrating, those vibrations pass into the surrounding air, causing the air to also vibrate. The sound travels through the air this way until it eventually reaches our ears. Sound is a type of a wave. The properties of a sound – for example, how loud the sound is or what its pitch is – are due to the shape of the sound wave. In glass bottles of water there are two different substances that can be vibrating. If the bottle is hit with something, then it is the glass that is vibrating. If the top of the bottle is blown across, then it is the air that is vibrating. The pitch of the sound in both cases will be determined by how much water is present in the bottle. If there is a lot of water, then hitting the bottle will produce a low-pitched sound. This is because the water slows down the vibrations of the glass. However, if there is a lot of water, then blowing across the bottle will produce a high-pitched sound. This is because the air has less distance to travel between the opening of the bottle and the top of the water.

NATIONAL CURRICULUM LINKS:
• **Year 4 programme of study:** Sound
   – Identify how sounds are made, associating some of them with something vibrating.
   – Find patterns between the pitch of a sound and features of the object that produced it.

MATERIALS NEEDED:
• Glass bottles
• Water
• Sticks for hitting musical instruments

 SAFETY AND TECHNICAL NOTES:
• Remind the children about how to work safely with glass.
• You may need to demonstrate the correct 'blowing' technique for blowing across the tops of the bottles.

METHOD:

TO BE DONE IN ADVANCE BY THE TEACHER:
You may wish to produce a 'tuned' xylophone by filling a set of water bottles with the required amount of water to use as a demonstration.

CHILDREN:

1 Tap your empty bottle with the stick. What does it sound like? Write down your observations.
2 Now try blowing across the top of the bottle. What does it sound like? Write down your observations.
3 Fill about ¼ of your bottle with water.
4 Tap your bottle with the stick. What does it sound like now? Write down your observations.
5 Blow across the top of the bottle. What does it sound like now? Write down your observations.
6 Keep adding water to your bottle and repeating the above. Write down your observations.

 ### DATA COLLECTION IDEAS:

Amount of water in the bottle	Observations	
	Tapping the bottle	Blowing across the bottle
Empty		
¼ full		
½ full		
¾ full		
Full		

DIFFERENTIATION:
- **Decrease the challenge:** The children may struggle with blowing across the top of the bottle so may need an adult to do this for them.
- **Increase the challenge:** The children could undertake a more systematic investigation and measure the exact volume of water in the bottle. They could also investigate a greater range of volumes.

USEFUL QUESTIONS TO ASK THE CHILDREN:
- What happened to the sound when we added more water and tapped the bottle? Why do you think this was?
- What happened to the sound when we added more water and blew across the bottle? Why do you think this was?
- How else could we change the sounds we produced with the bottles?

FURTHER WORK:
This investigation could be linked with cross-curricular work in music. The children could investigate how the pitch is changed on different types of instruments – for example, shortening or lengthening strings – and how this relates to the vibrations.

Making an ear trumpet

LEARNING OBJECTIVES:
Investigate the best design for an ear trumpet.

INTRODUCTION:
The children investigate the optimum size and shape for an ear trumpet by making their own ear trumpets and performing a fair test.

USEFUL PRIOR WORK:
The children should know that our ears allow us to hear and that sound travels as vibrations through the air to our ears.

 BACKGROUND SCIENCE:
Sound is a type of energy. A sound is made when an object vibrates. These vibrations then cause the surrounding air to vibrate. The sound is carried this way through the air by vibrations, eventually reaching our ears where it will cause our eardrum to vibrate. These vibrations are converted into an electrical impulse by the auditory nerve and carried to the brain. An ear trumpet can improve hearing by collecting or 'funnelling' the sound vibrations into the ear, increasing the vibrations against the eardrum and making the sound appear louder. The larger the funnel end of the ear trumpet, the more sound vibrations will be collected. Before modern-day hearing devices, ear trumpets were used by people with hearing difficulties.

NATIONAL CURRICULUM LINKS:
- **Key Stage 1 programme of study**: Animals, including humans
  - Identify, name, draw and label the basic parts of the human body and say which part of the body is associated with each sense.
- **Year 4 programme of study**: Sound
  - Recognise that vibrations from sounds travel through a medium to the ear.

MATERIALS NEEDED:
- Large pieces of cardboard and other types of paper – for example newspaper, sugar paper, thick wrapping paper – for making the trumpets
- Items for making sounds, for example a drum, xylophone, etc.
- Sellotape
- Scissors
- Rulers
- Photographs of modern hearing aids (optional)

 SAFETY AND TECHNICAL NOTES:
- Remind the children not to shout or make other very loud noises into each other's ears.
- Tell the children not to put the smaller end of the ear trumpet directly into their ear. It should just be held near to their ear.

METHOD:

TO BE DONE IN ADVANCE BY THE TEACHER:
Demonstrate to the children how to make an ear trumpet. The easiest method is to roll a piece of paper into a cone and then secure it with Sellotape. The ear trumpet can be made bigger or smaller by rolling the paper more or less tightly.

 CHILDREN:

1 You are going to perform a fair test to find out the best design for an ear trumpet. You can either make your ear trumpets from different types of paper or make your ear trumpets different sizes. Choose which of these two variables you would like to investigate.
2 Decide what other variables you will need to keep the same. Plan how you will carry out your investigation.
3 Make your ear trumpets and test them by following your plan. Remember what you need to do in order to make it a fair test.
4 When you have tested all your ear trumpets, decide which one you think was the best design. See if you can think about why that was the best design.

 DATA COLLECTION IDEAS:
The children can rank the ear trumpets they have made from the best to the worst. Those who have investigated size can measure the width of the large end of the cone. Those who have investigated the type of paper can record what paper each ear trumpet was made from. The results from the two types of investigation could then be brought together in order to establish what would be the best size and paper to make an ear trumpet.

DIFFERENTIATION:
- **Decrease the challenge:** The children can be helped measuring the width of the ear trumpet.
- **Increase the challenge:** The children could investigate both variables (size and type of paper) and then make the best design for an ear trumpet using both sets of results.

USEFUL QUESTIONS TO ASK THE CHILDREN:
- What was the best size for an ear trumpet? Why do you think this was?
- What was the best paper for an ear trumpet? Why do you think this was?
- What are the advantages of using hearing aids rather than using ear trumpets?

FURTHER WORK:
The children could research how modern-day hearing aids work and how these have developed and improved over time. Be sensitive to any children who may have hearing difficulties.

Soundproofing

LEARNING OBJECTIVES:
Make a soundproof box.

INTRODUCTION:
The children investigate how well different materials soundproof a box containing a ticking clock.

USEFUL PRIOR WORK:
The children should know that sound travels as vibrations, and can travel through solids, liquids and gases.

 BACKGROUND SCIENCE:
Sound is a type of energy. When an object vibrates, the vibrations cause neighbouring air particles to vibrate. These vibrations continue to pass through the air until they reach our ear where they make our eardrum vibrate. Sometimes we want to reduce sound levels if they are too loud or a nuisance. For this soundproofing can be used. Soundproofing materials can work by either absorbing or reflecting the sound. Materials that absorb sound allow a small amount of the sound energy to be transferred as heat energy (energy cannot be created or destroyed, only transferred from one type to another). Generally, thick, porous materials (such as towels) or materials with a high mass (such as rubber) are better soundproofers. The effectiveness of the material at soundproofing in this investigation can be done by the children using a subjective scale of 1–10. Alternatively a data-logger can be used that will measure the level of the sound in decibels.

NATIONAL CURRICULUM LINKS:
- **Year 2 programme of study**: Uses of everyday materials
  - Identify and compare the suitability of a variety of everyday materials – including wood, metal, plastic, glass, brick, rock, paper and cardboard – for particular uses.
- **Year 4 programme of study**: Sound
  - Identify how sounds are made, associating some of them with something vibrating.
  - Recognise that vibrations from sounds travel through a medium to the ear.
  - Recognise that sounds get fainter as the distance from the sound source increases.
- **Year 5 programme of study**: Properties and changes of materials
  - Give reasons, based on evidence from comparative and fair tests, for the particular uses of everyday materials, including metals, wood and plastic.

MATERIALS NEEDED:
- Cardboard box – shoe boxes are a good choice
- An object that makes a regular sound, for example a ticking clock
- Materials for soundproofing for example newspaper, cotton wool, tissue paper, tea-towels, plastic bags
- Sellotape
- Elastic bands
- Data-logger (optional)

SAFETY AND TECHNICAL NOTES:

• A data-logger could be used to measure the level of the sound.

METHOD:

TO BE DONE IN ADVANCE BY THE TEACHER:
Prepare the materials that the children will be testing. Try to make them similar sizes.

 CHILDREN:

1 Place your noisy object in the box and close the lid. Listen to how loud the object is.
2 Choose the first material you want to test. Cover the box with this material. You may need to use elastic bands or Sellotape to hold it in place.
3 Listen to how loud the sound is now. Give it a score between 1–10 or use your data-logger. Record this in your results table.
4 Repeat the investigation with the rest of the materials.

 DATA COLLECTION IDEAS:

Material	How loud the sound was (1–10 dB)

DIFFERENTIATION:

• **Decrease the challenge:** The boxes could be pre-made with the different materials covering them. The children can then listen to the boxes and rank them in order of how loud the sound is.
• **Increase the challenge:** The children could investigate the effect of using layers of the materials and seeing how many layers are needed to block the sound completely.

USEFUL QUESTIONS TO ASK THE CHILDREN:

• Which material was best at soundproofing? Why do you think this was?
• Which material was the worst at soundproofing? Why do you think this was?
• Where in everyday life might we need to use soundproofing?

FURTHER WORK:
The children could research the effect on our hearing if we are exposed to continuous high levels of sound or high frequency sound and how any damage can be prevented.

Build a steady-hand game

LEARNING OBJECTIVES:
Design and build our own steady hand game!

INTRODUCTION:
The children use their knowledge of circuits to design and build a steady-hand game using a coat-hanger and a margarine tub lid.

USEFUL PRIOR WORK:
The children should know how to build simple electrical circuit.

 BACKGROUND SCIENCE:
A steady hand game is a test of hand–eye coordination. It involves moving a rod with a metal loop on the end along a piece of wire, without touching the wire. The game is designed in such a way that the electrical circuit is not complete until the metal rod touches the metal wire. This usually results in some signal being given off, for example a light coming on or a buzzing sound. Electricity can only travel around a complete circuit, so until the rod is touching the wire there is effectively a break or 'gap' in the circuit. The casing and all other parts of the steady hand game will generally be built out of insulating materials. This helps to reduce any issues with overheating. Steady-hand games can run on batteries as they only need to power a small device, for example an LED light or a buzzer.

NATIONAL CURRICULUM LINKS:
- **Year 4 programme of study**: Electricity
  - Construct a simple series electrical circuit, identifying and naming its basic parts, including cells, wires, bulbs, switches and buzzers.
  - Identify whether or not a lamp will light in a simple series circuit based in whether or not the lamp is part of a complete loop with a battery.
  - Recognise some common conductors and insulators, and associate metals with being good conductors.
- **Year 6 programme of study**: Electricity
  - Compare and give reasons for variations in how components function, including the brightness of bulbs, the loudness of buzzers and the on/off position of switches.

MATERIALS NEEDED:
- Metal coat-hangers
- Rectangular lid from a plastic tub, for example margarine tubs
- Short strand of bare copper wire
- Components for building an electric circuit including wires, crocodile clips, batteries and LED lights or buzzers
- Craft knife
- Pliers (optional)

 SAFETY AND TECHNICAL NOTES:
- Only adults should use the craft knife for cutting the plastic tubs.
- Tell the children to be careful with the coat-hangers as the ends can be sharp.
- The coat-hangers can be shaped by hand or by using pliers. Supervise children if they are using pliers.

- Resources can be purchased from Better Equipped (www.betterequipped.co.uk) and Hope Education (www.hope-education.co.uk).
- Circuit symbols are provided in the back of the book.

METHOD:

TO BE DONE IN ADVANCE BY THE TEACHER:
Prepare the lengths of copper wire. These should be about 10cm long. Untwist the coat-hangers.

 CHILDREN:

1 Shape your coat-hanger into the shape you want your steady hand game to be! Think about how difficult you want it to be. Remember it needs to have enough space for the rod to go around.
2 Make your rod. Take a piece of copper wire and bend one end into a loop. It should be big enough to fit over the coat-hanger wire. Wrap an electrical wire along the length of the rod (not the loop) to insulate the rod for the person holding it.
3 Draw on your plastic lid where you want the ends of your coat-hanger and your LED light or buzzer to go. Have your teacher cut some slits into the lid.
4 Push the ends of the coat-hanger through the lid (don't put too much through or your game will not stand up by itself). Push the LED light or buzzer through the lid.
5 Build your electrical circuit. Think about what you will need to make it work. Remember to include your rod in your circuit. Your circuit should only be complete if the rod is touching the coat-hanger.
6 When your game is finished you can play it and see how steady your hand is!

 **DATA COLLECTION IDEAS:**
The children take photographs of their steady hand games and can try each other's steady hand games.

DIFFERENTIATION:
- **Decrease the challenge:** The children can be provided with a template or instructions for how to build the steady-hand game.
- **Increase the challenge:** The children can be challenged to design the circuit themselves.

USEFUL QUESTIONS TO ASK THE CHILDREN:
- Why did the light/buzzer work when the rod touched the coat-hanger?
- Why did we insulate the rod?
- How could we improve our steady-hand games?

FURTHER WORK:
The children can come up with rules for their steady-hand games and challenge each other to complete their steady-hand games.

EXPERIMENT 76

Testing urine!

LEARNING OBJECTIVES:
Analyse some urine samples.

INTRODUCTION:
The children analyse some fake 'urine', including testing to see which ones contain glucose and protein.

USEFUL PRIOR WORK:
The children do not need to have any particular prior knowledge before completing this investigation.

 BACKGROUND SCIENCE:
Urine is produced by the kidneys and stored in the bladder before it is excreted by the body. Urine is an important indicator of the health of the body. Simple properties, such as the colour, can indicate how concentrated the urine is (very concentrated urine can be an indicator of dehydration). Urine can also contain products from digestion. If urine contains protein, this could be a sign of kidney damage as the kidneys should not allow proteins to pass into the urine. If glucose is present this could be a sign of diabetes (it can also be a sign of pregnancy in women). The pH of urine is typically around 7 (neutral) with most people falling between 5 and 8. Higher or lower pHs can indicate certain diseases. The presence of protein in urine can be found by heating the urine and seeing if it goes cloudy. Glucose can be tested for by using Clinistix strips, which are available to purchase. pH can be tested for by using universal indicator paper.

NATIONAL CURRICULUM LINKS:
*   **Year 2 programme of study**: Animals including humans
    –   Describe the importance for humans of exercise, eating the right amounts of different types of food and hygiene.
*   **Year 3 programme of study**: Animals including humans
    –   Identify that animals, including humans, need the right types and amount of nutrition, and that they cannot make their own food; they get nutrition from what they eat.
*   **Year 6 programme of study**: Animals including humans
    –   Describe the way in which nutrients and water are transported within animals, including humans.

MATERIALS NEEDED:
*   Fake urine samples (see technical notes)
*   Universal indicator paper
*   Clinistix strips (pre-treated strips that test for the presence of glucose)
*   Beakers
*   Test tubes
*   Test tube racks
*   Water baths
*   Glucose powder
*   Albumin powder
*   Lemon juice
*   Yellow food colouring

 SAFETY AND TECHNICAL NOTES:
*   Make up four samples of fake urine. Use water with some food colouring added. You can also use tea to make the urine darker. Add 1 or 2 teaspoons of glucose powder to any urine samples you want to contain glucose. Add 1 or 2 teaspoons of albumin powder to any urine samples you want to contain protein. Add some lemon juice to any samples you want to make more acidic.
*   Set water baths to 50°C. Supervise children while they use the water baths.

- Resources can be purchased from Hope Education (www.hopeeducation.co.uk).
- Be aware of any allergies.

METHOD:

TO BE DONE IN ADVANCE BY THE TEACHER:
Make up the urine samples. Have a mixture of samples with different or no amounts of glucose and protein and different pHs.

 ### CHILDREN:

1 You are going to analyse four different urine samples. First, examine each sample. Write down the colour of the sample on your results table.
2 Use a piece of universal indicator paper to test the pH of each sample. Write down the results in your results table.
3 Pour half of the sample into a test tube and place the test tube in a water bath. Leave for 2 minutes.
4 Remove the sample and see whether it has gone cloudy. If it is cloudy that means there is protein present.
5 Use a Clinistix strip to test the other half of the urine sample. Dip the strip into the sample and see what colour it goes. Compare this with the chart to see if there is any glucose present.

 ## DATA COLLECTION IDEAS:

Urine sample	Colour	pH	Protein present?	Glucose present?
1				
2				
3				
4				

DIFFERENTIATION:
- **Decrease the challenge:** The children may need help deciding if the urine has gone cloudy for the protein test. Before and after photos could be taken for them to compare.
- **Increase the challenge:** The children could be challenged to match the urine samples with 'patients', for example 'Patient A has diabetes and has a diet high in acidic food'.

USEFUL QUESTIONS TO ASK THE CHILDREN:
- Which urine samples came from people who may have diabetes?
- Which urine samples came from people who may have kidney disease?
- What might cause someone's urine to become more acidic?

FURTHER WORK:
The children could research diabetes, including the causes, symptoms and treatment. Be sensitive to any children who may have diabetes.

Volcanic eruption!

LEARNING OBJECTIVES:
Make our own erupting volcano!

INTRODUCTION:
The children create a 'volcano' using baking soda and vinegar.

USEFUL PRIOR WORK:
The children should know what volcanoes are and that volcanoes can erupt, releasing lava.

 BACKGROUND SCIENCE:
A volcano is a mass of land that has a vent leading down through the Earth's crust to a pool of magma. When volcanoes erupt, the magma, volcanic ash and gases escape. When magma escapes from a volcano, it is referred to as lava. Volcanoes can be active (erupt regularly), dormant (has not erupted for a very long) or extinct (will not erupt again). A model can be made of an erupting volcano by using baking soda and vinegar. Baking soda is an alkali whereas vinegar is an acid. When the baking soda and vinegar are mixed, they react and produce carbonic acid. The carbonic acid, however, is unstable and quickly breaks down into the gas carbon dioxide. The build up of this gas is what causes the model volcano to 'erupt'. Adding a few drops of washing-up liquid helps to collect the bubbles of gas and makes the lava flow over the sides of the volcano.

NATIONAL CURRICULUM LINKS:
- **Year 5 programme of study:**
  Properties and changes of materials
  – Explain that some changes result in
    the formation of new materials (and
    that this kind of change is not usually
    reversible) including changes
    associated with burning and the
    action of acid on bicarbonate of soda.

MATERIALS NEEDED:
- Small plastic bottle (for example a water bottle or pop bottle)
- Baking soda
- Vinegar
- Washing-up liquid (optional)
- Water
- Modelling clay
- Red food colouring
- Teaspoon
- Beakers
- Paper towels

SAFETY AND TECHNICAL NOTES:

- The children can make the body of their volcano using modelling clay or any other art materials you wish. The model can be very detailed and could be made in advance of the actual experiment. The children could look at pictures of famous volcanoes and base their volcano on one of them, or they could come up with their own design.
- Make sure the plastic bottles have been thoroughly cleaned.
- Boiling water is not needed for this experiment. Water from the hot tap will be sufficient.
- This experiment is very messy and is best done on lots of paper towels or, if possible, outside.
- It is worth doing a trial before the experiment in order to check the best quantities of baking soda, vinegar and food colouring to use.

METHOD:

TO BE DONE IN ADVANCE BY THE TEACHER:
Perform a trial run to check the best quantities of vinegar, baking soda and food colouring to use. When you know the best quantities, pour the required amount of vinegar into the beakers so that the children have the correct amount when it comes time to pouring it into the volcano.

 CHILDREN:

1 You need to build your volcano first. Your empty bottle needs to be in the centre of your volcano. Build around the bottle but do not cover the opening of the bottle. This is where the lava will escape from.
2 When your volcano has been built and is ready to 'erupt', fill the bottle inside your volcano with warm water. Fill it about 1/2 full.
3 Add a few drops of food colouring and few drops of washing-up liquid to the bottle.
4 Add 2 teaspoons of baking soda to the bottle.
5 Your volcano is ready to erupt! Make sure you have put your volcano somewhere safe where it will not damage anything. Put lots of paper towels around it to soak up the mess.
6 When you are ready, very slowly pour the vinegar into your volcano.

 DATA COLLECTION IDEAS:
The children could video their volcanoes erupting or take photographs before, during and after the eruption.

DIFFERENTIATION:
- **Decrease the challenge:** The children can be helped with measuring out the ingredients.
- **Increase the challenge:** The children could perform a more systematic investigation and vary the amounts of baking soda and vinegar used (though within a pre-set range to avoid them using too much) and see what effect this has on the eruption.

USEFUL QUESTIONS TO ASK THE CHILDREN:
- How is our volcano similar/different to a real volcano?
- What do you think caused our volcano to erupt?
- Do you think we could get the vinegar and the baking soda back again?

FURTHER WORK:
This investigation could be linked with cross-curricular work in history and geography. The children could research famous volcanic eruptions – for example, Pompeii – and what happened during and after the eruptions. The children could also research where most volcanoes are located and produce a global map of volcanoes.

EXPERIMENT 78

Which is the best washing-up liquid?

LEARNING OBJECTIVES:
Investigate which is the best washing-up liquid.

INTRODUCTION:
The children investigate which is the best washing-up liquid for removing different stains on white tiles.

USEFUL PRIOR WORK:
The children do not need to have any particular prior knowledge before completing this investigation.

 BACKGROUND SCIENCE:
Washing-up liquids contain molecules of detergent. Detergents have a special chemical structure: they have a hydrophobic ('water hating') tail and a hydrophilic ('water loving') head. When these molecules come into contact with water, they form a spherical shape with the hydrophilic heads facing outwards and the hydrophobic tails on the inside. Oily substances are also hydrophobic. This means that when washing-up liquid is added to water with dirty plates, the grease will want to go inside the detergent structure where it can 'hide' from the water. This makes washing-up liquids particularly good at cleaning greasy foods from plates. The washing-up liquid is not the only factor that can affect how well plates are cleaned though. The water itself acts as a solvent and can dissolve many stains. Stains can also be physically removed by, for example, scrubbing with a sponge. Another factor to consider is whether the bacteria from the plates have been removed. Washing-up liquids are not normally antibacterial, although antibacterial versions are available.

NATIONAL CURRICULUM LINKS:
- **Year 5 programme of study**: Properties and changes of materials
  - Know that some substances will dissolve to form a solution, and describe how to recover a substance from a solution.

MATERIALS NEEDED:
- A selection of different washing-up liquids
- White tiles
- Non-latex gloves
- Substances for making stains: chocolate, butter and jam make good choices
- Washing-up bowls or large plastic tubs
- Timers
- Sponges (optional)

 SAFETY AND TECHNICAL NOTES:
- The children should wear non-latex gloves while carrying out this investigation.
- Warm water from the hot tap will be sufficient for this investigation.
- The dirty tiles need to be made in advance so that the stains can dry.

- A control tile could also be used that is cleaned with just water. This could be done by each group or one could be done by the teacher.
- The children can test the washing-up liquids by soaking the tiles in the washing-up liquid and water for a set time or by rubbing them with a sponge for a set amount of time. If children choose to rub the tiles, it is best to encourage the children not to rub too many times, once or twice with the smooth side of a sponge, will be enough.
- Remind children not to eat any of the food substances.
- Be aware of any allergies.

METHOD:

TO BE DONE IN ADVANCE BY THE TEACHER:
Have a selection of food items for making the white tiles dirty.
Remind the children that this is a fair test investigation, so they need to identify all the variables that they will have to control.

 CHILDREN:

1 You need to make your dirty tiles first. Think about what you will need to do to make it a fair test. Use the food provided by your teacher to make your dirty tiles. Put them somewhere safe to dry.
2 When your tiles are dry you can now start your investigation. Prepare your washing-up bowl. Again – remember what you need to do to make it a fair test.
3 Choose your first washing-up liquid to test. Add the washing-up liquid to the water or sponge.
4 Leave the dirty tile in the water for your chosen amount of time or wipe it with the sponge for your chosen number of times.
5 Place your dirty tile on a paper towel to dry.
6 Repeat the investigation with the rest of the washing-up liquids.

 DATA COLLECTION IDEAS:
The children can take photographs of their tiles and rank them in order of how well the washing-up liquids cleaned them.

DIFFERENTIATION:
- **Decrease the challenge:** The children may find it easier to cover the tile in the food stain and leave it to soak for a designated amount of time.
- **Increase the challenge:** The children could investigate how good the washing-up liquids are at cleaning different types of stains.

USEFUL QUESTIONS TO ASK THE CHILDREN:
- Which washing-up liquid was the best? Why do you think this?
- How do you think the washing-up liquid helped to remove the stains?
- What other features might we look for in a washing-up liquid?

FURTHER WORK:
The children could use this as part of a wider study on the best washing-up liquid. They could also look at other factors such as price, smell, how environmentally friendly it is, etc. before deciding on the best washing-up liquid.

Making a hovercraft

LEARNING OBJECTIVES:
Build and test our own hovercrafts!

INTRODUCTION:
The children make a hovercraft using a CD and balloon and investigate the factors that affect how fast it travels.

USEFUL PRIOR WORK:
The children should know what a hovercraft is and how it moves.

 ## BACKGROUND SCIENCE:
A hovercraft is a craft that is able to travel over flat land, water and ice. It travels on a cushion of air that is generated by propellers on the hovercraft. This cushion of air is directed below the hovercraft by fans. The hovercraft is usually surrounded by a flexible skirt that acts to trap the cushion of air underneath the hovercraft. This cushion of air reduces the friction between the hovercraft and the surface, allowing the hovercraft to move freely over the surface. The hovercraft is piloted and can be steered and directed by the pilot. Most modern day hovercrafts are used on water and are often commercial vehicles. As they can travel on both land and water they are referred to as amphibious vehicles.

NATIONAL CURRICULUM LINKS:
* **Year 3 programme of study**: Forces and magnets
    – Compare how things move on different surfaces.
* **Year 5 programme of study**: Forces
    – Identify the effects of air resistance, water resistance and friction that act between moving surfaces.

MATERIALS NEEDED:
* Sports-cap style plastic bottle lids
* New blank CDs or DVDs (or old ones that are no longer needed)
* Balloons
* Blu-Tack
* Timers

 ## SAFETY AND TECHNICAL NOTES:
* Use non-latex balloons in case of allergies.
* Some children may struggle to blow up balloons so extra adult help may be needed for this investigation.
* Tell children not to share balloons or blow into each other's balloons.

METHOD:

TO BE DONE IN ADVANCE BY THE TEACHER:
Prepare surfaces on which the hovercrafts can be tested. Table-tops are fine but they should be completely cleared and dusted with a dry cloth or paper towel before the investigation.

CHILDREN:

1 Put the bottle lid over the hole in the CD/DVD. Use Blu-Tack to hold it in place. Make sure it completely covers the hole and use plenty of Blu-Tack to hold it in place.
2 Blow up the balloon fully then pinch the neck so that no air can escape.
3 Make sure the bottle cap opening is in the closed position. Now place the neck of your balloon over the pop-up part of the bottle cap.
4 Place your hovercraft in the middle of a clear surface. Pop-up the bottle cap opening and start your timer. Watch your hovercraft and see how it moves! When it stops moving, stop the timer and record the result.
5 Now try the investigation again but only blow up your balloon about half-full. What happens this time?

 ### DATA COLLECTION IDEAS:

Trial	How long the hovercraft moved for (s)	
	Full balloon	Half-full balloon
1		
2		
3		

DIFFERENTIATION:
- **Decrease the challenge:** The children may need help to blow up the balloon and attach it to the hovercraft.
- **Increase the challenge:** The children could do a more systematic investigation about the amount of air in the hovercraft. They could investigate, for example, one breath of air, two breaths of air, three breaths of air, etc.

USEFUL QUESTIONS TO ASK THE CHILDREN:
- What do you think was causing your hovercraft to move?
- What happened when you put more air into your balloon? Why do you think this was?
- Can you think of any other factors that might make the hovercraft move for longer?

FURTHER WORK:
The children could research how real-life hovercrafts work and where they are used.

EXPERIMENT 80

Conker science

LEARNING OBJECTIVES:
Investigate whether some conker myths are true!

INTRODUCTION:
The children investigate whether different 'myths' about how to strengthen conkers are true, including freezing, soaking in vinegar and baking.

USEFUL PRIOR WORK:
The children do not need to have any particular prior knowledge before completing this investigation.

 BACKGROUND SCIENCE:
Conkers are the seeds of the horse chestnut tree and are generally dropped by the tree in September and October. There are some methods suggested for strengthening conkers so that they last longer in the traditional game of conkers. Three common methods are: soaking the conker in vinegar, freezing the conker and baking the conker. All of these methods are supposed to harden the outside of the conker shell, therefore making it less likely to crack when it is hit. There is not much evidence if any of these methods actually work, although soaking in vinegar has sometimes been found to weaken the conker by softening the outside. There is some anecdotal evidence that freezing and baking do help to strengthen the conker. By testing the three methods and comparing them to a 'control conker' the children can try to find out if any of these 'conker myths' are actually true.

NATIONAL CURRICULUM LINKS:
- **Year 2 programme of study**: Uses of everyday materials
  - Find out how the shapes of solid objects made from some materials can be changed by squashing, bending, twisting and stretching.
- **Year 3 programme of study**: Forces and magnets
  - Notice that some forces need contact between two objects, but magnetic forces can act at a distance.
- **Year 5 programme of study**: Forces
  - Identify the effects of air resistance, water resistance and friction that act between moving surfaces.

MATERIALS NEEDED:
- Conkers
- Brown vinegar
- Beakers
- Freezer
- Oven
- String
- Timers
- Paper towels
- Hand drill

 SAFETY AND TECHNICAL NOTES:

- Choose conkers that are firm and symmetrical with no obvious sign of damage.
- Adults should prepare the holes in the conker. A hand drill is one of the best ways of doing this.

- Adults should operate the oven. Children should be closely supervised if they are allowed to put the conkers into and out of the oven. Oven gloves should be worn.
- Have some conkers left over to act as 'control conkers'. These should not be treated in any way.
- Children should wash their hands after the investigation.

METHOD:

TO BE DONE IN ADVANCE BY THE TEACHER:
Collect enough conkers (you could have the children do this as well). The holes in the conkers should be put in after they have been 'strengthened'. Decide if you want the groups to investigate all three myths or have each group investigate one myth.

 CHILDREN:

Using vinegar:

1 Place your conker in a beaker.
2 Pour enough vinegar into the beaker to just cover the conker.
3 Start your timer. Leave it in the vinegar for 2 minutes.
4 When the time is up take out your conker and wipe it with a paper towel. Place it on a clean paper towel to dry.

Freezing:

1 Place your conker in a freezer and leave overnight.

Baking:

1 Have your teacher heat the oven to 250°C.
2 Place your conker on a baking tray. Place the baking tray into the oven. Make sure you are wearing oven gloves.
3 Start your timer. Leave the conker for 1 minute.
4 When the time is up, take the baking tray out of the oven. Place your conker onto a paper towel to cool down. Make sure you are wearing oven gloves.

 DATA COLLECTION IDEAS:
The children could test their conkers by playing a traditional game of conkers and seeing which conkers 'survive'. Alternatively a more fair test could be conducted by dropping the conkers from increasing heights to see if they crack.

DIFFERENTIATION:
- **Decrease the challenge:** The children can be helped when testing the conkers, particularly if they are playing conkers.
- **Increase the challenge:** The children could choose their own 'myths' to investigate.

USEFUL QUESTIONS TO ASK THE CHILDREN:
- Did we manage to prove that any of the myths were true? Why do you think this?
- What else would need to be controlled in order to make this a fair test?
- Why did we also have conkers that we did not strengthen in any way?

FURTHER WORK:
The children could research the history of the game of conkers, including the rules for playing.

Protect an egg!

LEARNING OBJECTIVES:
Protect an egg from a 1 metre fall.

INTRODUCTION:
The children investigate the best design for a device to protect an egg from breaking when it is dropped from a height of 1 metre.

USEFUL PRIOR WORK:
The children should know that objects fall to the Earth because of gravity and that different materials have different properties.

 BACKGROUND SCIENCE:
A force is something that can change the speed, direction or shape of an object. Gravity is an example of a force. Unsupported objects will fall towards the Earth because of gravity. As an object falls it accelerates (until terminal velocity is reached). When the falling object comes into contact with the ground it stops suddenly and the force of the contact with the ground can break the object. In order to protect the object, this force needs to be minimised. This can be done by slowing down the descent of the object, therefore allowing it to stop more slowly when it hits the ground. This can be achieved with parachute-style devices. Another method is to find something else to absorb some of the force, thereby reducing the amount of force that acts on the object. This can be achieved by using devices with lots of padding.

NATIONAL CURRICULUM LINKS:
- **Year 2 programme of study**: Uses of everyday materials
    - Identify and compare the suitability of a variety of everyday materials – including wood, metal, plastic, glass, brick, rock, paper and cardboard – for particular uses.
- **Year 5 programme of study**: Properties and changes of materials
    - Give reasons, based on evidence from comparative and fair tests, for the particular uses of everyday materials, including metals, wood and plastic.
- **Year 5 programme of study**: Forces
    - Explain that unsupported objects fall towards the Earth because of the force of gravity acting between the Earth and the falling object.
    - Identify the effect of air resistance, water resistance and friction that act between moving surfaces.

MATERIALS NEEDED:
- Eggs (soft-boiled in advance)
- A selection of materials for the children to build their egg protection devices, for example egg boxes, plastic bags, straws, newspaper, cotton wool, tissue paper, straw, yogurt pots, cut-up tights, rice, puffed cereal (for example Rice Krispies or Sugar Puffs) Sellotape, etc.
- Metre ruler

SAFETY AND TECHNICAL NOTES:

- Ensure that any containers that previously held food have been cleaned.
- Boiling the eggs in advance will prevent any mess caused if the eggs break when dropped.
- Remind children not to eat the egg.
- Be aware of any allergies.

METHOD:

TO BE DONE IN ADVANCE BY THE TEACHER:

Soft-boil the eggs that are to be used in the investigation. It is best to have a few more than is needed in case there are any breakages while the children are building the protection devices.

Have all the materials that the children can choose from ready. You may wish to give each group the same materials or provide a selection of materials from which the children can pick.

 CHILDREN:

1 You have been challenged with building a device to protect your egg so it doesn't break when it is dropped from a height of 1 metre!
2 Spend a few minutes looking at the materials you have been provided with. Discuss in your group what designs might work best. You may find drawing your designs helpful at this stage.
3 Choose your best design and select the materials you will need.
4 Build your egg-protecting device. Refer back to any drawings you made of your design as you build it. You may also wish to change or improve your design as you are building it.
5 When your device is ready, give it to your teacher ready for the big drop!

 DATA COLLECTION IDEAS:

The children can draw or take photographs of their design and then take a photograph of their egg after they have been dropped.

DIFFERENTIATION:

- **Decrease the challenge:** The children could be allowed to 'test' their design before the final drop by providing them with one or two 'practice eggs'. They can modify their design based on the results of the practice test.
- **Increase the challenge:** The children can be given a limited selection of materials to choose from.

USEFUL QUESTIONS TO ASK THE CHILDREN:

- Which designs were best at protecting the egg? Why do you think this was?
- Which materials were best at protecting the egg? Why do you think this was?
- How could we improve our designs, for example would making them waterproof make them better?

FURTHER WORK:

The children could research how similar systems work in real-life situations, for example crumple zones in cars.

CSI: Crime scene investigation

LEARNING OBJECTIVES:
Learn how to take fingerprints at a crime scene.

INTRODUCTION:
The children learn how to lift fingerprints from objects and take fingerprints from 'suspects'.

USEFUL PRIOR WORK:
The children do not need to have any particular prior knowledge before completing this investigation.

 BACKGROUND SCIENCE:
All humans (and some primates) are born with fingerprints that remain the same throughout their lives. The fingerprints are actually caused by ridges of skin and are thought to play a part in transmitting nervous impulses from the skin on our fingers. Fingerprints are unique to an individual, meaning that no two people have the same fingerprints – not even identical twins. This allows people to be identified from fingerprints that they leave behind at a crime scene. Fingerprints can be left on lots of different surfaces, but are most commonly found on smooth, shiny surfaces such as glass. The fingerprint that is left behind is caused by perspiration and grease from the fingers. It can be lifted off a surface by using a powder and special tape. In forensics, aluminium powder is used. This, however, is expensive so iron powder or flour can be used instead. Normal Sellotape can be used to lift the print. The tape can then be stuck onto a piece of card so the print can be viewed.

NATIONAL CURRICULUM LINKS:
- **Year 6 programme of study**: Evolution and inheritance
  - Recognise that living things produce offspring of the same kind, but normally offspring vary and are not identical to their parents.

MATERIALS NEEDED:
- Soft paintbrushes
- Flour
- Surfaces for taking prints from – ideally smooth surfaces such as plastic. Glass can be used but care would need to be taken in case of breakages
- Black card or sugar paper
- Sellotape
- Magnifying glasses
- Black ink pads or finger-paints
- White card or paper
- Fingerprint pattern sheet (available on the internet)

 SAFETY AND TECHNICAL NOTES:
- Care should be taken if using glass objects for this investigation. Ideally, use small, light objects such as beakers. Instruct children on what to do if there are any breakages.
- Aluminium powder gives very good results and can be used for this investigation but it is expensive.

METHOD:

TO BE DONE IN ADVANCE BY THE TEACHER:
Have a selection of objects available for the children to practise lifting fingerprints. Make sure they are clean and dry. Show children how to hold the objects so that they do not transfer fingerprints onto the surface until they are ready.

CHILDREN:

Lifting fingerprints:

1 Carefully hold the object you are going to lift fingerprints from so you do not put lots of fingerprints onto it until you are ready.
2 Press each fingertip firmly onto the object. Keep it as still as possible and hold it there for a few seconds. Try not to let your fingertips touch.
3 Dip a paintbrush into the flour. Gently shake off the excess. Carefully dab the flour over the spot where you put your fingerprints. You should find the flour sticks to the fingerprint.
4 When you think you have completely covered the fingerprint, take some Sellotape and carefully stick it over the fingerprint. Now peel it off slowly. The flour fingerprint will be stuck onto the Sellotape.
5 Stick the tape onto some black card or sugar paper to preserve your fingerprint.

Taking your fingerprints:

1 Make sure your hands are clean and dry.
2 Have your fingerprint recording sheet ready and close to you.
3 Gently press your finger into the ink or fingerprint. Try not to get your fingertip too wet.
4 Gently press your finger into the correct place on your fingerprint recording sheet.
5 Repeat with the rest of your fingers.
6 When all your fingerprints are taken, you can compare them to the pattern sheet to see what patterns you can spot on your own fingerprints.

 DATA COLLECTION IDEAS:

The children can take photographs of the fingerprints they lift from the surfaces.

My fingerprints – right hand				
Thumb	Index finger	Middle finger	Ring finger	Little finger

My fingerprints – left hand				
Little finger	Ring finger	Middle finger	Index finger	Thumb

DIFFERENTIATION:
• **Decrease the challenge:** The children could have their fingerprints taken by an adult.
• **Increase the challenge:** The children could investigate what other surfaces they could lift fingerprints from using this method.

USEFUL QUESTIONS TO ASK THE CHILDREN:
• What patterns did you find on your fingerprints?
• What other surfaces do you think you could take fingerprints from?
• Why are fingerprints useful at crime scenes?

FURTHER WORK:
The children could research the history of fingerprints being used as a means of identifying people.

Measuring photosynthesis

LEARNING OBJECTIVES:
Measuring the rate of photosynthesis.

INTRODUCTION:
The children investigate the rate of photosynthesis by observing the bubbles produced by pondweed in a beaker of water.

USEFUL PRIOR WORK:
The children should know that plants make their food via photosynthesis and that they give out oxygen.

 BACKGROUND SCIENCE:
Plants produce their own food via photosynthesis. To do this, they take in carbon dioxide from the atmosphere through small holes in their leaves called stomata. They also need water (which they take in from their roots) and energy in the form of light (which they absorb using chloroplasts in their leaves). Photosynthesis produces glucose, which the plant uses for energy. It also produces oxygen, although the plant does not need this in large quantities (it does require some for the process of respiration), so the oxygen is given off through the stomata. The process of the oxygen being given off by the plant can be easily observed by using water plants. Bubbles of gas can be seen in the water. These bubbles are the oxygen being given off by the plant. The more bubbles that are observed, the higher the rate of photosynthesis. In this investigation, the effect of the distance of the light from the plant is being investigated. The closer the light, the higher the rate of photosynthesis will be.

NATIONAL CURRICULUM LINKS:
- **Year 2 programme of study**: Plants
  - Find out and describe how plants need water, light and a suitable temperature to grow and stay healthy.
- **Year 3 programme of study**: Plants
  - Explore the requirements of plants for life and growth (air, light, water, nutrients from soil and room to grow) and how they vary from plant to plant.

MATERIALS NEEDED:
- Pieces of *Cabomba* pondweed for each group, about 5cm long
- Clear beakers
- Lamps or torches
- Timers
- Rulers
- Water

 SAFETY AND TECHNICAL NOTES:
- The best pondweed to use for this investigation is *Cabomba* pondweed. *Cabomba* is an aquatic plant and can be purchased quite easily from aquarium suppliers such as Aqua Essentials (www.aqua essentials.co.uk) and pet shops as it is used in home aquariums.
- Remind the children to be careful when using water around electrical lamps. Ensure there are lots of paper towels available for cleaning up any spills.

• Dispose of the pondweed in the normal rubbish or in a compost bin. Do not add it to ponds as it is not a native species.

METHOD:

TO BE DONE IN ADVANCE BY THE TEACHER:
Prepare the lengths of the pondweed for each group. Each length should have one cut end of stem and lots of leaves. The cut end of stem is where the bubbles of oxygen will come out. Store the cut lengths of pondweed in a beaker of water until needed.

 ### CHILDREN:
1 Fill a beaker with water.
2 Place a piece of pondweed into your beaker so the stem is at the top of the beaker and the leaves are at the bottom of the beaker. Make sure all of the pondweed is in the beaker.
3 Place your lamp or torch 30cm away from your beaker. Turn on the lamp or torch and start the timer.
4 Count how many bubbles you see in the beaker of water for 1 minute.
5 Repeat for the rest of the distances in your results table.

 ### DATA COLLECTION IDEAS:

Distance from lamp/torch (cm)	Number of bubbles produced in 1 minute
30	
25	
20	
15	
10	
5	

DIFFERENTIATION:
• **Decrease the challenge:** The children may find this investigation easier as a whole class investigation.
• **Increase the challenge:** The children could repeat each distance three times and work out an average for each distance.

USEFUL QUESTIONS TO ASK THE CHILDREN:
• What happened to the number of bubbles as the lamp/torch moved closer to the pondweed? Why do you think this happened?
• Did you notice any pattern in your results?
• What do you think would happen if we moved the lamp/torch 40cm away?

FURTHER WORK:
This investigation could be linked with cross-curricular work in geography. The children could research the rainforests and why they are so important in terms of providing oxygen and taking in carbon dioxide.

EXPERIMENT 84

Fussy woodlice

LEARNING OBJECTIVES:
Investigating what type of habitat woodlice prefer.

INTRODUCTION:
The children investigate what conditions
woodlice prefer by setting up a choice-chamber
with different environmental conditions.

USEFUL PRIOR WORK:
The children should know that different animals
live in different habitats.

 ## BACKGROUND SCIENCE:
A woodlouse is a crustacean (not an insect), with an exterior shell that provides the woodlouse with
protection. If the woodlouse is threatened it can curl up into a ball, exposing only the outer shell. There
are over forty different species of woodlice living in the United Kingdom. They are herbivores and
mostly feed on decaying leaves and plant materials. They prefer habitats that are dark and damp, such
as under stones and under logs. Their preferences for certain habitats can be investigated using a 'choice-
chamber'. This is where woodlice are placed into a container that has been artificially set up to recreate
particular habitats. After the woodlice have been in the container for a period of time (usually within
1 hour) they typically move over to the habitat that they prefer and remain there.

NATIONAL CURRICULUM LINKS:
- **Year 2 programme of study**: Living things and their habitats
  - Identify that most living things live in habitats to which they are suited and describe how different
    habitats provide for the basic needs of different kinds of animals and plants, and how they depend
    on each other.
  - Identify and name a variety of plants and animals in their habitats, including microhabitats.
- **Year 4 programme of study**: Living things and their habitats
  - Recognise that environments can change and that this can sometimes pose dangers to living things.
- **Year 6 programme of study**: Evolution and inheritance
  - Identify how animals and plants are adapted to suit their environment in different ways and that
    adaptation may lead to evolution.

MATERIALS NEEDED:
- Choice-chamber or small, see-through plastic containers with lids,
  for example Petri dishes. These can be purchased from Better
  Equipped (www.betterequipped.co.uk) and Hope Education
  (www.hope-education.co.uk)
- Black paper
- Water
- Paper towels
- Paintbrushes
- Scissors
- Woodlice

SAFETY AND TECHNICAL NOTES:

- Remind the children that the woodlice are living animals and should be handled carefully.
- The children should wash their hands after the investigation.

METHOD:

TO BE DONE IN ADVANCE BY THE TEACHER:

Collect the woodlice for the children to use in their investigation. They will typically be found under rocks and wood in damp places. About 3–5 woodlice per group of children will be sufficient.

 CHILDREN:

1 You need to divide your container into four different habitats. These habitats are:
- Dark and dry
- Dark and damp
- Light and dry
- Light and damp
2 Draw around your container onto a piece of black paper and cut this out. Cut this piece of paper in half. Stick one half onto the lid of your container so that it covers one half of your container.
3 Cut up some pieces of paper towel so that they will fit into one half of your container. Dip the pieces of paper towel quickly into some water so that they are damp but not soaking wet. Place these pieces of paper towel into the container so they cover one half of the bottom of the container. IMPORTANT: Make sure that half of the wet paper towel is covered by the black paper and that the other half is not.

 DATA COLLECTION IDEAS:

Number of woodlice	
Dark and dry	Light and dry
Dark and damp	Light and damp

DIFFERENTIATION:
- **Decrease the challenge:** The children may need help with setting up their choice-chamber.
- **Increase the challenge:** The children could be challenged to come up with how to make the different habitats themselves rather than being given the instructions.

USEFUL QUESTIONS TO ASK THE CHILDREN:
- Which conditions did the woodlice prefer? Why do you think this is?
- Where might we find woodlice outside?
- What might happen to the woodlice if they were not able to find the conditions they like to live in?

FURTHER WORK:

The children could use the results from this investigation to make predictions about where they would find woodlice living in the school grounds. They could then go on a 'bug-hunt' to see if they are correct.

Gummy bear science

LEARNING OBJECTIVES:
Investigate what happens to gummy bears when they are left in different solutions.

INTRODUCTION:
The children investigate what happens when gummy bears are added to water and other solutions.

USEFUL PRIOR WORK:
The children do not need to have any particular prior knowledge before completing this investigation.

 BACKGROUND SCIENCE:
Gummy bears are sweets that are contain a substance called gelatine. When gummy bears are made, the mixture is heated, which causes the gelatine to solidify and the water inside the gummy bear is removed. This means that there is very little water left inside the gummy bear. If the gummy bear is placed in water, the water will move into the gummy bear. The water moves due to the process of osmosis, where water moves from an area of low concentration to an area of high concentration through a permeable membrane. This will cause the gummy bear to become swollen. If the gummy bear is placed in water that contains salt, then the water from the gummy bear will move out of the bear and into the water, causing the bear to shrink slightly (as there is not much water in the bear). If the gummy bear is placed in water that contains vinegar, then the acid in the vinegar will dissolve the outer membrane of the gummy bear. If the gummy bear is placed in water that contains bicarbonate of soda it will expand but not usually as much as a gummy bear placed in just water.

NATIONAL CURRICULUM LINKS:
- **Year 1 programme of study**: Everyday materials
  - Describe the simple physical properties of a variety of everyday materials.
- **Year 5 programme of study**: Properties and changes of materials
  - Know that some materials will dissolve in a liquid to form a solution, and describe how to recover a substance from a solution.

MATERIALS NEEDED:
- Gummy bears
- Water
- Salt
- Vinegar
- Bicarbonate of soda
- Beakers
- Balance
- Rulers
- Labels
- Digital camera (optional)

 SAFETY AND TECHNICAL NOTES:
- Remind the children not to eat the gummy bears (unless they have permission).

METHOD:

TO BE DONE IN ADVANCE BY THE TEACHER:
* Have somewhere ready for the beakers to be stored overnight.

 ### CHILDREN:

1 Take one gummy bear. Measure how long it is using a ruler. Record this in your results table. Weigh the gummy bear using the balance. Record this in your results table.
2 Fill one of your beakers with water. Add the gummy bear you just measured to the beaker. Label the beaker 'water'.
3 Take another gummy bear and measure its length and mass. Record this on your table.
4 Fill another beaker with water and then add a teaspoon of salt and stir. Add the gummy bear you just measured to this beaker and label it 'salt water'.
5 Take another gummy bear and measure its length and mass. Record this on your table.
6 Fill another beaker with water and then add a teaspoon of bicarbonate of soda and stir. Add the gummy bear you just measured to this beaker and label it 'soda and water'.
7 Take a final gummy bear and measure its length and mass. Record this on your table.
8 Fill another beaker with water and then add a teaspoon of vinegar and stir. Add the gummy bear you just measured to this beaker and label it 'vinegar and water'.
9 Place your beakers somewhere safe and leave them overnight. Come back and observe them tomorrow.

 ### DATA COLLECTION IDEAS:

Solution	Length before (cm)	Mass before (g)	Length after (cm)	Mass after (g)	Observations
Water					
Salt water					
Soda and water					
Vinegar and water					

The children can also take 'before' and 'after' photos of their gummy bears.

DIFFERENTIATION:
* **Decrease the challenge:** The children may need help with measuring the length of the gummy bears.
* **Increase the challenge:** The children could come up with their own solutions and test the gummy bears in these.

USEFUL QUESTIONS TO ASK THE CHILDREN:
* What happened to the gummy bear in the water/salt water/soda water and vinegar water? Why do you think this was?
* What other liquids could we test out gummy bears in? What do you think would happen?
* Do you think we could get back the gummy bears back to their original size?

FURTHER WORK:
The children could investigate jelly and how it changes state from being a solid to a liquid and back to a solid and at what temperatures this happens.

Making waves

LEARNING OBJECTIVES:
Build a beach and see how waves are formed.

INTRODUCTION:
The children investigate how waves develop on a sandy beach.

USEFUL PRIOR WORK:
The children do not need to have any particular prior knowledge before completing this investigation.

 BACKGROUND SCIENCE:
A beach is a natural formation that occurs alongside a body of water. The beach itself can be made up of rock particles, sand, pebbles, gravel and shell fragments. This will depend on the natural geology of the area. The part of the beach that is mostly above water is called the berm. The part of the beach that slopes towards the water is called the face. Some beaches have a trough at the end of the face. The shape, structure and materials the beach is made from is influenced by the action of the waves moving over the beach. Particles can be moved and deposited, and surrounding cliffs can be eroded. The wind will also affect the beach further inland, for example blowing the sand and forming sand dunes.

NATIONAL CURRICULUM LINKS:
- **Year 3 programme of study**: Rocks
  - Compare and group together different kinds of rocks on the basis of their appearance and simple physical properties.
- **Year 5 programme of study**: Forces
  - Identify the effects of air resistance, water resistance and friction that act between moving surfaces.

MATERIALS NEEDED:
- Large plastic tubs, for example ice cream tubs
- Small, empty plastic bottle
- Sand
- Gravel or small stones
- Beaker
- Timers
- Water
- Digital camera (optional)

 SAFETY AND TECHNICAL NOTES:
- Use clean sand and gravel for the investigation. This can be purchased from garden centres.
- The children should wash their hands after completing the investigation.

METHOD:

TO BE DONE IN ADVANCE BY THE TEACHER:
Have large tubs of sand and gravel ready for the children to use. Make sure any plastic tubs being used are clean.

 CHILDREN:

1 Cover the bottom of the tub with sand. Build up the sand so that most of it is at one end of your tub. This is your 'beach'.
2 Pour a beaker of water into the other end of the tub. This is your 'ocean'.
3 Take a photograph of your beach and ocean.
4 Take the plastic bottle (make sure the lid is on) and float it in your ocean. It should be lying horizontally.
5 Start the timer. Gently push up and down on the bottle to create waves. The water should not come over the sides of the tub.
6 After 1 minute, stop making waves and take a look at your beach. What has happened? Take a photo of your beach.
7 Start the timer and push up and down on the bottle again. After 1 minute stop the timer and take a look at your beach. What has happened? Take a photo of your beach.
8 Smooth out the sand on your beach and take another photo.
9 Now add a handful of gravel to your beach. It should be in the middle of the beach, where the beach and ocean meet. Some of the gravel can go into the ocean.
10 Start the timer and push up and down on the bottle again. After 1 minute stop the timer and take a look at your beach. What has happened? Take a photo of your beach.
11 Start the timer and make the waves again. After 1 minute stop the timer and take a look at your beach. What has happened? Take a photo of your beach.

 DATA COLLECTION IDEAS:
The children can take photographs of the beach at the different stages.

DIFFERENTIATION:
• **Decrease the challenge:** This investigation could be done as a whole class investigation.
• **Increase the challenge:** The children could investigate the effect of putting the gravel in different places on the beach or having more than one pile of gravel.

USEFUL QUESTIONS TO ASK THE CHILDREN:
• What happened to the beach after the waves when there was no gravel on the beach?
• Was the beach any different between the first time you made waves and the second time you made waves? Why do you think this was?
• What happened to the beach after the waves when there was gravel on the beach? Why do you think this happened?

FURTHER WORK:
This investigation could be linked with cross-curricular work in geography. The children could research how sand, beaches and sand dunes are formed.

Call the surgeon!

LEARNING OBJECTIVES:
Practise being a surgeon!

INTRODUCTION:
The children perform a simple heart dissection on a lamb's heart in order to learn more about the function and structure of the heart.

USEFUL PRIOR WORK:
The children should know what the heart is and its role in the body.

 BACKGROUND SCIENCE:
The heart's primary role in the human body is to pump blood around the body. The heart itself is just a muscle; however, it is a myogenic muscle, which means that it beats by itself without us having to control it with our nervous system. Humans have a double circulatory system. This means that the heart first pumps deoxygenated blood to the lungs where it picks up oxygen before returning to the heart. The heart then pumps this oxygenated blood around the body. The heart is divided into four chambers. The top two chambers are called atria (right atrium and left atrium) and the bottom two chambers are called ventricles (right ventricle and left ventricle). The atria are very small in comparison to the ventricles. Between the atria and ventricles there are valves, which ensure that the blood can only flow in one direction. The left side of the heart (though it is the right side of the heart as you look at it) is much thicker and more muscular than the right side of the heart as it has to pump blood all around the body whereas the right side of the heart only has to pump blood to the lungs. The journey the blood takes through the heart is; right atrium, right ventricle, lungs (via pulmonary artery), left atrium (via pulmonary vein), left ventricle, rest of the body.

NATIONAL CURRICULUM LINKS:
• **Year 6 programme of study**: Animals including humans
  – Identify and name the main parts of the human circulatory system and describe the functions of the heart, blood vessels and blood.

MATERIALS NEEDED:
• Lamb hearts
• Scissors
• Magnifying lenses
• Non-latex gloves
• Aprons
• Paper towels or white tiles
• Bin liners
• Disinfectant (for cleaning up)

 SAFETY AND TECHNICAL NOTES:
• Dissections are safe to perform in primary schools if you use food quality meat purchased from butchers or shops. The meat should still be in its use by date and should be stored in a fridge until needed. Using lamb organs will help to avoid issues regarding religion. Refer to CLEAPSS guidelines available at www.cleapss.org.uk/attachments/article/0/Looking%20at%20(Dissecting)%20animal%20organs%20in%20primary%20schools,%20health%20and%20safety%20aspects.pdf?Conferences/ASE%202014/.
• Be sensitive to the wishes of any children who do not wish to participate in a dissection. Have an alternative activity available for them.

- Scissors are strong enough for dissecting most meat products as long as they are sharp. Round-ended scissors will work for this investigation.
- The children should wear non-latex gloves and aprons, roll up their sleeves and remove any watches or jewellery.
- Perform the dissection on several paper towels or a white tile.
- The dissected material, gloves and paper towels should be disposed of in bin liners as soon as the investigation has ended. If the waste collection will not take place soon then the bin liners should be sealed and stored in a fridge until they can be put out.
- The tables should be cleaned with a disinfectant after the investigation. If white tiles were used they should be washed in hot, soapy water.
- Aprons should be washed or wiped down with hot soapy water.
- The children should wash their hands after the investigation.

METHOD:

TO BE DONE IN ADVANCE BY THE TEACHER:
Purchase enough hearts for your class and ensure they are properly stored until needed. You may want to carry out a practice dissection before the class investigation.

 CHILDREN:

1 Make sure you are wearing gloves and an apron. Have paper towels or a white tile ready to place your heart onto.
2 When you have your heart, examine it closely. What does it look like? What colour is it? Is it the same colour everywhere? What does it feel it? Does it feel the same everywhere? Write down your observations.
3 Use your scissors to carefully cut the heart open. Start at the top of the heart and cut downwards. Only cut through the top side of the heart so that you can open the heart like a book.
4 Examine the inside of the heart. What can you see? Use your magnifying glass to examine the inside of the heart in detail. What structures can you see? Feel the walls of the heart. What do they feel like? Write down your observations.
5 When you are finished, dispose of your heart and gloves according to your teacher's instructions.

 DATA COLLECTION IDEAS:
The children can draw and make notes of what they do and observe. Photographs could also be taken.

DIFFERENTIATION:
This investigation is best carried out with older children. Younger children however could watch a demonstration of the dissection. They can still 'dress up' as surgeons in gloves and aprons and advise you on what to do next as you dissect the heart.

USEFUL QUESTIONS TO ASK THE CHILDREN:
- What observations did you make about the heart?
- Was the heart similar or different to what you expected?
- Do you think our hearts would be similar to this heart? Why do you think that?

FURTHER WORK:
The children could research the history of heart surgery, including the first heart transplant that took place in South Africa in 1967.

Making a bouncy ball

LEARNING OBJECTIVES:
Make a bouncy ball!

INTRODUCTION:
The children make a bouncy ball using Epsom salts and PVA glue and investigate how well they bounce.

USEFUL PRIOR WORK:
The children do not need to have any particular prior knowledge before completing this investigation.

 BACKGROUND SCIENCE:
Bouncy balls are usually made from plastic or rubber. These materials are polymers, which means they are made up of many smaller units (called monomers) joined together into long chains. These chains can be stretched out or squashed together, which makes the material elastic. In this investigation, the polymers in the PVA glue form cross-links when reacted with the Epsom salts. The bouncy balls from this investigation will start to lose their elasticity over time and therefore will stop being 'bouncy' – this can be slowed down by keeping the ball in a sealed plastic bag.

NATIONAL CURRICULUM LINKS:
- **Year 2 programme of study**: Uses of everyday materials
  - Find out how the shapes of solid objects made from some materials can be changed by squashing, bending, twisting and stretching.
- **Year 5 programme of study**: Properties and changes of materials
  - Compare and group together everyday materials on the basis of their physical properties including their hardness, solubility, transparency, conductivity (electrical and thermal) and response to magnets.
  - Give reasons, based on evidence from comparative and fair tests, for the particular uses of everyday materials, including metals, wood and plastic.
  - Explain that some changes result in the formation of new materials (and that this kind of change is not usually reversible) including changes associated with burning and the action of acid on bicarbonate of soda.

MATERIALS NEEDED:
- Epsom salts
- PVA glue
- Beakers or plastic cups
- Bowls
- Measuring spoons
- Stirrers
- Paper towels
- Plastic sandwich bags
- Water
- A rubber bouncy ball for comparisons (optional)

SAFETY AND TECHNICAL NOTES:

- The water in this investigation does not have to be boiling, water from the hot tap will be sufficient.
- The ball is best kept in a plastic bag after it is made.

METHOD:

TO BE DONE IN ADVANCE BY THE TEACHER:
Prepare bowls containing the water, Epsom salts and PVA glue.

 CHILDREN:

1 Put 1 tablespoon of PVA glue into a beaker.
2 In a different beaker, put 1/2 teaspoon of water and 1/2 teaspoon of Epsom salts. Stir so that the Epsom salts dissolve. It is ok if some of the Epsom salts do not dissolve.
3 Pour the water and Epsom salts mixture into the beaker with the PVA glue. Stir the mixture.
4 Keep stirring until you have a big clump.
5 Take the clump out and roll it for a bit, and then place it on some paper towels. Use the paper towels to gently squeeze out any excess water. Knead the clump in your hands until it forms a smooth ball.
6 Try bouncing your ball.
7 Store your bouncy ball in a plastic bag to help keep it bouncy.

 DATA COLLECTION IDEAS:

The children can test their balls and see how high they bounce. A class table could be made to show how high each ball bounced.

Name of child	How high the ball bounced

DIFFERENTIATION:

- **Decrease the challenge:** The children can have the ingredients already measured out for them.
- **Increase the challenge:** The children could investigate how changing the amount of Epsom salts and PVA glue in the mixture affects how bouncy the ball is.

USEFUL QUESTIONS TO ASK THE CHILDREN:

- Why do you think the ball you made is able to bounce?
- How does your bouncy ball compare to a bouncy ball made from rubber?
- Which surface does your ball bounce best on? Why do you think this is?

FURTHER WORK:

The children could compare the bouncy balls they make with plastic and rubber bouncy balls and carry out a comparative fair test.

Make a mini-rocket

LEARNING OBJECTIVES:
Design and make a mini-rocket.

INTRODUCTION:
The children make a miniature rocket
using a film canister. A reaction between
water and Alka-Seltzer creates a build-
up of gas that causes the 'rocket' to
take off.

USEFUL PRIOR WORK:
The children should know how the
particles are arranged in a gas.

 ### BACKGROUND SCIENCE:
This investigation works due to the reaction between water and Alka-Seltzer tablets. As the Alka-Seltzer
dissolves in the water, it produces carbon dioxide gas. This gas starts to build up in the enclosed space
of the film canister. Eventually the gas will have filled all the available space in the film canister and
the pressure inside the film canister will increase as the gas continues to be produced. Finally, the
pressure inside the film canister will be so great that the lid of the canister is pushed away and the
rocket will be able to take off from the force of the gas. This occurs due to Newton's Third Law of
Motion, which states that every action has an equal and opposite reaction. The force of the gas pushing
downwards causes the rocket to take off upwards. The film canister can be modified to look more like
a rocket by rolling it in a tube of cardboard and adding a tail and fins. These modifications can also
help the film canister's flight. A parachute could also be added to the top of the canister for its eventual
descent.

NATIONAL CURRICULUM LINKS:
- **Year 5 programme of study**: Properties and changes of materials
  - Give reasons, based on evidence from comparative and fair tests, for the particular uses of
    everyday materials, including metals, wood and plastic.
  - Explain that some changes result in the formation of new materials (and that this kind of change
    is not usually reversible) including changes associated with burning and the action of acid on
    bicarbonate of soda.
- **Year 5 programme of study**: Forces
  - Explain that unsupported objects fall towards the Earth because of the force of gravity acting
    between the Earth and the falling object.
  - Identify the effects of air resistance, water resistance and friction that act between moving surfaces.

MATERIALS NEEDED:
- Empty film canisters
- Alka-Seltzer tablets
- Water
- Cardboard
- Sellotape
- Materials for building a parachute for example, small
  sandwich bags, string, tissue paper (optional)
- Timers

SAFETY AND TECHNICAL NOTES:

- Make sure the canister is placed lid downwards on the ground.
- The lid must be firmly on the canister otherwise the gas will leak out and they will not take off.
- Have the children stand at least 2 metres away from the canisters when they are taking off.
- Do not allow the children to approach any canisters that have not taken off. Wait at least 1 minute before approaching.
- Children should wash their hands after the investigation.
- Remind children not to drink the water.

METHOD:

TO BE DONE IN ADVANCE BY THE TEACHER:
Choose a suitable place for launching the rockets. This should be outside, on flat ground, away from anything that may be damaged by stray rockets.

 CHILDREN:

1 Make a rough sketch of the design for your rocket. When you are happy with your design, choose the materials you will need.
2 Build your rocket! Make sure that the film canister can sit flat on the ground, lid first.
3 When you have built your rocket, carefully fill the film canister with water halfway.
4 Put the lid on your rocket.
5 When you are ready to launch, (your teacher will tell you when) put an Alka-Seltzer tablet in the film canister, put the lid on firmly and place the film canister on the ground, lid first. You will need to do all of this quickly!
6 Stand back and watch your rocket take off! When it launches, start your timer and time how long it takes for your film canister to land back on the ground again. Watch how your rocket travels. Did it travel straight up? Did it come straight back down again?

 DATA COLLECTION IDEAS:
The children could take videos of their rockets taking off and record how long they take to land after taking off.

DIFFERENTIATION:
- **Decrease the challenge:** The children could have an adult set up their rocket for launching as they may not be quick enough putting the lid back on the canister.
- **Increase the challenge:** The children could investigate the effect of adding different amounts of Alka-Seltzer to their rockets, for example 1/4 of a tablet, 1/2 tablet, 1 tablet.

USEFUL QUESTIONS TO ASK THE CHILDREN:
- Why do you think our rockets took off?
- What design did you choose for your rocket? Why did you choose this? What effect do you think it had?
- Can you think of any other ways we could make our rockets go higher when they take off?

FURTHER WORK:
The children could research actual space rockets and how they take off from Earth and land again.

Extracting DNA

LEARNING OBJECTIVES:
Extract some DNA from a strawberry!

INTRODUCTION:
The children extract DNA from strawberries using a homemade DNA extraction solution.

USEFUL PRIOR WORK:
The children should know that living organisms inherit certain characteristics from their parents.

 BACKGROUND SCIENCE:
All living things contain DNA (deoxyribonucleic acid), which is found in every cell of the organism. DNA contains all the genetic information, like an instruction manual, ensuring that the organism develops and functions as it is supposed to do. DNA contains many genes: each gene codes one particular characteristic of the organism, for example eye colour. It is a very small molecule in the shape of a double helix (two separate strands wrapped around each other giving the appearance of a twisted ladder) and cannot normally be seen with the naked eye. It is possible to extract DNA from cells. Strawberries are particularly good for this as they have a large number of chromosomes. This makes the chromosomes easier to extract and see. The extraction solution consists of washing-up liquid (which breaks down the cell membranes allowing the DNA to be released), and salt, which breaks down the bonds that hold the two DNA strands together. DNA is insoluble in alcohol (even more so when the alcohol is cold), which is why alcohol is used instead of water.

NATIONAL CURRICULUM LINKS:
- **Year 6 programme of study**: Evolution and inheritance
  - Recognise that living things produce offspring of the same kind, but normally offspring vary and are not identical to their parents.

MATERIALS NEEDED:
- Strawberries
- Washing-up liquid
- Salt
- Ethanol (cold)
- Water
- Zip-lock freezer bag
- Measuring cylinder
- Beaker
- Funnel
- Filter paper
- Teaspoon
- Lolly sticks

 SAFETY AND TECHNICAL NOTES:
- Supervise the children at all times when they are using the ethanol.
- Ethanol is flammable. Keep away from all naked flames and sources of heat.
- The ethanol should be as cold as possible so store in a freezer or fridge until it is needed.

- If ethanol is not available, hand-sanitiser can be used instead.
- You may wish to make up a batch of the DNA extraction solution yourself and have the children take what they need. If so, mix 900ml of water with 100ml of washing-up liquid. Add 3 teaspoons of salt to the mixture and stir. Alternatively the children can make their extraction solution. They should use 90ml of water, 10ml of washing-up liquid and 1/2 teaspoon of salt.

METHOD:

TO BE DONE IN ADVANCE BY THE TEACHER:
Chill the ethanol. Make up the extraction solution if the children are not doing this themselves.

 CHILDREN:

1 Put one strawberry into your zip-lock bag.
2 Add 100ml of the extraction solution to the bag.
3 Close the bag and mash up your strawberry until no big pieces remain.
4 Place the funnel into the beaker. Fold a piece of filter paper (your teacher will show you how to do this) and place this inside your funnel.
5 Pour your mashed-up strawberry into the funnel so that all the juices flow into the beaker. Try to get as much of the strawberry and liquid into the funnel as possible.
6 Use the teaspoon to mash up any remaining pieces of strawberry in the funnel so that as much juice goes into the beaker as possible.
7 Remove the funnel from the beaker. Slowly pour 5ml of the cold alcohol into the beaker.
8 Observe the beaker closely. What can you see happening?
9 You should see some white strands floating on your solution. This is the DNA! Use the lolly stick to try and lift out the DNA.

 DATA COLLECTION IDEAS:
The children can take photographs of the DNA they have collected and the different steps of the investigation.

DIFFERENTIATION:
- **Decrease the challenge:** The children may benefit from having the extraction solution made up for them so that they only have to measure out the volume that they need.
- **Increase the challenge:** The children could be challenged with extracting DNA (using the same method) from different fruits and see which one yields the best sample of DNA. Bananas and kiwi fruits work well whereas grapes tend to work less well.

USEFUL QUESTIONS TO ASK THE CHILDREN:
- What did you observe when you added the alcohol to the strawberry solution?
- What did the DNA that you extracted look like? Was it what you expected?
- Why do you think the strawberry needs to have DNA?

FURTHER WORK:
The children could investigate how DNA was discovered, including the different scientists that were involved.

Making lemonade

LEARNING OBJECTIVES:
Make our own fizzy lemonade!

INTRODUCTION:
The children make a fizzy lemonade drink using baking soda.

USEFUL PRIOR WORK:
The children should know that some substances can dissolve in water.

 BACKGROUND SCIENCE:
Normal fizzy drinks are fizzy because they contain carbon dioxide gas. The carbon dioxide gas is pumped into the drinks at high pressure. This is why, when you open a fizzy drink, it fizzes to the top and sometimes comes over the top of the bottle. The carbon dioxide gas can also dissolve in the drink itself forming a weak acidic solution (carbonic acid). This is another reason why fizzy drinks are not good for your teeth (as well as the high amounts of sugar) as this acid can damage the enamel on our teeth. In this investigation the carbon dioxide is formed by mixing together a base (alkali) and an acid. The base is the baking soda and the acid is the lemon juice.

NATIONAL CURRICULUM LINKS:
- **Year 2 programme of study**: Animals, including humans
  - Describe the importance for humans of exercise, eating the right amounts of different types of food and hygiene.
- **Year 3 programme of study**: Animals, including humans
  - Identify that animals, including humans, need the right types and amount of nutrition, and that they cannot make their own food; they get nutrition from what they eat.
- **Year 4 programme of study**: States of matter
  - Compare and group materials together according to whether they are solids, liquids or gases.
- **Year 5 programme of study**: Properties and changes of materials
  - Know that some materials will dissolve in liquid to form a solution, and describe how to recover a substance from a solution.
  - Explain that some changes result in the formation of new materials (and that this kind of change is not usually reversible) including changes associated with burning and the action of acid on bicarbonate of soda.

MATERIALS NEEDED:
- Lemons
- Large jugs or beakers of water
- Sugar
- Baking soda
- Teaspoons
- Knife for cutting the lemons

SAFETY AND TECHNICAL NOTES:

- Ensure that all the food preparation areas are clean and that the children wash their hands before the experiment.
- Supervise the children if they are cutting the lemons in half themselves. Use metal knives rather than plastic ones.
- Check for allergies.
- Avoid using glass jugs or beakers if possible.
- Rolling the lemons firmly across a hard surface before they are cut will help to release the juice when they are squeezed.
- You may wish to run a trial to find out how much lemon juice you need for the size of your beakers or jugs.
- Ensure parental permission has been given for this experiment.

METHOD:

TO BE DONE IN ADVANCE BY THE TEACHER:
Cut the lemons in half if the children are not doing this themselves. Perform a trial run so you can check how much lemon juice you need to use.

 CHILDREN:

1 Fill your jug or beaker with water.
2 Squeeze both halves of your lemon over your water. Try to get as much of the lemon juice into the water as possible. You may need to use more than one lemon. Your teacher will tell you how many you need.
3 Add a teaspoon of baking soda and stir until it has dissolved.
4 Add a teaspoon of sugar. Test your lemonade. You can add some more sugar if it is not sweet enough yet.
5 What does your lemonade taste like? What can you see in your lemonade?

 DATA COLLECTION IDEAS:
The children can draw or take photographs of the ingredients and the method and make an illustrated recipe for making lemonade. They can annotate this with a description of the science behind the investigation.

DIFFERENTIATION:
- **Decrease the challenge:** The children could have the ingredients already measured out for them.
- **Increase the challenge:** The children could make different types of fizzy drinks, such as limeade and orangeade, and compare them in terms of how fizzy they were and how much sugar needed to be added to them to make them sweet.

USEFUL QUESTIONS TO ASK THE CHILDREN:
- What does your lemonade look/taste like? Is it the same as normal lemonade or is it any different?
- Do you think we could get the lemon juice and the sugar back from the lemonade?
- Do you think this is the best way of making lemonade? Why do you think that?

FURTHER WORK:
The children could research the effect that fizzy drinks have on our teeth. A demonstration could be set up with a hard-boiled, white-shelled egg being soaked in cola overnight to see the effect on the shell.

EXPERIMENT 92

Making a lava lamp

LEARNING OBJECTIVES:
Make our own lava lamp!

INTRODUCTION:
The children make a lava lamp using a plastic bottle and Alka-Seltzer tablets.

USEFUL PRIOR WORK:
The children do not need to have any particular prior knowledge before completing this investigation.

 BACKGROUND SCIENCE:
This investigation works on the basis of liquids having different densities and the reaction of Alka-Seltzer with water. The vegetable oil and water have different densities so form two separate layers in the bottle, with the water on the bottom and the oil on the top. The food colouring falls through the cooking oil and mixes with the water at the bottom. When the Alka-Seltzer tablets are added, they react with the water, forming bubbles of carbon dioxide gas. This carbon dioxide rises up through the vegetable oil and carries some blobs of the coloured water with it, forming the 'lava lamp'. When the carbon dioxide reaches the top of the bottle it escapes, causing the coloured water to fall back down again. The lava lamp will keep working as long as Alka-Seltzer tablets are added to the bottle.

NATIONAL CURRICULUM LINKS:
• **Year 4 programme of study**: States of matter
  – Compare and group materials together according to whether they are solids, liquids or gases.
• **Year 5 programme of study**: Properties and changes of materials
  – Compare and group together everyday materials on the basis of their physical properties including their hardness, solubility, transparency, conductivity (electrical and thermal) and response to magnets.

MATERIALS NEEDED:
• Small plastic bottles
• Alka-Seltzer tablets
• Vegetable oil
• Food colouring
• Funnels
• Pestle and mortar or small plastic bags
• Water
• Digital camera (optional)

 SAFETY AND TECHNICAL NOTES:
• The children should wash their hands after the investigation.
• The lid should not be put on the bottle while the lava lamp is working but can be put on afterwards.

METHOD:

TO BE DONE IN ADVANCE BY THE TEACHER:
Make sure all the plastic bottles are empty and clean.

CHILDREN:
1 Place a funnel into the neck of your bottle. Pour the cooking oil into the bottle until it is 1/2 full.
2 Pour water into the bottle until it is almost full.
3 Leave the bottle for a couple of minutes so that the oil and water form separate layers in the bottle.
4 Add ten drops of food colouring to the bottle.
5 Crush up an Alka-Seltzer tablet using a pestle and mortar or place it in a plastic bag and hit it gently with a ruler.
6 Add the crushed up Alka-Seltzer to the bottle and watch the lava lamp!
7 When you want your lava lamp to work again, add another crushed up Alka-Seltzer tablet.

DATA COLLECTION IDEAS:
The children can take photographs or videos of their lava lamps.

DIFFERENTIATION:
• **Decrease the challenge:** The children could have the ingredients already measured out for them.
• **Increase the challenge:** The children could investigate the effect of using water at different temperature in the lava lamp, for example cold water, room temperature water, water from the hot tap.

USEFUL QUESTIONS TO ASK THE CHILDREN:
• Why did the vegetable oil and water form separate layers in the bottle?
• What happened when you added the Alka-Seltzer tablets to the bottle? Why do you think this was?
• What do you think would happen if we added more Alka-Seltzer tablets to the bottle?

FURTHER WORK:
The children could investigate how real lava lamps work. Lava lamps contain wax suspended in a liquid. The wax rises and falls due to the heating of the liquid by the bulb in the lava lamp.

Making slime

LEARNING OBJECTIVES:
Make our own slime!

INTRODUCTION:
The children make 'slime' using PVA glue and cornstarch.

USEFUL PRIOR WORK:
The children do not need to have any particular prior knowledge before completing this investigation.

 BACKGROUND SCIENCE:
The 'slime' that is produced in this investigation is an example of a non-Newtonian fluid. This means that it does not behave in the same way as normal liquids. A non-Newtonian fluid has properties of both solids and liquids. It can be poured like a liquid and will take the shape of its container but it can also be formed into a solid ball and if hit it will form into a solid rather than splashing everywhere. This is because a non-Newtonian fluid responds to force. If no forces are acting on it, such as when it is in a bowl, it will act like a fluid. However, when a force is applied to it, such as when it is picked up and squeezed, it will act like a solid. This is because the force causes the particles in the fluid to lock together. Custard is another example of a non-Newtonian fluid.

NATIONAL CURRICULUM LINKS:
- **Year 2 programme of study**: Uses of everyday materials
  - Find out how the shapes of solid objects made from some materials can be changed by squashing, bending, twisting and stretching.
- **Year 5 programme of study**: Properties and changes of materials
  - Compare and group together everyday materials on the basis of their physical properties including their hardness, solubility, transparency, conductivity (electrical and thermal) and response to magnets.
  - Explain that some changes result in the formation of new materials (and that this kind of change is not usually reversible) including changes associated with burning and the action of acid on bicarbonate of soda.

MATERIALS NEEDED:
- PVA glue
- Cornstarch
- Food colouring (optional)
- Beakers
- Tablespoons
- Sandwich bags
- Digital camera (optional)

 SAFETY AND TECHNICAL NOTES:
- The children should wash their hands after completing the investigation.
- The slime is best kept in a plastic bag after it is made.

METHOD:

TO BE DONE IN ADVANCE BY THE TEACHER:
Prepare bowls of PVA glue and cornstarch.

 CHILDREN:

1 Half fill a beaker with PVA glue.
2 Add 1 tablespoon of cornstarch to the PVA glue and stir.
3 Keep adding 1 tablespoon of cornstarch to the PVA glue and stirring until the mixture is firm but can still be stirred.
4 Add a few drops of food colouring to the PVA glue and stir until it is evenly mixed through the glue. You may need to add some more cornstarch if the mixture becomes too wet.
5 Wait for 1 minute to allow the slime to 'set', then remove it from the beaker. What properties does your slime have?

 DATA COLLECTION IDEAS:
The children can take photographs of their slime and also record properties of the slime, for example, how far will it stretch, is it bouncy? can it be squashed, can it be poured, etc.

DIFFERENTIATION:
- **Decrease the challenge:** The children could have the ingredients already measured out for them.
- **Increase the challenge:** The children could vary the amounts of PVA glue and cornstarch in the mixture to see what effect this has on the slime.

USEFUL QUESTIONS TO ASK THE CHILDREN:
- What properties does your slime have?
- What do you think would happen if we added more glue/cornstarch to the mixture?
- Do you think we could get the PVA glue and the cornstarch back from the slime?

FURTHER WORK:
The children could investigate other non-Newtonian fluids such as custard and oobleck (cornstarch and water).

Extracting 'plastic' from milk

LEARNING OBJECTIVES:
Extract some plastic from milk.

INTRODUCTION:
The children extract plastic (casein) from hot milk using white wine vinegar.

USEFUL PRIOR WORK:
The children should know that plastic is a type of material.

 BACKGROUND SCIENCE:
A plastic is a type of material called a polymer. A polymer is made up from many smaller units (called monomers) joined together. Milk contains a protein polymer called casein. The casein can be removed by heating the milk and adding an acid. The heat and acid cause the casein polymers to unfold. These polymers can then be removed from the milk and allowed to set. Casein plastic has been around for over a hundred years and has been used to make small plastic items such as jewellery. It is not as strong or durable as normal plastic so is not good for making products that need to last a long time.

NATIONAL CURRICULUM LINKS:
- **Year 1 programme of study**: Everyday materials
  - Identify and name a variety of everyday materials, including wood, plastic, glass, metal and rock.
- **Year 2 programme of study**: Uses of everyday materials
  - Find out how the shapes of solid objects made from some materials can be changed by squashing, bending, twisting and stretching.
- **Year 5 programme of study**: Properties and changes of materials
  - Explain that some changes result in the formation of new materials (and that this kind of change is not usually reversible) including changes associated with burning and the action of acid on bicarbonate of soda.

MATERIALS NEEDED:
- Milk
- White wine vinegar
- Thermos or other closed container
- Beakers or mugs
- Funnels
- Filter paper
- Teaspoons
- Paper towels

 SAFETY AND TECHNICAL NOTES:
- Only adults should heat the milk.
- The milk does not need to be boiling. The temperature needed for a warm drink will be sufficient.
- Use a thermos or other closed container to hold the hot milk.
- The children should be supervised at all times when using the hot milk.
- Remind the children not to drink the milk.
- Be aware of any allergies.

METHOD:

TO BE DONE IN ADVANCE BY THE TEACHER:

Measure out the required amount of milk (approximately one cup per child or group). Heat the milk until it is hot but not boiling. Put the hot milk into a thermos or closed container.

 CHILDREN:

1 Add 4 teaspoons of the white wine vinegar to a beaker.
2 With an adult's help, carefully pour the hot milk into the beaker with the vinegar.
3 Use a teaspoon to stir the milk. Observe what happens.
4 Set up a funnel with filter paper and place the funnel into another beaker.
5 When you have lots of lumps in your milk, carefully pour the milk into the funnel to separate out the lumps.
6 Leave the lumps on the filter paper to cool down for a few minutes. When they have cooled, carefully remove the filter paper and shake the lumps onto some paper towels. Press a paper towel on top of the lumps to help dry them out.
7 Squeeze the lumps together so that you have a ball. This is your plastic!
8 You can use your plastic like play-dough and shape it and then paint it when it is dry.

 DATA COLLECTION IDEAS:

The children could use the plastic extracted from the milk to make shapes, which can then be dried and painted or decorated. The plastic usually takes between 24 and 48 hours to dry.

DIFFERENTIATION:

- **Decrease the challenge:** The children may find it easier to do this investigation in small groups with an adult helper. The investigation could be done on a bigger scale with the resulting milk poured through a vegetable strainer over a sink and the casein cooled down with cold water. The lumps can then be squeezed together and moulded as normal.
- **Increase the challenge:** The children could try the investigation with different types of milk (for example soya milk, goat's milk) and see what results they obtain.

USEFUL QUESTIONS TO ASK THE CHILDREN:

- What properties does the milk plastic have?
- What sort of objects are normally made from plastic?
- What are the advantages and disadvantages of getting plastic from milk?

FURTHER WORK:

The children could investigate what objects have been made from milk plastic and what other unusual plastics there are, for example vegetable plastics.

Cleaning pennies

LEARNING OBJECTIVES:
Clean some dirty pennies.

INTRODUCTION:
The children clean dirty pennies using a mixture of vinegar and salt.

USEFUL PRIOR WORK:
The children should know that vinegar is an acid.

 BACKGROUND SCIENCE:
Pennies contain the metal copper. Over time, the pennies become dull and dirty due the formation of copper oxide, and everyday dirt and grime building up on the penny. In this investigation, white wine vinegar is mixed with salt. Vinegar is an acid and when it reacts with salt it produces sodium acetate (the sodium comes from the salt and the acetate comes from the acetic acid in the vinegar). There is also a small amount of hydrochloric acid formed. These two chemicals are able to clean pennies (and other metals). If the vinegar and salt are washed off the pennies, then the pennies will be clean as the copper oxide has been removed. However, if the pennies are removed from the vinegar and salt but they are not rinsed with water, the residual vinegar and salt will cause the penny to react with oxygen in the air, causing copper oxide to form quickly on the pennies. This leaves a blue/green coating on the pennies, called verdigris. Additionally, the solution of vinegar and salt will contain some copper from the pennies. If a steel nail is placed into the vinegar and salt, a coating of copper will form on the nail. This is because the copper in the solution is attracted to the steel in the nail.

NATIONAL CURRICULUM LINKS:
• **Year 4 programme of study**: States of matter
  – Compare and group materials together according to whether they are solids, liquids or gases.
• **Year 5 programme of study**: Properties and changes of materials
  – Explain that some changes result in the formation of new materials (and that this kind of change is not usually reversible) including changes associated with burning and the action of acid on bicarbonate of soda.

MATERIALS NEEDED:
• Dirty pennies
• Steel nail
• White wine vinegar
• Salt
• Beakers
• Tablespoons
• Teaspoons
• Paper towels

 SAFETY AND TECHNICAL NOTES:
• The children should wash their hands after completing the investigation.

METHOD:

TO BE DONE IN ADVANCE BY THE TEACHER:
Have enough dirty pennies for each child/group.

CHILDREN:

1 Add 2 tablespoons of the vinegar to a beaker.
2 Add 1 teaspoon of salt to the vinegar. Stir the mixture.
3 Put the pennies into the beaker and leave them for 1 minute.
4 Fill another beaker with water.
5 Use the tablespoon to remove the pennies from the beaker. Try not to touch the pennies with your hands.
6 Put half of the pennies into the beaker of water to wash off the vinegar and salt solution. Stir them around for a few seconds.
7 Put the other half of the pennies onto a paper towel and leave them for a few minutes. Do not wash off the vinegar and salt solution.
8 Remove the pennies from the beaker of water and compare them to how they looked before. Take a look at the pennies on the paper towel. What has happened to them?
9 Now place a nail into the beaker that contains the vinegar and salt solution. Leave it for a few minutes.
10 Use the tablespoon to remove the nail from the beaker. What has happened to it?

 DATA COLLECTION IDEAS:
The children can take 'before' and 'after' photographs of their pennies and nails.

DIFFERENTIATION:
• **Decrease the challenge:** The children may find it easier to handle 2p coins.
• **Increase the challenge:** The children could investigate different acids (for example, lemon juice, brown vinegar, etc.) to see if there is any difference in how well they clean the pennies.

USEFUL QUESTIONS TO ASK THE CHILDREN:
• What happened to the pennies that were washed/not washed after being put in the vinegar and salt solution? Why do you think this happened?
• What happened to the nails that were put into the vinegar and salt solution? Why do you think this happened?
• Can you think of anything else we could clean with our vinegar and salt solution?

FURTHER WORK:
The children could investigate copper statues and why they often develop a greenish colour over time.

Colourful milk

LEARNING OBJECTIVES:
Observe the effects of surface tension in milk.

INTRODUCTION:
The children investigate what happens when food colouring and washing-up liquid are added to milk.

USEFUL PRIOR WORK:
The children do not need to have any particular prior knowledge before completing this investigation.

 BACKGROUND SCIENCE:
This investigation is all to do with surface tension. Surface tension is something that exists in all liquids that contain water. Milk is used in this investigation instead of water as the colour of milk helps to show up the colours of the food colouring better (similar results would be obtained with water). Surface tension is due to the tendency of water molecules to 'stick' to each other, especially at the surface where there are fewer water molecules to adhere to. This forms a skin-like layer on the surface of the water and is, for instance, what allows water-skimming bugs to seemingly walk on water. Washing-up liquid has been designed to break down the surface tension of water, meaning that it will cause a breakdown in the surface tension of the milk, allowing the water molecules to move more freely and therefore carry the food colouring around the surface of the milk.

NATIONAL CURRICULUM LINKS:
- **Year 5 programme of study**: Properties and changes of materials
  - Compare and group together everyday materials on the basis of their physical properties including their hardness, solubility, transparency, conductivity (electrical and thermal) and response to magnets.

MATERIALS NEEDED:
- Milk
- Washing-up liquid
- Food colouring in different colours
- Droppers
- Small bowls
- Cotton wool buds

 SAFETY AND TECHNICAL NOTES:
- Remind the children not to drink the milk.
- Be aware of any allergies.

METHOD:

TO BE DONE IN ADVANCE BY THE TEACHER:
You may wish to pour the milk and washing-up liquids into jugs so the children can take what they need.

CHILDREN:
1 Pour enough milk into your bowl so that it just covers the bottom of the bowl.
2 Add a few drops of food colouring to your milk. Use four different colours and drop them into places in your milk.
3 Dip your cotton wool bud into some washing-up liquid. Now touch your cotton wool bud into your milk and see what happens. Compare what happens when you touch the milk and when you touch the food colouring.
4 Experiment and see what patterns you create. Can you mix the colours together to create new colours?

 DATA COLLECTION IDEAS:
The children can take a photograph of their final 'milk design'.

DIFFERENTIATION:
• **Decrease the challenge:** The children could use a cotton wool ball stuck onto the end of a straw.
• **Increase the challenge:** The children could be set a challenge to create a particular design or a design in the style of a particular artist. They can practise before attempting their 'masterpiece'.

USEFUL QUESTIONS TO ASK THE CHILDREN:
• What did you observe happening when you touched the milk/food colouring with the cotton wool bud?
• Why do you think this was happening?
• Do you think we would get similar results if we used other liquids? Why do you think this?

FURTHER WORK:
The children could research insects such as water skaters to see how they are able to use surface tension to enable them to walk on water.

Homemade ice cream

LEARNING OBJECTIVES:
Make our own ice cream without a freezer!

INTRODUCTION:
The children make their own ice cream using ice, milk and rock salt.

USEFUL PRIOR WORK:
The children do not need to have any particular prior knowledge before completing this investigation.

 BACKGROUND SCIENCE:
Ice cream is made by freezing the milk or cream mixture that it is made from. This would normally be achieved by using a freezer or an ice cream maker. In this investigation, ice cubes and rock salt are used instead. In order for the ice to freeze the ice cream mixture, it has to absorb heat energy from the ice cream mixture. This heat energy will cause the ice to melt, changing it from a solid to a liquid. By adding rock salt, the freezing point of the ice, normally 0 degrees Celsius, is lowered. This means that the ice has to absorb even more heat energy than normal in order to melt. This makes the ice cream mixture freeze faster than if the rock salt was not being used. This is also why salt is spread over pavements and roads in winter. The temperature has to become even colder for the water to be able to freeze into ice.

NATIONAL CURRICULUM LINKS:
- **Year 4 programme of study**: States of matter
  - Observe that some materials change state when they are heated or cooled and measure or research the temperature at which this happens in degrees Celsius (°C).

MATERIALS NEEDED:
- Milk
- Ice
- Vanilla extract
- Caster sugar
- Rock salt
- Zip-lock bags – large and medium-sized
- Strong Sellotape
- Ice cream toppings of your choice

 SAFETY AND TECHNICAL NOTES:
- Ensure that all the food preparation areas are clean and that the children wash their hands before the experiment.
- Check for allergies. Soya milk can be used instead of normal milk for children who cannot have dairy. The method is the same.
- Ensure parental permission has been given for this experiment.

METHOD:

TO BE DONE IN ADVANCE BY THE TEACHER:

Measure out the rock salt and ice for each group or student in advance. They will need 6 tablespoons of rock salt and 1kg of ice each. You may want to measure out the other ingredients in advance as well depending on your group. They will need 300ml of milk, 1 tablespoon of caster sugar and 1/4 teaspoon of vanilla extract.

 ### CHILDREN:

1 Put the ice and the rock salt into the large zip-lock bag.
2 Put the milk, caster sugar and vanilla extract into the medium zip-lock bag. Close the bag and seal it with some Sellotape to make sure it does not open.
3 Place the medium-sized bag filled with your ingredients inside the large bag filled with the ice. Close the large bag and seal it with some Sellotape.
4 Mix your ingredients together by squeezing the bag and throwing it from one hand to another.
5 After about 15 minutes your ice cream should be ready! Open up the bags (you may need an adult to help you with this part) and scoop out your ice cream.

 ### DATA COLLECTION IDEAS:

The children can take photographs of the ingredients and the different stages of making the ice cream and produce a display.

DIFFERENTIATION:

- **Decrease the challenge:** The children will find this easier if all of the ingredients are measured out for them so they only have to mix them together.
- **Increase the challenge:** The children could conduct a 'taste test' and see which ice cream topping is the most popular.

USEFUL QUESTIONS TO ASK THE CHILDREN:

- What does your ice cream look/taste like? Is it the same as normal ice cream or is it any different?
- Do you think we could get the milk and the sugar back from the ice cream?
- Do you think this is the best way of making ice cream? Why do you think that?

FURTHER WORK:

The children could research what people did with food before fridges and freezers were invented. They could look at how other ways of preserving food were used, for example pickling, salting, smoking, etc.

Eating iron for breakfast!

LEARNING OBJECTIVES:
Investigate which breakfast cereals contain iron.

INTRODUCTION:
The children extract iron from breakfast cereal using a pestle and mortar and a magnet. Once the cereal is ground up, the iron is easy to remove.

USEFUL PRIOR WORK:
The children should know that iron is magnetic and that it can be attracted by a magnet.

 BACKGROUND SCIENCE:
A lot of breakfast cereal has added iron in order to make it more nutritious. We need iron for our red blood cells so that they can carry oxygen around our body. The iron in breakfast cereals is usually added as a fine powder of food-grade iron, which means that it is safe to eat. It also makes it relatively easy to remove the iron from the cereal as it is not chemically bonded with the other ingredients (therefore it can be removed by a physical separation process). Once the cereal is ground up the iron can be removed using a strong magnet. Different cereals have different amounts of iron added to them. This information can be found by looking at the nutrition label on the box. It is best to use cereal that contains a lot of iron as this will maximise the chances of iron being collected from the cereal.

NATIONAL CURRICULUM LINKS:
- **Year 2 programme of study**: Animals, including humans
  - Describe the importance for humans of exercise, eating the right amounts of different types of food and hygiene.
- **Year 3 programme of study**: Animals, including humans
  - Identify that animals, including humans, need the right types and amount of nutrition, and that they cannot make their own food; they get nutrition from what they eat.
- **Year 4 programme of study**: Forces and magnets
  - Observe how magnets attract or repel each other, and attract some materials and not others.
- **Year 6 programme of study**: Animals, including humans
  - Recognise the impact of diet, exercise, drugs and lifestyle on the way their bodies function.

MATERIALS NEEDED:
- A selection of different breakfast cereal (read the nutrition label and select ones with different amounts of added iron)
- Plastic beakers
- Magnets
- Pestle-and-mortars, or something to crush the breakfast cereal
- White paper

 SAFETY AND TECHNICAL NOTES:
- Strong magnets are needed for this investigation. Use the strongest magnets that you have available.
- Wrap the magnets in cellophane. This makes it easier to remove the iron from the magnets and to compare how much iron was removed from each cereal.
- Remind the children not to eat the breakfast cereal.

METHOD:

TO BE DONE IN ADVANCE BY THE TEACHER:
Fill bowls with the different types of cereal. Make a note of which cereal is in which bowl but do not let the children know. Wrap the magnets in cellophane.

 ### CHILDREN:
1 Put some of the breakfast cereal you are testing into the pestle-and-mortar.
2 Crush up the cereal into a powder. This may take some time.
3 Use the magnet to try to remove the iron from the cereal. You should see the iron on your magnet. 'Stir' the magnet in the crushed-up cereal until no more iron is being picked up by the magnet.
4 Now repeat the investigation with the other cereal. Use a new magnet each time. Do not remove the cellophane from your magnet. Place your magnet gently down onto a piece of white paper.
5 When you have finished, put your magnets in order of how much iron has been removed. Check with your teacher if you were right.

 ### DATA COLLECTION IDEAS:
The children can rank the cereal in order of how much iron has been removed. They can do this visually be inspecting their magnets and judging how much iron has been removed.

DIFFERENTIATION:
- **Decrease the challenge:** The children may find it easier to use horseshoe-shaped magnets.
- **Increase the challenge:** The children could attempt to measure how much iron has been removed by using a balance to find out the mass of the iron. Unwrapping the cellophane from the magnet will allow the iron to fall off (so this would need to be done over the balance). Only small amounts will be being removed, however, so a sensitive electronic balance would be needed.

USEFUL QUESTIONS TO ASK THE CHILDREN:
- Which cereal did you find contained the most iron? How do you know this?
- Which cereal did you find contained the least iron? How do you know this?
- Why do you think iron is added to breakfast cereal?

FURTHER WORK:
The children could look at what other foods have minerals added to them and why this is done. They could also look at water and how in some parts of the country fluorine and chlorine are added to the water.

EXPERIMENT 99

Compost in a cup

LEARNING OBJECTIVES:
Make a mini compost heap.

INTRODUCTION:
The children make their own compost using green and brown organic matter in a plastic cup.

USEFUL PRIOR WORK:
The children should know that plants need a medium such as soil to grow in and that the medium should contain minerals that the plant needs to grow.

 BACKGROUND SCIENCE:
Compost is formed from the breakdown of organic matter. It produces a soil-like substance that can be used on its own as a growing medium for plants or it can be added to soil in order to improve the nutrient levels and the condition of the soil. Compost is made from organic matter that can be broken down into two groups. These are: green waste (contains high levels of nitrogen) such as vegetable peelings, grass clippings and tea bags; and brown waste (contains high levels of carbon), such as newspapers, cardboard and leaves. A compost heap can be built in a container or can be a free-standing heap on the ground. Bacteria then break down the organic matter into compost. As bacteria are involved, the compost heap needs to be moist and turned regularly in order to add oxygen to it. The compost is ready when it is a dark brown colour and crumbly in texture.

NATIONAL CURRICULUM LINKS:
- **Year 2 programme of study**: Plants
  – Observe and describe how seeds and bulbs grow into mature plants.
- **Year 3 programme of study**: Plants
  – Explore the requirements of plants for life and growth (air, light, water, nutrients from soil and room to grow) and how they vary from plant to plant.

MATERIALS NEEDED:
- Small plastic cups – ideally clear cups
- A selection of compostable materials including green and brown waste – good choices are: leaves, grass clippings, plant clippings, tea bags, coffee grounds, newspaper, and vegetable and fruit peelings
- Water, tablespoons, cling film, elastic bands, soil from the garden

 SAFETY AND TECHNICAL NOTES:
- Children should wash their hands after the investigation.
- This is a long-term investigation. The amount of time it takes the material to break down will vary according to the material used, the amount of water and the temperature. It is best set up at the beginning of a topic and revisited regularly.
- The material in the cup should not be too wet. It should just remain damp throughout the investigation.

METHOD:

TO BE DONE IN ADVANCE BY THE TEACHER:
Collect together the material that can be used in the cups and divide into both green and brown waste. Allow the children to choose what they want to put into the cup, but ensure they use a mix of both types.

Collect some soil from the garden, enough for each child to have approximately 1 tablespoon of the soil. This soil helps to provide the bacteria that will break down the organic materials.

You may wish to pre-cut squares of cling film for the children to put over their cups.

 CHILDREN:

1 Choose what materials you want to use for your compost. Choose from both green and brown waste materials.
2 Add the materials to your cup. Try to build up the material in layers and alternate between green and brown waste material.
3 When your cup is full, add a tablespoon of soil and a tablespoon of water on top.
4 Place a piece of cling film over your cup and hold it in place with an elastic band. Make sure the top of your cup is completely covered.
5 Now shake your cup gently to mix in the soil and the water.
6 Label your cup with your name and place it somewhere warm. A windowsill is ideal.
7 Check on your cup every few days to see what is happening. When you check your cup add a teaspoon of water and give it a gentle shake. Your compost is ready when it is dark brown and crumbly.

 DATA COLLECTION IDEAS:
The children can take photographs of their compost as it develops and make a 'timeline' for their compost.

DIFFERENTIATION:
- **Decrease the challenge:** The children may need help filling their cups with the materials. It may be better for them to use larger cups and work in small groups.
- **Increase the challenge:** The children could make three different types of compost – one with a mix of green and brown waste, one with just green waste and one with just brown waste – and compare the difference.

USEFUL QUESTIONS TO ASK THE CHILDREN:
- What do you think will happen to the materials we put in the cup?
- What do you think the difference is between 'green' and 'brown' waste?
- Why do you think compost is good for plants?

FURTHER WORK:
The children could grow a plant in their compost. The cup would be a good size to initially grow a plant such as a runner bean. Another plant could be grown in normal soil to compare with the plant grown in the compost.

Growing crystals

LEARNING OBJECTIVES:
Grow our own crystals using Epsom salts.

INTRODUCTION:
The children grow their own crystals using Epsom salts.

USEFUL PRIOR WORK:
The children do not need to have any particular prior knowledge before completing this investigation.

 BACKGROUND SCIENCE:
A crystal is a solid mineral that is arranged of repeating geometric shapes. Some crystals are naturally occurring, for example gemstones such as diamonds and sapphires. Crystals can also be formed from salt. Epsom salts are basically magnesium sulphate, a type of salt. The salt is initially dissolved in hot water. As the water cools, the particles of magnesium sulphate 'bump' into each other and start to form a crystallised structure. This experiment can take a few days to complete so it is best started at the beginning of the week so the children can monitor their crystals every day.

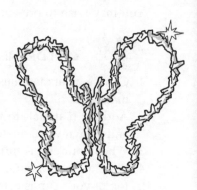

NATIONAL CURRICULUM LINKS:
- **Year 1 programme of study**: Everyday materials
  - Identify and name a variety of everyday materials, including wood, plastic, glass, metal and rock.
- **Year 3 programme of study**: Rocks
  - Compare and group together different kinds of rocks on the basis of their appearance and simple physical properties.

MATERIALS NEEDED:
- Epsom salts
- Beakers or empty glass jars, for example jam jars
- Petri dishes or lids from glass jars
- Wooden stirrers
- Hot water (recently boiled is fine)
- Food colouring
- String
- Small pebbles or stones

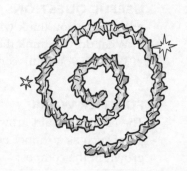

 SAFETY AND TECHNICAL NOTES:
- Boiling water should always be carried out in the classroom in a sealed container such as a kettle. Have an adult fill the beakers and jars with the boiling water. Do not use plastic containers as they may deform due to the heat of the water.

METHOD:

TO BE DONE IN ADVANCE BY THE TEACHER:
Half fill the beakers or jars with boiling water from the kettle and distribute one beaker or jar per child.

 CHILDREN:

1 Add some Epsom salt to your water and stir using your wooden stirrer. Keep adding the salts slowly to your water and stirring until the crystals stop dissolving. You will see some salt crystals at the bottom of your beaker or jar.
2 Add a few drops of food colouring.
3 Have an adult pour some of this water into three Petri dishes or jam jar lids.
4 Add some string to one of your dishes or lids. You can arrange it any way you want. Be careful though as the water will still be hot.
5 Add some pebbles to one of the other dishes or jars. You can arrange them any way you want.
6 Place your dishes or lids somewhere safe.
7 Check your dishes the next day to see what crystals you have grown.

 DATA COLLECTION IDEAS:
Children can take photographs of their crystals over time to see how they are growing. These can then be arranged into a 'timeline' of their crystals. Alternatively, children could draw the 'final' crystals (after a few days of growing) with cross-curricular links to art.

DIFFERENTIATION:
- **Decrease the challenge:** The children may need an adult's help with arranging the string in jars.
- **Increase the challenge:** The children could be challenged to investigate what happens to the crystals if you cool the water down at different rates. They could place one dish in a fridge (be careful to avoid contamination of food), one on a cool windowsill and one somewhere warm such as near a radiator.

USEFUL QUESTIONS TO ASK THE CHILDREN:
- What observations have you made about your crystals?
- What shapes can you see in your crystals? Are they regular or irregular shapes?
- What happened when you included string and stones into your crystals?

FURTHER WORK:
Children could look at crystals that occur naturally such as minerals and gemstones and compare how these have formed to how they grew their own crystals.

Appendix 1
National Curriculum grid

How the Really Useful Science Experiments link to the 2014 National Curriculum

	Plants	Animals, including humans	Living things and their environments	Evolution and inheritance	Seasonal changes	Everyday materials	Uses of everyday materials	Properties and changes of materials	States of matter	Rocks	Sound	Light	Electricity	Forces and magnets
Reaction times		✓												
Decomposing			✓											
Keeping warm							✓							
Heartbeats		✓												
Big feet, big hands?		✓												
Taste vs. smell		✓		✓										
Catch the ball!		✓												
How sensitive are you?		✓												
Time to get sweaty		✓												
Food testing		✓												
All about yeast			✓											
What do plants need to grow?	✓													
What's growing where?			✓	✓										
Brushing our teeth		✓												
Design a seed!	✓		✓											
Find the stomata	✓													
Chewing food		✓												
Green worms!			✓	✓										
How varied are we?		✓		✓										
Colourful carnations	✓													
Moving water	✓													
Bird beaks		✓	✓	✓										
Mouldy bread			✓											
Germinating seeds	✓													
Fertilisers	✓													

	Plants	Animals, including humans	Living things and their environments	Evolution and inheritance	Seasonal changes	Everyday materials	Uses of everyday materials	Properties and changes of materials	States of matter	Rocks	Sound	Light	Electricity	Forces
Making an indicator								✓						
M&M chromatography								✓						
Time to separate!								✓						✓
Dissolving sugars								✓	✓					
Find the solvent!								✓						
Let's get saturated!								✓						
Cleaning water								✓						
Diffusion rates								✓	✓					
The best straw	✓													
Let's make an emulsion						✓		✓	✓					
Salty water									✓					✓
Observing melting								✓	✓					
Observing burning								✓	✓					
A rusty problem						✓		✓						
Conductor or insulator?							✓	✓					✓	
The strongest thread							✓	✓						✓
Design a bag							✓	✓						
Keep it dry!					✓	✓		✓						
Drying the washing					✓	✓	✓	✓	✓					
Comparing soils	✓									✓				
Testing rocks								✓		✓				
Acid rain!								✓		✓				
Ice cube challenge								✓	✓					
Where did the water go?								✓	✓					
Make a fossil				✓						✓				

	Plants	Animals, including humans	Living things and their environments	Evolution and inheritance	Seasonal changes	Everyday materials	Uses of everyday materials	Properties and changes of materials	States of matter	Rocks	Sound	Light	Electricity	Forces
How strong is your magnet?														✓
Making an electromagnet														✓
Let's make a switch								✓					✓	
Fruit circuits!													✓	
Brighter bulbs													✓	
Floating and sinking						✓	✓							✓
Density, density						✓								✓
Friction								✓						✓
How much force?							✓							✓
Bouncy balls!						✓	✓	✓						✓
Speedy cars														✓
Let's make a helicopter														✓
Let's make a parachute														✓
Taking the heat						✓	✓	✓	✓					
Swinging time!														✓
Stretching springs							✓	✓						
Making a rainbow												✓		
Colourful light						✓	✓	✓				✓		
Designing curtains												✓		
Mirror, mirror on the wall												✓		
In the shadows												✓		
Musical water											✓			
Making an ear trumpet		✓					✓				✓			
Soundproofing								✓			✓			
Build a steady hand game														✓

Activity	Plants	Animals, including humans	Living things and their environments	Evolution and inheritance	Seasonal changes	Everyday materials	Uses of everyday materials	Properties and changes of materials	States of matter	Rocks	Sound	Light	Electricity	Forces
Testing urine!		✓												
Volcanic eruption!								✓						
Which is the best washing-up liquid?								✓						
Making a hovercraft							✓							✓
Conker science							✓							✓
Protect an egg!							✓	✓						✓
CSI: Crime scene investigation				✓										
Measuring photosynthesis	✓													
Fussy woodlice			✓											
Gummy bear science						✓		✓						
Making waves										✓				✓
Call the surgeon!		✓												
Making a bouncy ball						✓	✓	✓						
Make a mini-rocket								✓						✓
Extracting DNA		✓		✓										
Making lemonade								✓	✓					
Making a lava lamp								✓	✓					
Making slime								✓	✓					
Extracting 'plastic' from milk							✓	✓						
Cleaning pennies								✓	✓					
Colourful milk								✓						
Homemade ice cream									✓					
Eating iron for breakfast!		✓												✓
Compost in a cup	✓					✓								
Growing crystals										✓				

Appendix 2
Circuit symbols

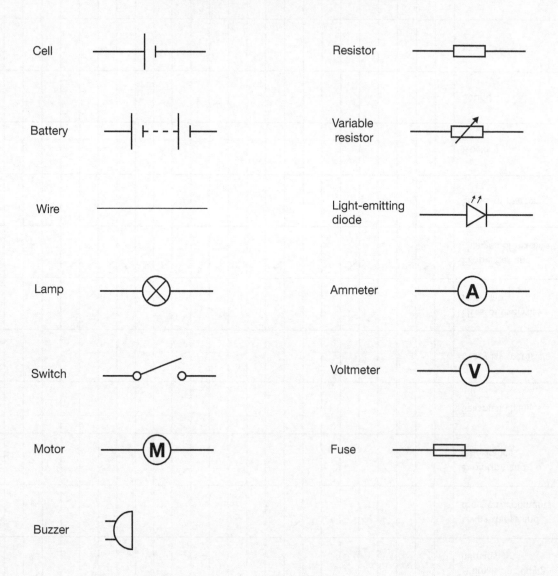

Cell	Resistor
Battery	Variable resistor
Wire	Light-emitting diode
Lamp	Ammeter
Switch	Voltmeter
Motor	Fuse
Buzzer	

Index